THE JAPAN-US ALLIANCE

Dedicated to my late elder brother
Shri S. Amravathi

THE JAPAN-US ALLIANCE

A History of its Genesis

MALLAPPA AMRAVATI

CONCEPT PUBLISHING COMPANY, NEW DELHI

The Indian Council of Historical Research, New Delhi, gave the financial support towards the publication of this work. The Council, however, is not responsible for the views expressed therein.

First Published 1985

Mallappa Amravati (*b.* 1935-)

Published by

Naurang Rai
Concept Publishing Company
H-13, Bali Nagar
NEW DELHI-110 015 (India)

Printed in India by

Kiran Mudran Kendra
Mayapuri, Phase I,
NEW DELHI-110 064

FOREWORD

THE Occupation of Japan began on 28 August 1945 with the arrival of General Douglas MacArthur at the Atsugi military airport. Formally it was terminated on 28 April 1952, though in reality it had become meaningless after the San Francisco Conference held in September 1951. Those 80 months saw the forging of a new relationship between, and an alliance of, two nations which had fought one of the greatest wars in the Asian-Pacific area. The birth of an American-Japanese order in the area was the outgrowth of that Occupation.

In name the Occupation was a collective endeavour but in fact it was an exclusive concern of the United States of America with General MacArthur exercising almost unlimited authority in the name of the Allied Powers. The eleven-nation Far Eastern Commission, set up to advise and guide MacArthur, remained ineffective due to the right of veto held by the United States, the Soviet Union, China and Britain. Though they were not accepting docilely whatever was being done in Japan, others had no option but to go along with the decisions made by MacArthur and his aides regarding Japan.

The objectives of the Occupation were to carry out a thorough reform of Japan's society, economy and polity, to change the system of land ownership, to introduce a new educational programme, give a new constitution (in which there was no place for the divinity of the Emperor) and free labour from all manner of restrictions. Reflecting their faith in the universality of their own system, and guided by a measure of idealism, the American reformers of Japan wanted to make Japan "safe for democracy". What they were embarking upon was by no means easy as there was subtle resistance from vested interests within Japan which sought to salvage as much of the old order as possible. Other Allies questioned the manner in which the reforms were to be carried out. Even the contents of the reforms did not go uncontested.

Towards the end of 1947 there was a reversal of policy from reform to rehabilitation, partly in response to the Cold War and largely to stop Japan from becoming a total economic liability. Punishing and weakening Japan was no longer the objective of the Occupation. The more important purpose was first to make that country self-reliant and then help it to transform itself into the "workshop of Asia". This reversal of policy left many Japanese in confusion, save those who had been working for slowing down the speed of reforms or subverting them completely. Nor were the Allies unanimous about the shift in policy.

An early peace settlement was the logical result of the reversal of policy. Japan was no longer to be treated as an "enemy" but looked upon as a friend and built into an ally. That meant the termination of Allied presence in Japan through the signing of a peace treaty. Since the restoration of peace to a country which had been demilitarized, and without the means to defend itself, was risky a bilateral security arrangement was also conceived. The result was a package which neatly tied together a peace settlement, rearmament by Japan and a bilateral security treaty between Japan and the United States. On the procedure to be adopted for a settlement and the desirability of integrating Japan with a security network in the Pacific there were important differences among the Allies but none had the power to stop either.

Many scholars have tried to tell the story of the Occupation of Japan and the peace settlement which followed it. Naturally there are divergent views on the subject. Dr. Amravati Mallappa has tried in this book to present ably a non-Western approach to the subject. Using the scholarly writings of others, and through his own independent research in India, Japan and the United States, he has succeeded in producing a coherent and meaningful picture out of tricky material. One may not agree with all his conclusions but they certainly deserve thoughtful attention. Consider, for example, the following : (1) War-time decisions by the great powers concerning post-war arrangements assume questionable validity in peace time; (2) a foreign power can achieve only limited socio-economic objectives in the country which it occupies; (3) one-nation, one-man control of an ex-enemy nation seems to work better than a collective control; (4) peace conferences are usually looked upon by the great powers as occasions for propaganda; (5) a country which occupies another country hands over the reins of power to groups which are likely to follow the general policy laid down by the occupying nation; and (6) the conservative leadership in an occupied country finds it convenient to align itself with the occupying nation.

Those who know less about Japan's American interlude as well as those who already know something about it will find Dr. Mallappa's book equally interesting.

Centre for East Asian Studies
School of International Studies
Jawaharlal Nehru University
NEW DELHI.

P.A. NARASIMHA MURTHY
Professor

ACKNOWLEDGEMENTS

THIS dissertation is a product of several years of research in India, Japan and the United States. The author spent a year at Tokyo University during 1961-62 with the help of a field-trip grant made available by the Indian School of International Studies at New Delhi. The author also had an opportunity to work on the dissertation at the East Asian Institute of Columbia University in New York during spring and summer of 1963. Deep appreciation is owed to many for assistance in this dissertation. Dr. P.A. Narasimha Murthy my principal advisor was most helpful and encouraging from the earliest to the very final stages of this thesis. The author is grateful to Professor.

Jun-ichi Kyogoku of Tokyo University for his guidance in selection of Japanese materials and for his patient explanation of Japanese reactions and responses to the occupation, during the author's stay in Tokyo. Grateful thanks go to Dr. James W. Morley of Columbia University for reading the manuscript and for making many constructive suggestions. The author also wishes to thank Dr. Willard Range of University of Georgia and Professor Quincy Wright for inspiration and help when lights seemed to be dim. The reference librarians at the Indian School of International Studies, Columbia University, University of North Carolina at Chapel Hill, Duke University at Durham, North Carolina, National Diet Library at Tokyo and the Library of Congress in Washington always were eager to ferret out material. Grateful thanks are due to all these librarians. Special thanks go to Mrs. Sylvander for proof reading the typescript, and Dr. William Keech of the University of North Carolina for assistance in the tabulation of sample surveys. Needless to say all errors of omission and commission are the author's alone.

MALLAPPA AMRAVATI

INTRODUCTION

THIS dissertation is concerned with the allied occupation of Japan in general and the peace treaty and the security pact of 1951 in particular. The central thesis of the dissertation is that repenting little for their past deeds and resenting much the occupation of the country by foreign powers the Japanese ruling conservative party decided on the day of the surrender to preserve the ancient regime at all cost. They also hoped to regain for their country its pre-war position as a great power. They tried to achieve their first objective by consistently and persistently wrecking Supreme Commander for Allied Powers reforms from within and without. On the other hand the Japanese oligarchs attempted to realize their second objective by exploiting the cold war between the great powers. Through manoeuvering and secret diplomacy the conservative leaders succeeded in signing a peace treaty which helped to preserve the ruling authority for the conservative elements in the country. The dissertation also deals with the changing and shifting attitude of the United States towards Japan. Americans tried to remodel the occupied country in their own image by demolishing the country's political, economic, and social structure then after a while they decided to rehabilitate Japanese economy and a bulwark against communism and finally American policy-makers struck an alliance with the very elements in Japanese society which they wanted to destroy. This alliance between

Washington policy-makers and Japanese conservative leaders facilitated in bringing Japan into a western alliance in the Pacific.

The first three chapters are concerned with the surrender, organization of Supreme Commander for Allied Powers, reforms, and an evaluation of the impact of allied reforms on Japanese society. The fourth chapter deals with the shift in American policy vis-a-vis Japan and its implications for the occupied country. The fifth chapter is devoted to American views on the Japanese peace settlement and the security problem in the Far East. The sixth chapter is concerned with the stands taken by the members of the Far Eastern Commission on the peace settlement. The seventh chapter deals with the peace conference held in San Francisco in September 1951. It also contains a critical review of the peace treaty and the security pact. The eighth chapter is concerned with the divisions in Japanese society on the peace settlements. The concluding chapter deals with some tentative conclusions reached by the author regarding foreign occupations, reforms, peace conferences and content of peace treaties. These conclusions are relevant to international relations.

CONTENTS

1

THE UNCONDITIONAL SURRENDER AND ITS AFTERMATH

FOR THE sake of convenience, the Allied occupation of Japan could be divided into three successive phases which might be described as periods of : (1) Reform, (2) Rehabilitation and (3) Revision. These phases were not separated by a sharp division of time—each phase was characterized by certain types of activity and attitude on the part of both the Americans and the Japanese.[1] The present and the following two chapters deal with the first phase. This chapter is concerned with the unconditional surrender, Japanese reaction to it, and, the organization of the occupation. The second chapter deals with the reforms. The third chapter is devoted to an evaluation of Japanese response to the reforms and their impact on Japanese society. The first phase of the occupation started with the formal surrender of Japan on 2 September 1945, and concluded with the unsuccessful efforts of the United States to call a peace conference in the autumn of 1947. It was the period in which the most extensive and drastic reforms were undertaken to ensure Japanese democratization. Japan was thoroughly defeated before its formal surrender on 14 August 1945. Neither the atomic bomb nor the Russian declaration of war against Japan basically changed the course of the war. According to a Japanese diplomat :

Japan would have surrendered in due time even without the

> terrific chastisement of the bomb or the terrible shock of the Russian attack.[2]

However, it cannot be denied that both these events accelerated the surrender.

The movement in Japan toward surrender had begun as early as 1944 when the Co-ordinating Bureau of the Cabinet concluded that the war was lost. The Bureau reached this conclusion after a careful consideration of the military and economic resources of the nation and the war situation. When Saipan fell in early July, 1944, the war was as good as lost.[3]

Industrial activity was decreasing at an accelerated rate. Such vital industries as electric power and coal had dropped to forty per cent of peak production, and ship-building had fallen to twenty-five per cent of the pre-war level.[4] Civilian goods were practically non-existent. The food situation was very critical. The caloric intake had fallen from a pre-war daily per capita average of 2000 calories to 1680 calories.[5] Sugar and soap became so rare that they were more precious than jewels, as one Japanese has put it.[6]

The air attacks brought direct and immediate pressure on a large segment of the population, causing an abrupt decline in morale and doubt in ultimate victory. A cross-section survey of Japanese civilians showed that the air attack was the most important single factor causing them to have doubts about victory.[7] Forty-three of Japan's sixty-six largest cities were destroyed as a result of the American air offensive against Japan.[8] The mass movement from cities began after the great fire raids on Tokyo in March, 1945. These evacuees went everywhere, spreading news of disaster. Civilian morale fell and deterioration of the social fabric became general. People became critical of their leaders and lost confidence in one another. The conservative faction in the ruling oligarchy saw in the disintegration of the morale of the people a threat to the structure of the Japanese state.[9] In other words the oligarchs were more afraid of a socio-economic revolution than defeat at the hands of a foreign enemy. The Japanese propagandists made elaborate attempts to hide the progress of the war from the people, but they were betrayed by events.

Unconditional surrender and Japanese reaction to it

On 14 August 1945, Japan surrendered unconditionally to the Allied powers on the basis of the Potsdam Declaration. The Declaration was signed on 26 July 1945 at Potsdam by the President of the United States, the Prime Minister of the United Kingdom, and was concurred in by the President of the Nationalist Government of China. A little later, the Soviet Union subscribed to the principles. In this Declaration, the Allies set forth minimum terms for Japanese capitulation. It said among other things that :

(1) The authority and influence of militarists and ultra-nationists should be eliminated, and that a new order of peace, security and justice should be established.

(2) Stern justice should be meted out to all war criminals.

(3) Japanese sovereignty should be limited to the four main islands and such minor islands as might be determined later.

(4) Japanese armed forces abroad, after being completely disarmed, were to return home.

(5) Freedom of speech, of religion, of thought, and other fundamental human rights were to be established in Japan.

(6) Japan was to be permitted to maintain such industries as would sustain her economy and allow the extraction of a just reparation in kind. To this end, Japan was to be permitted to have access to raw materials, and to be allowed to eventually participate in world trade.

(7) The occupying forces were to remain in Japan until these objectives were accomplished and there had been established in accordance with the freely expressed will of the Japanese people a peacefully-inclined and responsible government.[10]

The Emperor took an unprecedented step when he broadcast a message to the nation. The Emperor said that :

> After pondering deeply the general trends of the world and the actual conditions obtaining in our Empire today, we have decided to effect a settlement of the present situation by resorting to an extraordinary measure . . . the war situation has developed not necessarily to Japan's advantage, while the general trends of the world have all turned against her interest. Moreover, the enemy has begun to employ a

> new and most cruel bomb, the power of which to do damage is indeed incalculable, taking the toll of many innocent lives....

Anticipating some trouble from the militarists, the emperor said:

> Having been able to safeguard and maintain the structure of the Imperial State, we are always with ye, our good and loyal subjects, relying upon your sincerity and integrity. Be aware most strictly of any outburst of emotion that may endanger needless complications, and any fraternal contention and strife that may create confusion, lead ye astray cause ye to lose confidence of the world...[11]

The Emperor's reference to the war situation seemed to be a masterpiece of understatement. First, the Emperor did not use the word surrender at all in his message. Second, he implied that Japan was not forced to surrender by saying that "we have decided to effect a settlement...; the war situation has developed not necessarily to Japan's advantage." In fact, Japan was not only defeated, but, for the first time in its long history, came under the control of a foreign country. Lastly, the phrase, "having been able to safeguard and maintain the structure of the Imperial State," gave the impression that the acceptance of the terms of the Potsdam Declaration would enable Japan to preserve the Imperial structure. On the contrary, the Potsdam Declaration made it clear that the Japanese people would decide the future structure of the state by their free will.

The defeat was complete, yet the military hotheads still persisted in their illusions and refused to recognize the fact of defeat. On the night of the 14th of August a group of young military officers led by a lieutenant colonel Hatanaka attempted to destroy the recorded speech of the Emperor in order to prevent the impending announcement of capitulation. They believed that the decision to surrender was forced upon the Emperor by his unpatriotic advisors. General Tanaka, commander-in-chief of the Eastern Army, after three hours argument with the rebels, convinced them of the futility of their action.[12] The abortive revolt fizzled out.

The Emperor's voice was heard in every hamlet throughout the land. People were so overcome by emotion that at first they could hardly concentrate on the message. Since radio reception in many districts was extremely poor and since the word 'surrender' was not used in the transcript, the fact of surrender did not sink into the consciousness of many people for many days. Very few understood what acceptance of the terms of the Potsdam Declaration meant. But the core of the message was clear—Japan has been defeated. The surrender announcement dazed and saddened the Japanese people. Though most of them long since suspected that Japan could not win, they held on to a last desperate hope. The Kamikaze, that is the Divine Wind, had been counted upon to accomplish a miracle for the Japanese people. The atom bomb proved the real Kamikaze since it saved Japan from further useless slaughter and destruction. On the other hand, the news of the surrender came as a god-sent relief to the weary people of Japan. It was a relief from the ever-present fear of death from the skies, for the horror of air raids had stopped. According to the report of the United States Strategic Bombing Survey, the predominant reaction of the people to the Emperor's announcement of surrender was one of "sorrow, misery, surprise and disillusionment".[13] The Table 1.1 indicates the mood of the general mass of the people on surrender.[14]

Some of the typical comments of the common people on the Imperial announcement of surrender were as follows :

> *A housewife's reactions* . I was greatly disappointed and was not able to do any work. I heard the Emperor's proclamation at noon, but it was not clear. So I did not know definitely until that afternoon. My daughter and I heard this later report together. We were shocked. We cried for a long time. I crawled into bed with a headache and stayed there all the rest of the day We had worked hard, refrained from buying what we wanted, given up many things, all because I believed that we would win. Then came the letdown. I cannot find words to express myself, for the thought of win-

ning was uppermost in my mind all the time. Then to have lost the war was the biggest disappointment in my life.[15]

TABLE 1.1 : **Immediate reaction to the surrender**

	per cent
Regret, misery, disappointment	30
Surprise, shock, bewilderment	23
Feeling of relief or happiness that the war was over and suffering at an end	22
Anxiety, worry about treatment under occupation	13
Shame followed by relief, acceptance with regret, expected it but felt it a blot on national record	10
Expected it, knew it was coming, resignation	4
Emperor, sorrow for him	4
No answer or miscellaneous reactions	6
Some people gave more than one answer, therefore the total is 125.	125

Even on the last day of surrender many people were still hoping for some last-minute Divine Wind to save the day. The following was a typical comment :

> I was greatly surprised, I felt just like one feels when a sick friend suddenly dies, even though one knew his case was hopeless.

A Japanese psychiatrist characterized the reactions of the following fashion :

> They lost their grip on reality and in many cases became quite apathetic. They were dazed and this feeling has persisted up to the present.[16] (Up to December, 1945, when the interview was conducted.)

The minority who felt relief or happiness immediately upon hearing that the war was over spoke in the following terms :

> I was glad and quite relieved. I felt that with the war's

> end, my soldier son would be able to return home and things would not be so difficult.[17]

Military defeat did not come as a surprise to the ruling oligarchy in Japan. They knew that it was inevitable long before the day of actual surrender. Nevertheless, it was a day of humiliation to the ruling group.

The cessation of the hostilities did not mean the end of suffering and privation for the Japanese. As has been pointed out, the war destroyed the nation's economic system. Food was extremely short, black marketeering was ripe, and severe inequities existed in the distribution of the limited supplies of all necessities. In the chaotic conditions the mass of the population had little time for or interest in the political affairs of the country. From the political point of view the nation as a whole was a disorganized mass of people, seeking individual solutions to their desperate personal problems and conscious only of the immediate day-to-day task of staying alive.

On 2 September 1945, the Instrument of Surrender was signed by Mamoru Shigemitsu on behalf of the Emperor and the Japanese government on board the battleship 'Missouri' in Tokyo Bay. Japan entered upon a new and unfamiliar phase of its history.

Organization and personnel of the occupation

The United States Initial Post-surrender Policy for Japan provided that "The Supreme Commander will exercise his authority through the Japanese governmental machinery and agencies, including the Emperor . . . ."[18] In accordance with the directive the occupation machinery was organized in Tokyo.

At the apex of the occupation was the General of the Army, Douglas MacArthur, Supreme Commander for Allied Powers. Both General MacArthur and the organization over which he presided came to be known as SCAP. General Headquarters of the Supreme Commander for Allied Powers was divided into two main categories: (i) Four General Staff sections to deal with military affairs, and (ii) Nine special staff sections to deal with non military matters such as political, economic and resource problems. As new functions and duties arose, new sections were added. By August, 1947, there were fourteen non-military sections. These sections were given broad responsibility in their respective areas. The government section headed by Brigadier General Whitney was the most important; it was established to advise SCAP on policies concerning military government in Korea and the political matters regarding the occupation of Japan including demilitarization and decentralization. Contact with the Japanese Government was maintained through the Central Liaison Office (CLO), established by the Ministry of Foreign Affairs. The functions of the Central Liaison Office were to receive the directives, orders, and requests from the various sections, and forward them to the Japanese Government for action.[19]

At the lower levels of administrations—that is, in prefectures, cities, towns, and villages, the implementation of directives issued to the Japanese Government by SCAP was supervised by the Military Government Teams of the Eighth Army deployed throughout Japan. Initially, this surveillance was extensive. Progress in achieving occupation objectives later permitted sizable reduction in the number engaged in this activity.[20] The relationship between the policy forming staff section of General Headquarters in Tokyo and the Military Government teams was tenuous and indirect and often led to confusion. Military officers in the prefecture were often embarrassed by local Japanese officials who had been informed by their colleagues of American policy decisions in Tokyo, long before word was transmitted to the concerned officers on the Military Government teams.[21]

The predominant role of the United States in the Pacific war made it logical for that country to play a paramount role in the occupation of Japan. Nevertheless, the United States realized that its allies would seek some participation in the administration of the occupied country. On 21 August 1945, the United States submitted to China, the Soviet Union, and the United Kingdom, a proposal for the establishment of a Far Eastern Advisory Commission to make recommendations to the participating governments on the policies and steps which should be taken to ensure Japanese compliance with the surrender terms.[22] China and the Soviet Union promptly accepted the American proposal. The United Kingdom objected to the advisory character of the commission and suggested that a Control Council should be set up in Japan. Australia and New Zealand also wanted a share in the occupation. In the face of British objections and American unwillingness to share authority with the Allied Powers, nothing could be done.

At the London Conference of the Council of Foreign Ministers in September, 1945, the Soviet Foreign Minister, Molotov, requested that the question of the control of Japan be placed on the agenda and expressed his government's dissatisfaction with the implementation of surrender terms in Japan by General MacArthur. He particularly objected to the fact that the demobilized Japanese troops were not treated as prisoners of war and were not made to work.[23] He urged the establishment of a control commission for Japan in which the Soviet Union would have an equal voice with any other member. During his stay in London, the United States Secretary of State, Byrnes, was able to persuade the British government to agree to the establishment of a Far Eastern Commission by conceding a place on the proposed Commission to India and by agreeing that the Commission should be authorized to meet in Tokyo as well as in Washington. Consequently, the United States announced that the first meeting of the Commission would be held in Washington on 30 October 1945. Meanwhile the Soviet Union decided to reverse her position and complained that she was neither informed nor consulted about Japan and that her representative in Tokyo, Lieutenant-General Kuzuma Derevyenko, had been treated like a piece of furniture.[24] Consequently, he was recalled to Moscow. The Soviet Union refused to belong to a purely advisory body and again suggested the formation of a four-power control commission for Japan.

The Far Eastern Advisory Commission held its first meeting on 13 October 1945 in Washington. Without the Soviet Union participating and after electing Major General Frank R. McCoy as the Chairman, it adjourned for a week in the hope that the Soviet Union would change her mind and attend the Commission, but Russia ignored the meeting. The fact of the matter was that the United States, though willing to share the responsibility of the occupation of Japan with those Allies who had fought against the former enemy in the Pacific, was not prepared to forfeit the favoured position which she had won during the war. General MacArthur, who was designated as the Supreme Commander for the Allied Powers, was responsible to the United States Government. The United States insisted that this relationship be recognized. It also insisted that MacArthur be given the power to act directly in time of emergency. Finally, it expressed a fear that a Control Council in Tokyo would complicate the occupation of Japan and impinge on the Supreme Commander's authority.[25] Many conferences and long debates took place before the Allies finally agreed upon a draft proposal for a Far Eastern Commission and an Allied Council for Japan.

At the Council of Foreign Ministers in Moscow in December of 1945, the Ministers agreed to the formation of a Far Eastern Commission which would meet in Washington and which would be empowered to formulate policy for the occupation. They also agreed to form an Allied Council for Japan in Tokyo to advise the Supreme Commander.

The Far Eastern Commission was composed of representatives of Australia, Canada, China, France, India, the Netherlands, New Zealand, the Philippines, the Soviet Union, the United Kingdom, and the United States. Later Pakistan and Burma were also included. Under its terms of reference, the Far Eastern Commission had two principal functions :

(1) "To formulate the policies, principles and standards in conformity with which the fulfilment by Japan of its obligations under the terms of surrender may be accomplished."

(2) "To review on the request of any member, any directive issued to the Supreme Commander or any action taken by the Supreme Commander involving policy decisions within the jurisdiction of the Commission," and

(3) "To consider other matters as may be assigned to it by agreement among the participating governments reached in accordance with the voting procedure

provided for in Art. V2."[26]

Military operations or territorial assignments were beyond the scope of the Commission's activities. The Commission had to respect the existing central machinery in Japan, including the chain of command from the United States to the Supreme Commander and the Supreme Commander's command of the occupation forces. The task of the United States was to issue directives for the guidance of the Supreme Commander in accordance with the policy decisions of the Commission.

The Commission was designed to put certain limitations upon the freedom of the United States to formulate policies for Japan. But within these limitations, the United States had considerable freedom of action which enabled it to retain a predominant position in the ruling of Japan. The possibility of a considerable deviation of the eventual executive act from the policy decision was anticipated, and, therefore each Commission member was given the right to ask for a review of any directive or implementation. However, not only did such a review not suspend the directive or the Supreme Commander's act, but a review decision changing either of them was again to be considered a policy decision, which in turn had to pass through the process of voting and forever frustrate the influence of the Commission. Furthermore, the United States was allowed to issue 'interim directives' to the Supreme Commander pending action by the Commission when urgent matters arose not covered by policies already formulated by the Commission. The United States could not issue 'interim directives' without the Commission's previous approval on matters which involved: (i) fundamental changes in the Japanese constitutional structure or (ii) in the regime of control, or (iii) matters dealing with a change in Japanese government as a whole.

The Big Four China, the Soviet Union, the United Kingdom, and the United States enjoyed veto power in the Commission. Unanimity was not necessary, provided a majority of the representatives, including the Big Four, concurred. The voting method constituted both the Commission's strength as well as its weakness. This procedure was particularly valuable for the United States, as it ensured that only those policies which it approved would be adopted. The disadvantages of the veto were obvious. It was resented by many of the smaller countries. For example, at one of the earliest sessions of the Commission, Herbert Evatt, Australian Minister of External Affairs, protested against this method of voting. In addition, the veto retarded speedy action by the Commission, and, in some cases, notably that of reparations, postponed a decision indefinitely.[27] This situation, perhaps more than any other, led to the gradual ineffectiveness of the Commission. It eventually became a debating club.

The Allied Council for Japan consisted of four members, China, the Soviet Union, the United States, and a member representing jointly the United Kingdom, Australia, New Zealand and India. It was essentially consultative and advisory. The Supreme Commander of his deputy was to be the chairman of the Council. The terms of reference of the Council reiterated the Supreme Commander's authority to issue and implement orders concerning the surrender and occupation of Japan. He was required to "consult and advise with the Council in advance of the issuance of orders on matters of substance," the exigencies of the situation permitting. It was provided that the "Supreme Commander's decisions upon these matters shall be controlling."[28]

At the Council's first meeting in Tokyo, on 3 April 1946, MacArthur made it clear that he considered the Council to be exclusively consultative and advisory. He told the Council members that they should not make "sharp and illconceived criticism of our occupation policies."[29] At the next session on 17 April, an inquiry by the Soviet member on the elimination of militarists and ultranationalists elicited a comprehensive reply from a SCAP's spokesman, which lasted three hours and was presented in a sarcastic and contemptuous tone. In the words of one of the members of the Committee :

> At its inception, General MacArthur's representative treated it with frivolous derision."
>
> and
>
> The representative of Supreme Command for Allied Powers

> showed exceptional sensitiveness to any question or comment which might be construed as a criticism of any aspect of the occupation. In these circumstances, it was inevitable that the Council should have been on balance a failure, and at times, a fiasco.[30]

As the occupation neared its end, the Council's proceedings became shorter. In fact, they lasted exactly for one minute. The official report noted soberly that the session opened at 10.03 a.m. and closed at 10.04 a.m.

The Far Eastern Commission and the Allied Council could not function properly because of the strained relations between the two major powers, the United States and the Soviet Union. Moreover, MacArthur and his representatives further reduced the usefulness of the two international bodies by treating them in a cavalier fashion. The Supreme Commander denied the Commission its responsibility and had his own concept of what the Commission should do. For example MacArthur completely bypassed the Far Eastern Commission by drafting a constitution for the Japanese and then by ignoring the Commission's policy decision of 20 March 1946 which stated that the SCAP should keep the Far Eastern Commission informed on the progress of the draft constitution in the Diet and that the Supreme Commander should instruct the Japanese Government that the Commission should be given a chance to 'pass the final draft'.[31] However, it was to the credit of the representatives in the Far Eastern Commission that, notwithstanding many controversial questions with which they had to deal, a great number of agreements were reached. The Commission adopted the American 'post-surrender policy directive' as the Far Eastern Commission's Post-Surrender Policy in September, 1947.

The foregoing account makes it clear that it was an Allied occupation only in theory. In reality, it was an American undertaking. "From start to finish it was an American show," as Reischauer has put it.[32] General MacArthur was not only the Supreme Commander for the Allied Powers, but was also the Commander-in-Chief of all the United States' forces in the Far East. United States troops had the primary responsibility for taking over and policing Japan. The only non-United States force which occupied Hiroshima prefecture and a small portion of Yamaguchi prefecture under the operational control of the commanding general was the British Commonwealth Force of the Eighth Army. But they were only a minority element among the tactical troops in Japan and without any direct involvement in the execution of the all-important reform programme.

MacArthur's huge staff of experts and advisors were always overwhelmingly American. The presence of a British or a French civilian here and there in General Headquarter, of SCAP only enhanced the American predominance. More important than the personnel in Japan was the fact that all important occupation policies originated from the State Department of the United States.

The man in the street in Japan, unaware of the international agreements concerning his country, and in view of the omnipresence of the Americans throughout the islands, perhaps never thought of the occupation as being international. In view of this fact, perhaps it would not be incorrect to say that the study of Japan under the occupation is mainly a study of American policy towards that country and the Japanese reaction to it.

Since the occupation was military, the defense department took an increasing responsibility in the administration of the occupied country. MacArthur himself was a top military commander. At various times, the Pentagon sent its important officers to Japan for an on-the-spot inspection. The State Department remained in the background.

General MacArthur, who guided the occupation, and who made all the policies originating in Tokyo and executed them, was a man of strong character and a controversial figure in American politics. He had his own concept of the occupation and did not like the idea of supervision of his work by superior authorities. As a result, he was in constant conflict with the Allied Council for Japan, the Far Eastern Commission, and sometimes with his superiors in Washington. He treated the two international organs as nuisances to be tolerated,[33] MacArthur was extremely sensitive to criticism and had an exaggerated view of himself.[34] He claimed a knowledge of Japanese psychology, history, tradition, almost everything concerning the occupied country, and considered himself the guardian of the Japanese people. In his own words :

> They come to regard me not as a conqueror, but as a protector. I had a deep responsibility as guardian of those people so dramatically brought under my charge.[35]

His sense of pride did not allow him to seek advice on matters of policy. He once boasted that his major advisers were George Washington and Abraham Lincoln.[36] He gathered around him mostly those who were loyal to him and then relied heavily upon them. These officers went to extreme lengths to protect him from supposed criticism.

The Supreme Commander tried to build Japan in his own image. America and democracy were synonyms for him. In his opinion, the operative democratic set up and the capitalistic economy of the United States were equally valid for Japan.[37] By advocating individualism in economics and politics, MacArthur unwillingly aligned himself with the conservative ruling group and took a position against the declared policy of the Social Democratic Party. It is questionable whether the Potsdam Declaration intended the Supreme Commander for Allied Powers to take sides in the domestic politics of the occupied country. MacArthur's anti-Communist and anti-Soviet feelings were strong, and often he used rather undignified language in his denunciation of Soviet policies toward Japan.[38] He was reported to have told President Truman's special ambassador Harriman, when the latter visited Tokyo in 1950, that the United States should fight the communists "everyplace—fight them like hell."[39]

The Supreme Commander did have some sterling qualities. His devotion to duty was unquestionable. During his five-year rule in Japan, MacArthur left the country only twice and never visited his homeland despite many invitations from high-ups in Washington. His dignity, aloofness, and authority won him the respect and admiration of the Japanese. He provided the Japanese with the leadership and also the hope they so desperately needed in their hour of defeat and demoralization.[40] His contacts with Japanese politicians were, however, limited to very few persons at the top. In this respect, MacArthur acted like the Emperor. In fact, it was often said that during the occupation, the Supreme Commander was the real Emperor of Japan. An analogy closer to precedent would be that the Japanese royal family had temporarily reverted to the position it had held between 489 and AD 1858 under the Tokugawa Shogunate, when the shoguns ruled the country in the Emperor's name.

MacArthur greatly overrated the achievements of the occupation and claimed too much credit for himself. For example the Supreme Commander said that.

> The occupation had almost overnight torn as-under a theory and practice of life built upon two thousand years of history and legend and tradition.[41]

The personnel in the General Headquarters came from both civilian and military branches of the United States Government. Almost every important section in the General Headquarters was headed by the top brass who were loyal to General MacArthur. The staff of the section chiefs for the most part consisted of civilians recruited in Washington for the specific purpose of the occupation. Some of the civilians came to Japan for adventure, some out of curiosity, and yet others for study and service. As a result, quality and efficiency of these persons varied widely. A few of the non-military officials were experts in Japanese affairs. But these experts were in subordinate positions and, therefore, could not exert any influence on the course of the occupation. Moreover, the captains and generals did not have-much liking for academic people. The army considered non-military jobs unimportant and appointed its least capable officers to civilian affairs.[42] Many of the civilians in the General Headquarters, unaccustomed to military protocol, became dissatisfied with army discipline and resigned. The task of the occupation was great, but the trained people were few.

Since SCAP was essentially a military set-up, hierarchy was strictly maintained. Although some of the officials were dedicated people and worked for a thorough reform of the occupied country, there seemed to be little or no opportunity for free discussion and individual initiative. The captains and generals regarded the sections they headed as personal empires, but remained ignorant of the nature of their empires.[43] Interdepartment jealousies and lack of co-ordination led to a great deal of overlapping and confusion. The conduct of certain chiefs in the General Headquarters was not above reproach. Some high-ranking officers were accused of accepting favours from prominent Japanese.[44] But such cases seemed to be few and far between.

SCAP's officials claimed too much too quickly.[45] In this respect, they were led by the Supreme Commander. The officers, in their anxiety to please MacArthur, tried to anticipate his wishes and echoed his propaganda. MacArthur's henchmen spared him the pain of reading contradictory material and disturbing news. The subordinates in the various sections quickly learned from their superiors to delete unpleasant facts from their memoranda to their chiefs. In short, it was a world of make-believe. The public relations section in the headquarters seemed to place little confidence in the art of understatement.[46]

REFERENCES

1. Edwin O. Reischauer, *Japan : Past and Present* 2nd ed. (Tokyo, 1962), p. 209.
2. Toshikazu Kase, *Journey to Missouri* (New Haven 1950), p. 217.
3. *Ibid.*, p. 77.
4. F.C. Jones, Hugh Borton and B.R. Pearn, *Survey of International Affairs 1939-1946 : The Far East 1942-1946* (London, 1955) p. 315.
5. *Ibid.*
6. Kase, op. cit. p. 197.
7. U.S. Strategic Bombing Survey, Morale Division, *The Effects of Strategic Bombing on Japanese Morale* (Washington D.C., 1947) p. 1.
8. *Ibid.*
9. This position is abundantly clear from the statement Prince Konoye is reported to have made in February 1945 that he felt disturbed by the fact that there was a leftist faction in the Army which was planning a revolution. See Shigeru Yoshida, *The Yoshida Memoirs : The Story of Japan in Crisis* (London, 1961) p. 25.
10. Supreme Commander for the Allied Powers, Report of Government Section, *Appendice A : Political Reorientation of Japan : September 1945 to September 1948* (Washington, D.C. 1949) p. 413. Henceforth this document will be cited as SCAP.

11. Robert J.C. Butow, *Japan's Decision to Surrender* (Stanford, 1954) p. 248.
12. Kase, op. cit., p. 258-9.
13. United States Strategic Bombing Survey, n. 7, p. 149.
14. *Ibid.*
15. *Ibid.*, p. 150.
16. *Ibid.*, p. 151.
17. *Ibid.*
18. SCAP, op. cit., p. 423.
19. SCAP, *Selected Data on the Occupation of Japan* (Washington, D.C., 1950) p. 1.
20. *Ibid.*, p. 2.
21. Jones *et al*, op. cit., p. 323.
22. George H. Blakeslee, *The Far Eastern Commission : A Study in International Co-operation 1945 to 1952*, Department of State Publication 5138 (Washington, D.C. 1953) p. 12.
23. James F. Byrnes *Speaking Frankly* (New York, 1947) p. 214.
24. *Ibid.*, p. 217.
25. Jones *et al*, op. cit., p. 339.
26. Art. V2 deals with the voting procedure which is explained in subsequent pages.
27. Jones *et al*, op. cit., p. 343.
28. SCAP, op. cit., p. 422.
29. *Ibid.*, p. 746.
30. W. MacMahon Ball, *Japan, Enemy or Ally* ? (New York, 1949) p. 33.
31. Hugh Borton, Preparation for the occupation of Japan, *The Journal of Asian Studies* 25 (February 1966) p. 210-1.
32. Edwin O. Reischauer, *The United States and Japan* (New York, 1965) p. 46.
33. Douglas MacArthur, *Reminiscences* (New York, 1964) 291-3.
34. John Gunther, *The Riddle of MacArthur* (New York, 1950) (23-4 also see Russel Brines, *MacArthur's Japan* (New York, 1948) p. 68.
35. MacArthur, op. cit., p. 283.
36. Brines, op. cit., p. 63.
37. MacArthur, op. cit., p. 283.
38. In a statement MacArthur charged the Soviet representative on the FEC of hipocracy, brutality, vulgarity and so forth. See MacArthur, op. cit., p. 293.
39. Harry S. Truman, *Memoirs, Years of Trial and Hope* 2 (New York, 1956) p. 353.
40. Reischauer, op. cit., 225, according to a Japanese author "when faced by crisis, rather than thinking out rational solutions for themselves, Japanese tend to look to a hara type leader for guidance." Hajime Shinohara, "The Conservative Party," *Journal of Social and Political Ideas in Japan* 2 (December 1964) p. 45. Henceforth this periodical will be cited as *JSPIJ*.

41. SCAP, op. cit., p. 756.
42. Brigadier—General Ken R. Dyke who had no college education and had served as an advertising manager before he joined the army was in charge of schools, religion, the press and cultural activities in GHQ, SCAP. Another military official on without any research and writing experience was appointed as the official historian of the occupation. See Harry Emerson Wildes, *Typhoon in Tokyo* (New York, 1954) p. 8-9.
43. Brines, op cit., p. 77.
44. Wildes, op. cit., p. 37.
45. "They were sure of astonishing success of directives before they were issued. General Willoughby was so sure of this that before the occupation had more than opened, he hailed it as 'the greatest achievement of its kind since Napoleonic days'." Wildes, op. cit., p. 23.
46. *Ibid.*, p. 27.

2

POLITICAL AND SOCIO-ECONOMIC REFORMS

THE AIMS and objectives of the occupation were found in the United States Initial Post-Surrender Policy for Japan. It was an elaboration of the general principles enunciated at Potsdam and incorporated in the Instrument of Surrender. This document covered the entire range of political, economic, financial, and administrative activities. It set forth three basic objectives for Japan : (1) demilitarization, (2) democratization, and (3) decentralization.[1] These objectives found their concrete expression in the various political and socio-economic reforms sponsored by the SCAP.

The immediate problem facing the allied occupation after the formal surrender was the actual demobilization of the Japanese armed forces. Over two million officers and men in Japan were demobilized in the opening months of the occupation. The Imperial Army and Navy Ministers were transformed into the first and second Demobilization Ministers. Arsenals and factories engaged in producing military weapons were all closed at once by the occupation. Naval bases were destroyed. An international tribunal was set up in Tokyo to punish those guilty of war crimes. The work of breaking up Japan's ultranationalistic setup, which at the outset seemed a little difficult, was carried out rather smoothly, to the surprise of even the occupation authorities.[2]

THE PURGE

The Allied Powers recognized that the successful operation of a democratic government in Japan would depend on the political attitude of that country's leadership. The militarists who had led Japan into the war were obviously not qualified to serve as spokesmen for democracy. Also, in pursuance of the stipulation contained in the Potsdam Declaration that :

> There must be eliminated for all time the authority and influence of those who have deceived and misled the people of Japan on embarking on world conquest, for we insist that a new order of peace, security and justice will be impossible until irresponsible militarism is driven from the world.[3]

A thoroughgoing purge of Japanese leadership was undertaken. The purge programme as a whole was divided into two parts, the (i) political purge, and (ii) its extension in January, 1947 to include local officials and leaders in industry and in the media of expression.

On 4 January 1946, two directives were issued by the SCAP which began the political purge. One of these directives ordered the abolition of political parties, societies, and other organizations which advocated Japanese militarism, sponsored Japanese hegemony over Asia, or contributed to the growth of Japanese ultranationalism. It listed twenty-seven of the most prominent terroristic and nationalistic societies and ordered the seizure of their property.[4]

The second directive was entitled "Removal and Exclusion of Undesirable Personnel from Public Office." This directive was the basis for all the subsequent purges in Japan. It resulted in the removal and expulsion of 1,067 incumbents of and candidates for important positions in the national government. This phase included a preliminary screening of all Diet candidates in the April, 1946 elections and final screening of successful candidates in June of that year.[5]

The operation of this directive created confusion in the rank and file of Japanese political parties as pre-war leaders fell one after another under the successive interpretation of the purge, and as their followers and partisans sought new political standards to save themselves. The Shidehara cabinet sustained a severe blow in January, 1946. Only three cabinet members were exempted from the purge. All the 257 Diet members of the Progressive Party were estimated to fall under the purge and the Chief Secretary of the party announced that only three of the party's leaders were unaffected by the directive.[6] *The Asahi Shimbun* in discussing the effects of the announcement on purge stated, "The application of the purge categories was so wide that they are unable to find successors to the president, managers and other members".[7] The officials of the Home Ministry and the Imperial Household, and the members of the House of Peers suffered heavily under this directive.

In 1947, the purge policy was further extended to local bodies. A number of Imperial ordinances were issued in January, 1947, which ordered the removal and exclusion of undesirable personnel from public office in local assemblies and other organizations of the cities, prefectures, towns, villages and hamlets. The ordinance also provided the removal of the top executives, directors, and other officials who exercised authority or influence commensurate therewith, from companies specifically listed. Finally, the purge was extended to include the leaders in the field of public information and propaganda.[8]

The purge policies were so broad in scope that they covered men of letters, journalists, teachers, civil servants, former members of the Imperial Rule Assistance Association, businessmen, and all categories of people in public life. By May, 1948, 200,000 persons had been purged. The Japanese government resisted the purge policy, and, through open protests and questionable means, tried to ignore some of the directives. So much so that the government section of general headquarters rebuked the Japanese government for evasion of its duty. It said that "the Japanese government has shown an increasing tendency not only to ignore the spirit and intent of the basic directive, but to evade and circumvent the liberal provisions of the purge directives by extremely legalistic and liberal interpretations which in many instances are specious to the point of obvious political dishonesty".[9] The political purgees, like their counterparts in business and industry, continued to visit their offices and guided their subordinates and followers from behind the scene. Some got wind of what was coming and resigned just before the directive was issued. In some other cases, operation was comic. For instance, SCAP's officials ordered prompt arrest of a member of the Black-Dragon Society who had been dead for four years, and ignored the president of the group.[10]

The scope and ramification of the purge policy brought sharp rejoinders from the conservative element in Japan. Critics maintained that the removal of tens of thousands of professional people at the lower echelon of government, such as mayors of cities and towns, heads of administrative branches and so forth, who worked within the framework of a policy laid down by their superiors, was indiscriminate and arbitrary.[11] Further, it was pointed out that SCAP made no distinction between those who questioned the aggressive policies of the militarists, but remained in their positions with the hope of moderating the government's actions from within, and those who expressed agreement with the militarists.[12] Moreover, the original objective of the purge was to remove those who had misled the Japanese people into embarking on world conquest. SCAP went beyond this term of reference by purging all those whom it regarded as inimical to the growth of democracy. Conservative spokesmen described these measures as punitive and political.[13] For example, the critics said that the motive behind the purge of two Democratic party leaders, Ken Inukai and Wataru Narahashi, in March, 1947, just prior to the April 1947 elections, was to weaken the Democratic party. It should be noted in this connection that Wataru Narahashi was reported to have reminded his constituents in 1942 elections that he took part in the reconstruction of East Asia and co-operated with the Japanese army in North China.[14] Another famous purge case was that of Tanzan Ishibashi, who was Finance Minister in 1946. It was alleged that he was purged because he made disdainful remarks on the professional competence of SCAP's economic planners. Again it should be pointed out that Ishibashi had written articles in favour of Italian fascism after a pre-war visit to Italy.[15] When facts concerning past political activities were brought to the fore, the conservative leaders accused SCAP's officials of being under the influence of Japanese communists, leftists, and their sympathizers.[16] There was nothing new in this charge. The post-war conservative leaders, like their predecessors in the pre-war days, used anti-communism as a weapon to discredit their opponents.

On the other hand, the supporters of the purge measures pointed out that the removals were selective and not drastic. In fact, ninety-seven per cent of the purgees consisted of militarists, ultranationalists, and the officials of the Imperial Rule Association Society. They agreed that some innocent people suffered along with the culprits. The purges cleared the political atmosphere of the country by removing the old discredited elements and their accomplices. It enabled the new generation of leaders to gain a foothold in the political and economic life of the country. In this sense, the purge made a notable contribution to the process of democratization intended by SCAP.[17] Supporters regarded it as the moral rearmament of Japan.

In due course of time there developed differences of opinion among the rank and file of SCAP's officials on the implementation of the purge directives. The Civil Intelligence Section, headed by General Willoughby, advocated mild interpretation of the directives. He maintained that it would be unwise to antagonise a large section of influential Japanese who would be useful allies against communism in the future. On the other hand, the government section in general headquarters, headed by General Whitney, preferred strict application of the policy.[18]

In 1948, when the United States began to fashion an anti-communist policy in Japan, purge measures, like other SCAP's reforms, were altered accordingly. In 1949, the second Appeal Board set up by the Japanese government re-examined 32,000 cases and over 10,000 people were depurged. In 1950, shortly after the outbreak of the Korean war, 3,250 former army and navy officers were released from the purge.[19] At the same time, the occupation took a reverse step by ordering the 'red purge.' The editors of the *Akahata* (the Communist Party Daily) were purged and later the paper itself was suspended. All this was done in the name of the original directives. General MacArthur pointed out in his directive of June, 1950, to Prime Minister Yoshida, that there was a strong similarity between the methods and threats of the pre-war militarists and those of the post-war Communists. He thus suggested that there was no fundamental change in occupation policy. SCAP, which brought about a reorientation of the purge programme from one extreme of the political spectrum to the other, stretched its imagination too far. For whatever activities the Japanese Communists might have been responsible for in the past, war was certainly not one of them. What actually happened was that American objectives in Japan changed from time to time. The original aim of the purge was to facilitate the rise of liberal leadership in Japan; later the objective was changed to accommodate leaders who were willing to work within the parliamentary framework designed by the United States. Finally, the occupation authorities decided to encourage only those who were well-disposed toward the West in general and the United States in particular, to obtain position of power in Japanese Government.[20]

PROMULGATION OF THE NEW CONSTITUTION

The new constitution promulgated on 3 May 1947 was perhaps the single most important achievement of the occupation. For it brought to the Japanese people those basic human freedoms and privileges which had been denied to them by the militarists for decades. The Potsdam Declaration stated :

> The occupying forces of the Allies shall be withdrawn from Japan as soon as these objectives have been accomplished and there has been established in accordance with the freely expressed will of the Japanese people a peacefully inclined and responsible government.[21]

A fundamental change in the law of the land was imperative not only for the establishment of a democratic form of government, but also for the changes in the social and economic life of the country envisaged by the Post-Surrender policy. Therefore, early in the occupation, SCAP made informal suggestions to the Japanese leaders to take steps towards a revision of the Meiji Constitution.

Shortly after the surrender, on a reported suggestion by General MacArthur, Prince Konoye, a member of the Imperial family, took upon himself the task of revising the constitution.[22] He established an office in the Imperial Palace for this purpose. SCAP's officials denied the reported assignment given to the Prince by General MacArthur. Meanwhile, the Japanese Government constituted a committee known as the 'Constitutional Problem Investigation Committee' under the chairmanship of Joti Matsumoto, Minister without portfolio. The name of the committee explained its task. Matsumoto gathered around him a group of Japanese educationists and jurists and set to work.

The motley group that ruled Japan following the surrender knew that a revision of the Meiji constitution was inevitable and had prepared itself for a minor modification in the system.[23] Their main objective as has been observed was to preserve the Kokutai or the National polity, which actually meant the imperial institution.[24] The emperor system was the nerve center of Japanese politics. It had perpetuated the privileges of the ruling oligarchy over the centuries. Any change in the constitution for the better would mean the curtailment of the privileges of the ruling class. Therefore, the Matsumoto committee desired minimum alteration in the body politic. The conservative leaders also decided to employ all their mental and material resources to contain the political revolution set in motion by the occupation. They wrongly calculated that SCAP would be satisfied with a mere shuffling of the cards. After a protracted and scholarly discussion, the constitutional pundits made an interesting modification in the phraseology of the Meiji constitution. For instance, the Meiji constitution described the emperor as 'sacred and inviolable'; the committee decided to insert the words 'most exalted' in the place of 'sacred'.[25] It left the Privy Council untouched and retained the armed forces. The Matsumoto report did not include a Bill of Rights as was required by the Potsdam Declaration. In fact, it took away some of the few rights that had already existed by making them subordinate to statutory law. Briefly, what the

Committee did was to liberalize the language of the country's fundamental law. It left the body of the system in its loose and flexible form, open to such application and interpretation as the ruling group might see fit to apply.[26] This half-hearted attempt of the ruling party revealed the mind of its leaders.

While the Matsumoto committee was investigating the possibilities of a revision, other political parties and groups in Japan formulated their own views on the problem and published them in the newspapers and periodicals. The Progressive Party advocated continuance of the Imperial institution. Sovereignty remained in the emperor. It favoured a bicameral legislature and the responsibility of the cabinet to the parliament. In short, the Progressives proposed many structural changes in the body politic, retaining the organic law.[27]

The Social Democratic Party proposed that sovereignty should reside in the people. It provided for an extensive Bill of Rights with some economic guarantees and championed the supremacy of the parliament.[28] The Communists were in favour of abolition of the emperor system and the establishment of a republic.[29]

The reactionary proposals of the Matsumoto Committee perhaps came as a surprise to SCAP's officials. The Matsumoto committee's work was also sharply criticised by the Japanese press. On 3 February 1946 even a conservative paper like the *Nippon Times* made the following comment on the Matsumoto draft.

> Thus it is seen that all drafts made by political parties and others are demanding the democratization of the constitution, but the government plan, adopted by Dr. Matsumoto, has shown no intention to democratize it. If the government insists upon the adoption of the Matsumoto draft, public opinion will rise against it.[30]

Another conservative paper, *Nihon Keizai,* said on 1 March 1946 that :

> Shidehara Cabinet . . . is actually the champion of conservatism, and are carrying on the revision of the constitution

in such a manner as to maintain the National polity.[31]

Needless to say, all progressive groups in the country desired a drastic reform in the old system.

Without wasting further time on advice and directives, SCAP decided to write a draft constitution for the Japanese. The Government Section in the General Headquarters constituted a committee of highranking American officials for this purpose. Within the space of a few weeks, this curious constitutional convention of military and naval officers, lawyers, professors, and writers, produced a completely new constitution for the country.[32] Then a delegation headed by General Whitney, Chief of the Government Section, went to see the Japanese cabinet members, presented them with a few copies of the draft, and urged its adoption. The Japanese leaders were shocked and disturbed by the draft submitted by SCAP. It was reported that Dr. Matsumoto gave a veiled warning to SCAP's officials that fundamental revision in the constitution would shock the moderate elements in Japan severely and cause them to assume an antagonistic attitude toward democracy itself.[33] According to Yoshida Shigeru his colleagues in the cabinet and the party were not prepared to accept such a 'revolutionary document'.[34] However, out of sheer helplessness, the Shidehara government accepted the model constitution, translated it into Japanese, and said it was its own creation.

The new constitution was a document of cardinal importance. It was designed to reform political, judicial, and social systems of Japan along liberal-democratic lines. The twin objectives of the occupation—demilitarization and democratization found their concrete expression in it. Article Nine of the constitution renounced war as a 'sovereign right of the nation' and forbade the maintenance of 'land, sea and air forces' as well as other war potential.[35] This provision made a profound impression on the Japanese and was regarded by many in that country as a weapon of peace. The document also contained a detailed 'Bill of Rights.' Article 11 in Chapter III described these rights as 'eternal and inviolate'.[36] Thirty Articles out of the total of one hundred and three dealt with this matter. The right to life, liberty, and the pursuit of happiness was guaranteed. Academic freedom and the privilege to receive an education was assured. The significance of this right lies in the fact that it recognized the equality of sexes in matters of education. Safeguards were provided against unwarranted arrest and detention without adequate cause. Special emphasis was laid on the right of workers to organize and bargain collectively. The inclusion of these rights in the body of the Constitution was a revolutionary departure from the old system, in which duties, rather than rights, were more important. The 'Bill of Rights' was indeed a Japanese version of its American counterpart.

The Constitution was based on the conception of popular sovereignty. The preamble of the Constitution began with the words "We, the Japanese people, . . . do proclaim that sovereign power resides with the people and do firmly establish this constitution . . . ."[37] The emperor lost to the people his political powers and his sovereignty. He became the symbol of the state and of the unity of the people. The Constitution established a parliamentary system in which the Diet was the supreme law making body. The cabinet was responsible to the legislature. The House of Representatives was given precedence over the House of Councillors. The organic law also created an independent judiciary headed by a Supreme Court. Another innovation of the Constitution was the introduction of popular elections in local administration. Article Ninety-three, paragraph two, stated that "The chief executive officers of all local entities, the members of their assemblies, and other such officials as may be determined by law, shall be elected by direct popular vote within their several communities.[38] This, and other provisions regarding local government, reduced the supremacy of the National Government in local affairs.

Critics of the Constitution have maintained that it was dictated by the victors to the vanquished.[39] And the foregoing account leads us to the conclusion that it was mainly written by SCAP. The Japanese intelligentia knew that its origin was foreign. Certain expressions such as 'we, the Japanese people', and so on, were alien to Japanese traditions. At the same time, it should be noted that the Japanese also had a hand in shaping the Constitution. For instance, Article nine on the renunciation of war was incorporated on the suggestion of Baron Shidehara.[40] Secondly, the original draft issued by SCAP provided for an unicameral legislature. The House of Peers, through an amendment, succeeded in making the Diet a bicameral legislature. Moreover, the ideas and ideals expressed in the Constitution had been for long the platform of all progressive elements in Japan. In this sense, the Constitution was an expression of the free will of a majority of the Japanese people.

In May 1946, the *Maimichi Shimbum*, one of the leading newspapers of the country, conducted a survey of public opinion on the 'Draft of the New Constitution.' Two thousand intellectuals of both sexes were questioned on some of the important issues in the Constitution. Eighty-five percent of those questioned expressed satisfaction over the emperor system described in Articles 1 and 2 of the draft. (Table 2.1) Only eleven percent were in favour of abolishing the Imperial Institution.[41] Seventy-two percent thought the provision concerning the renunciation of war (Table 2.2) was necessary, while twenty-eight percent regarded it unnecessary.[42] Seventy-nine percent favoured a bicameral legislature and seventeen percent opposed it. On the issue of executive veto forty-seven percent agreed that the government of the emperor should enjoy a veto power over the legislative enactment; on the other hand, fifty-two percent were against giving any veto power to the executive. (Table 2.3)[43]

TABLE 2.1 : **The emperor system**

answers	persons	percentage
Those in favour of emperor system	1,702	85
Those favouring the abolition of the emperor system	215	11
Those opposing the abolition of the emperor system	1,711	86
Undecided	74	3.7
	2,000 n=2,000	100%

TABLE 2.2 : **On renunciation of war**

answers	persons	percentage
Necessary	1,395	72
Unnecessary	605	28
Some of the reasons given were : (1) there is no need of surrendering the right of self-defence, although agressive wars should be abandoned. (2) it is too utopian (3) such matters should be fixed by international treaties	n=2,000	100%

TABLE 2.3 : **On the power of the executive**

answers	persons	percentage
Favoured veto power to the executive	932	47
Opposed any veto power to the executive	1,034	52
Undecided	34	1
	2,000 n=2,000	100%

FREEDOM OF EXPRESSION

Freedom of expression was basic to all SCAP's programmes designed to introduce democracy in Japan. In the hey-day of militarism, the rulers of Japan tightly controlled the press and all other media of expression. When the allied powers occupied the country, the Japanese expected that the freedom of expression and the press would be restored. Informed people understood that this freedom would have to be used judiciously, especially with regard to the policies of SCAP in the country. However, on 10 September 1945, SCAP issued a press code prohibiting the publication of untruthful statements, destructive criticism of the allied powers, inviting mistrust and resentment of the occupation forces, and unauthorized discussion of troop movements.[44] It further stated that there should be absolute minimum restriction upon freedom of speech. Though the press was free to discuss domestic politics, it was not permitted to voice criticism of the occupation. Two weeks later SCAP issued another directive which ordered the Japanese government to lift barriers to dissemination of news and open communication facilities to all nations and international news agencies. At the same time the directive stated that the distribution of news within Japan would be permitted under strict censorship.[45]

According to the directive, the Japanese press was not supposed to publish any material which would be detrimental to the objectives of the occupation. What exactly the word 'detrimental' meant was left to the censors to decide. SCAP's officials in charge of censorship interpreted it variously depending on their mood and political outlook. Sometimes the officials carried censorship to absurd lengths. For example, they required the press to submit for approval such items as want ads, baseball scores, and weather forecasts.[46] The new officers who replaced the older and experienced people in SCAP's headquarters had very little knowledge of their jobs. Unsure of themselves, they would often refer news stories to the men upstairs. While half a dozen colonels looked into the matter, the news items became too stale to be published.[47] Sometimes the censors would take issue with a news story which originated from their compatriots in one of the military units in the country. Most of the censored items were of American origin. Walter Lippman's syndicated column was a frequent victim of SCAP's censorship.[48] A more serious charge against the censorship was that it did not allow the Japanese press to discuss freely such important reforms as the new constitution and dissolution of the zaibatsu in which the Japanese people had vital interest. Moreover the Japanese editors had no access to the officers in General Headquarters, and censors treated the Japanese working newsmen with polite disdain. Therefore, the press had to depend for news solely on official release. Under these meaningless pinpricks the fourth estate became highly cynical about its freedom and seriously doubted many of SCAP's claims of success in occupation policies. The Japanese newspapermen, out of despair and with a slight exaggeration, said that SCAP's 'censorship was worse than the old Japanese military censorship.'[49]

MacArthur's subordinates and admirers in General Headquarters being highly sensitive to any criticism of their supreme commander and anxious to protect the General from alleged criticism at times over-reached themselves. For instance on 11 October 1946 the *Jiji Shimpo*, an evening newspaper of Tokyo, wrote an editorial commenting on the book *The Life of General MacArthur*, which had been a best seller in Japan since the end of the war. The editor pointed out that there was a danger in the extreme adoration in which MacArthur was held by some Japanese. Further, the editorial stated that the hero-worshippers might search for a living god after the General had left the country. Finally it concluded by saying that:

> The way to express the gratitude of the Japanese people to General MacArthur for the wisdom with which he is managing post-war Japan and for his efforts to democratize the nation is not to worship him as a God or as a hero, but to cast away that very servile spirit and to gain self-respect that would bow the head to no one, and to take hold of the power of government themselves. Only thus would General MacArthur rest content that the aims of the occupation have been achieved."[50]

The censors approved the editorial. The following day the *Nippon Times*, an English daily, reprinted the new article on MacArthur. As soon as the morning edition was out, the head of the G2 section, General Willoughby, mounted his horse and went in all directions ordering the burning of 50,000 copies of the newspaper. He also prohibited its later publication. For General Willoughby, MacArthur was no less than a demi-god. Even foreign correspondents, who were mostly Americans, frequently complained about the intolerance of the censors. No foreign correspondent with a critical eye on the occupation could live in peace in Tokyo.[51] Surprisingly enough, when General MacArthur was questioned on the issue, he denied the very existence of censorship.[52] In this way SCAP provided useful lessons in democracy to Japanese bureaucrats, pressmen, and all others who were closely watching the performance of the occupation authorities. The Japanese newspapers took full advantage of the new but restricted freedom and came out with sensational stories mixing rumour with fact. The Civil Information and Education section in General Headquarters made elaborate arrangements for distribution of news on occupation policies and foreign affairs. The National Press Association of Publishers and Editors adopted a code of journalism modelled on a similar code in the United States.

SCAP dug a gold mine in radio. The State-controlled radio network was re-organized into a corporation. Within a short time the radio artists made broadcasting lively and interesting by adopting the American techniques of interviews and comments from the listeners. Between them the press and the radio contributed substantially to the re-education of the Japanese.

FREEDOM OF RELIGION

In the pre-war days a close relationship existed between *Shintoism* and ultranationalism. The Emperor was the high priest of the State-sponsored shinto.[53] The ultranationalistic militarists distorted shinto and turned it into a virile militaristic philosophy. It described the sovereign as a divine human being and stated that it was the sacred mission of Japan to rule Asia.[54] The problem before SCAP was to expurgate ultranationalistic preachings from Shintoism.

SCAP established the freedom of religious belief through a directive issued on 4 October 1945. Another directive issued on 15 December 1945 called for the separation of Shinto from the State, the prevention of misuse of religion for political ends, and the establishment of the equality of all religions.[55] Accordingly, the Japanese Government expunged all Shinto preaching from public school text book and removed all Shinto symbols from public buildings. SCAP ordered the government to remove the portraits of the emperor and the empress from school premises. It also eliminated the imperial chrysanthemum from postage stamps and currency. With a view to root out all vestiges of connection between the state and religion the government began the complex task of transferring land titles from the state to religious organizations. It involved 200,000 acres of state-owned land occupied by approximately 110,000 Shinto Shrines and 40,000 Buddhist temples.[56] Also under order from SCAP, the Japanese Government displaced 8,000 monuments with ultranationalistic connotations.[57]

The Emperor took an unusual step by denouncing his divinity in a rescript issued on the New Year Day, 1946. He stated that :

> The ties between us and our people have always stood upon mutual trust and affection, they do not depend upon mere legends and myths. They are not predicted on the false conception that the Emperor is divine and that the Japanese people are superior to other races and fated to rule the world.[58]

At the same time, MacArthur gave encouragement to foreign Christian missionaries to spread the Christian faith in Japan. He believed that the propagation of the Christian ideal of brotherhood of man and the dignity of the individual would strengthen democratic movement in the country.[59] At his request, the Pocket Testament League distributed 10,000,000 Bibles in Japanese.[60] In view of this overt encouragement given to the Christian missionaries, perhaps it would not be incorrect to say that MacArthur was partial to the Christian faith. By June 1950 there were approximately 2,500 Christian missionaries in Japan.[61] The indigenous religions also set out to revive the faith of their followers. The well-organized Tenrikyo faith under the leadership of Shozen Nakayama seriously challenged the aspirations of Christianity to become the leading religion of Japan.[62]

LABOUR REFORMS

The zeal of the occupation authorities to demoralize Japan was never more apparent than in the case of the development of the trade union movement. SCAP's officials wanted labour to have a greater stake and an influential voice in Japanese politics. The Initial Post-Surrender policy for Japan laid down that encouragement should be given and favour shown to the "development of organizations in labour, industry and agriculture organized on a democratic basis."[63] In accordance with this directive, SCAP called on the Japanese government to encourage the organization of labour unions. Thereupon the Diet passed a series of laws concerning labour problems. The Trade Union Law, promulgated in December 1945, gave the unions the right to organize, to bargain, and to strike. The Labour Relation Adjustment Law provided means for the peaceful settlement of disputes. It created committees consisting of the representatives of management and labour for this purpose at the central and prefectural level. The task of these labour bodies was to investigate working conditions, summon witnesses, hold public hearings, and so forth. The labour standard law abolished feudal customs regarding the working conditions of the labour class and incorporated the minimum standards for labour, such as eight-hour working days, weekly rest, and paid holidays.[64] These laws were progressive in nature and together constituted a charter of freedom for Japanese workers. With these new opportunities, and under eager encouragement from SCAP's officials, trade unions had a mushroom growth. In little more than a year labour had grown from complete obscurity into a force capable of exerting a considerable influence on the government. During 1945-46 membership in labour unions grew from 126,000 to nearly four and one-half million.[65] The organization of two labour federations during the summer of 1946 both stimulated the awakening of a political consciousness among the workers and produced a clearer demarcation between progressive and conservative Labour groups. The first of these groups was the all-Japan Federation of Labour, with 905,000 members at the time of its inception. It gave strong political support to the Social Democratic Party. The rival organization, the Congress of Industrial Union, was set up at approximately the same time with a membership of 1,600,000. Its sympathies were reported to be with the Communist Party.[66]

In the unsettled economic conditions of Japan following the surrender, the working class was hard pressed. Especially 1946 was a turbulent year for Japanese labour. The rising cost of living, due to lack of food and inflation, forced the workers to improve their economic condition through strikes. Four hundred and fifty-four strikes occurred in one year.[67] It is interesting to note that the Japanese added some of their own innovations to the standard practices. For example, workers in the *Yomiuri Shimbun*, one of the leading newspapers of Japan, took over the management. Street car employees struck without quitting work, they continued service as a public duty, but refused to accept fares until their demands were met. One railroad union protested by blowing the whistles on all trains in Japan for one minute at the same time.

Representing the industrialists and big business, the Japanese Government sought to retard the growth of labour unions from the beginning. Knowing the unsympathetic attitude of the ruling party toward the working people's movement, SCAP's officials in General Headquarters closely supervised the labour legislation, showing interest even in minor details.[68] The conservative leaders did not have the strength to oppose SCAP's directives; therefore, they grudgingly accepted them. When the unions demanded better working conditions and higher wages, the government named them trouble makers. It was alleged by the oligarchs that the unions were not so much interested in developing a healthy trade union movement as in creating a political and social revolution in the country.[69] The ruling party's hostility to the workers was so strong that in 1946 the conservative government, headed by Shigeru Yoshida, refused to organize a labour ministry despite repeated suggestions by SCAP to that effect. The same year the government rejected the recommendations of the Central Labour Relation's Committee on the demands of the Electric Power Workers Union. This stubborn attitude of the government created tension and uneasiness among the workers. When the union threatened to strike in the face of refusals, the government leaders called them irresponsible and rebellious and likened the labour leadership to the military cliques of the old days.[70] It also employed police force to break up demonstrations.

A National Struggle Committee was formed by the major trade unions in the country to fight the government's refusal to accept their grievances. The committee (NSC) decided to call a general strike on 1 February 1947. As the date of the proposed strike approached and preparation began, tension in the country mounted. The government tried to upset the strike by adopting various questionable means. When these attempts failed to discredit the labour leaders, the ruling liberal party began to organize a counter-offensive against the unions. The chairman of the strike committee, received letters threatening his life. The oligarchs tried to revive the old methods of intimidation by hiring gangsters to do the job. For instance, the president of the National Congress of Industrial Union was stabbed by two men belonging to the "Shin-ei Taishuto, a reactionary organization run by a known gangster with strong arm men for hire".[71] A few hours before the scheduled strike, MacArthur issued a statement prohibiting the proposed strike. He said :

> Under the authority vested in me as supreme commander for the Allied Powers, I have informed the labour leaders whose unions have federated for the purpose of conducting a general strike that I will not permit the use of so deadly a social weapon in the present impoverished and emaciated condition of Japan, and have accordingly directed them to desist from the furtherance of such action.[72]

It was alleged by the opponents of labour that the strike was more political than economic; further, the right to strike did not include political strike.[73] The defenders of labour pointed out that if strikes employed by labour are labelled political then it would be impossible to use the weapon effectively. Also, it was hard to separate economics from politics. Moreover, labour's economic condition was determined by political policy in most countries.[74] Incidentally, it is interesting to note that the Far Eastern Commission in its recommendation on principles for Japanese trade unions said among other things that "trade unions should be allowed to take part in political activities and support political parties".[75] The *Far Eastern Economic Review* made the following comment on the issue.

> The truth of the matter is that Japanese labour has recently been forced to take what is termed political

action only because specific political action has been taken against it both by the Japanese government and by general headquarters.[76]

The abortive strike was followed by a so-called democratization movement in the various labour unions. This movement was inspired by SCAP, and it was in reality an anti-communist campaign. The postal union workers planned a general strike in June, 1948. Once again SCAP stepped in and ordered that the strike be called off.

In July of the same year General MacArthur wrote a letter to Prime Minister Ashida, suggesting that the National Public Service Law should be amended and a distinction be made between the public servants and other employees.[77] In addition, certain generals in General Headquarters gave specific oral instructions to the Japanese Prime Minister concerning steps to be taken against organized labour.[78] Accordingly on 31 July the Japanese Government issued an ordinance which outlawed all types of disputes in all branches of government activity, terminated all collective bargaining agreements existing between the government workers' unions and various agencies of the Japanese Government. It also established drastic jail sentences and military fines for anyone violating the terms of the ordinance. In November 1948 the Japanese Government, through an amendment to the Public Service Law, finally deprived public servants, who represented over one third of organized labour, of their right to collective bargaining and their right to strike. This act terminated SCAP's liberal labour policy in Japan. In June 1949 the Labour Union Law was revised. It made violent activities on the part of both employers and employees illegal. The amended law also stated that justifiable actions should be respected. However, it did not say what constituted justifiable actions. James S. Killen, Chief of the labour division in General Headquarters, resigned in protest against SCAP's anti-labour policy.

In a statement Killen said :

Officials in the American occupation forces publicly ruled that where two or more workers simultaneously terminated

> their employment with the government they are committing an act of dispute and are subject to the penalties of the cabinet order; and there are today countless warrants of arrest circulating throughout Japan, against workers who sought to improve their wages and working conditions by voluntarily terminating their government employment.... I certainly would be in great error were I to seek to minimize the efforts of the communists to touch not only the government workers' unions, but many of the unions in Japan. I submit, however, that this action so taken serves not to weaken or cripple the communist influence in those unions but gives the communists ammunition for their propaganda campaign against the occupation. It strengthens their hand in accusing the United States government of being anti-labour and not desirous of advancing the interest of Japanese workers.[79]

A wave of protest was raised both in the United States and Japan against SCAP's reversed policy toward labour. The Americans for Democratic Action condemned "General MacArthur's reactionary labour policy".[80] The American Federation of Labour called on the United States to "discontinue repressive action, which is being carried on under the guise of anti-Communism against the legitimate trade union objectives and practices, and move against the Japanese Communist party itself by exposing and prosecuting the illegal and anti-democratic activities of the party".[81] John W. Gibson, the United States Assistant Secretary of Labour said that "I have no hesitancy in saying that the National Public Service Act went too far in some fields".[82]

In Japan the Socialist and Communist Parties violently opposed the restrictions on Labour. Even conservative leaders described the measure as repressive.[83] It was a serious blow to the labour movement in the country. The rank and file of the unions were dumbfounded. The disappointment of the workers slowly hardened into distrust and resentment of the occupation. With the passage of time the traditional hostility of the Japanese conservative elements toward labour, which had been restrained earlier by occupation policies, began to reassert itself. In the summer of 1949, the emphasis of the Japanese Government shifted from illegal activities to political activities by trade unions. In June 1950, the Labour Ministry was reported to have sent instructions to prefectural governors to put down all political activities of the unions.[84] This step of the Japanese Government violated the Far Eastern Commission's instruction to Supreme Commander for Allied Powers, which stated that "no police or other government agencies should be employed in spying on workers, breaking strikes, or suppressing legitimate union activities".[85] The Japanese Government's aggressive attitude toward the unions and the employers' resistance to labour's demands resulted in disunity and dislocation in the working class movement. A large number of local unions died and by June 1950 union membership dropped to 5,839,000.[86]

By the end of 1950, the five-year-trade union movement brought very little improvement in the economic conditions of labour. But it had achieved for the working class a position of power and strength in the political life of the country.[87] Despite all the repressive measures taken by the government against the unions, labour remained as a force to be reckoned with.

DISSOLUTION OF THE ZAIBATSU

Throughout the modern history of Japan the Zaibatsu had dominated the industrial, financial, and commercial life of that country. Ten main family combines controlled ninety per cent of the nation's industry.[88] Enjoying preferential treatment from the government, these business houses held down wages, blocked labour unions, directed the political parties, and became active partners in the imperial adventure of the Japanese army. They were practically an arm of the government, and through their control of financing and marketing they exercised the power of life and death over small business.[89] Since domestic consumption could not keep pace with the increased productivity of the nation's industry because of low wages and concentration of profits, the surplus industrial goods created a need for the expansion of foreign markets and the drive for exports had been an outstanding motive behind Japanese imperialism.[90]

The United States government report on reparation described the Zaibatsu as "the greatest potential of Japan's conquest and aggression".[91] On the other hand, Reischauer and others questioned this contention.[92] It is beyond the scope of this work to discuss the chief reasons for Japanese imperialism. Nevertheless, the Zaibatsu system was undoubtedly uncongenial to the growth of political and social democracy in Japan.

The initial United States Post-Surrender Policy for Japan called for the encouragement of democratic organizations in industry and favoured a wider distribution of income and of the ownership of the means of production and trade. It further stated that "To this end it shall be the policy of the supreme commander:

(a) To prohibit the retention in or selection for places of importance in the economic field of individuals who do not direct future Japanese economic effort solely towards peaceful ends; and

(b) To favour a program for the dissolution of the large industrial and banking combines which have exercised control of a great part of Japan's trade and industry."[93]

The programme for dissolution of the Zaibatsu and the deconcentration of economic power, therefore, was an integral part of the larger programme for the demilitarization of Japan.

In September 1945, SCAP directed the Japanese Government to prepare a report on all industrial, manufacturing, and mining companies which had transacted business worth more than a million yen prior to the surrender. The four big companies, Mitsui, Mitsubishi, Yasuda and Sumitomo, took a cue from this directive and after consulting the officials of SCAP and the Japanese Government submitted a proposal for voluntary dissolution of the combines. Supreme Commander for Allied Powers (SCAP), in its directive issued on 6 November 1945, approved the proposal in general, and directed the Japanese Government to supervise its operation. It also instructed the Japanese government to prepare a plan which would eliminate the large trusts and combines with inter-locking directorates.[94] The government was to set up a Holding Company Liquidation

Commission. This commission was to take over the securities held by those holding companies of the Zaibatsu beginning with the big four, designated for dissolution. The securities were to be sold to the public. The idea was to provide for wider ownership in industry and wider distribution of income. Compensation was to be paid to the Zaibatsu owners of the securities.

Meanwhile the State and War Departments jointly sent a mission of experts on financial and industrial problems to Japan. Its assignment was to study the Zaibatsu problem and recommend to the two departments standards, policies, and procedures for carrying out the basic objectives concerning the combines. The next important step in the dissolution of the Zaibatsu was the extension of the purge in January, 1947 to include prominent persons in the financial and business world.[95]

In order to prevent the emergence of a new Zaibatsu, the Diet passed a series of laws prohibited private monopoly in trade, defined fair trade practices, and made mergers, interlocking of directorates, and other old Zaibatsu practices, illegal. The legislation also provided for a commission to enforce the new laws and to establish industry-wide codes. The most significant aspect of these legislative enactments was the law on the "measures for decentralization of industries with excessive economic power". It was based on Directive 230 presented to the Far Eastern Commission by the United States. It came to be known by its file number FEC 230.[96] As the contents of FEC 230 became known, its recommendations came under sharp criticism in the United States. A prominent New York lawyer, after visiting Japan on behalf of his business clients, described the measure as un-American and socialistic. He also claimed that the economic purge had drained the country of its business brain and had made the economic recovery of Japan difficult.[97] Senator Knowland of California demanded a congressional investigation of the economic policy of the occupation.

In December 1948 the United States withdrew its support of the draft directive FEC 230 in the commission on the ground that the programme might do more harm than good. And the officials of the Defense Department openly expressed opposition to the deconcentration measures.[98] This denunciation of

SCAP's policy in the United States immensely pleased the critics of the occupation in Japan.

Prime Minister Yoshida and his friends in the Zaibatsu were opposed to the programme right from the beginning. In a statement to foreign correspondents in Tokyo in 1945 Yoshida said that:

> it would be a great mistake to regard Japan's financial leaders as a bunch of criminals, that the nation's economic structure was built by such old-established and major financial concerns as Mitsui and Mitsubishi, and that modern Japan owed her prosperity largely to their endeavours, so that it was most doubtful whether the Japanese people would benefit from the disintegration of these concerns.[99]

The industrial magnates and the government leaders employed dubious means to circumvent the deconcentration programme. For instance, Supreme Commander for Allied Powers directives were deliberately distorted and linguistic difficulties were offered as reasons for misunderstanding.[100] The purged captains of industry retired to their villas in the countryside. But their subordinates in the office frequently visited them for instructions which were scrupulously carried out. As one author has put it:

> In the spirit of the bamboo philosophy, bending to the storm, they feigned acceptance of orders dissolving the Zaibatsu combines and cartels, but with an eye to the future they fitted the ownership and controls into a colossal jigsaw whose pattern was visible only to its authors.[101]

The purgees privately admitted that reforms had little effect on the Zaibatsu.[102] It was business as usual.

The cold war that developed between the United States and the Soviet Union in late 1947 quickly gave business leaders the opportunity to regain their position. They began to lobby in the occupation circles in Tokyo for support in building their assets under the guise of economic recovery, and had their sympathizers in Washington work for cessation of the programme.

Incidentally, it is interesting to note that, in February 1947, SCAP extended more than three billion yen credit to seventeen Zaibatsu companies for the extension of their chemical fertilizer plants. The Showa Electric industry, one of the designated holding companies with sixteen subsidiaries, received nearly half of the credit.[103] Also, at the same time, the great Zaibatsu concerns were contracting for the supply of materials to the occupation forces.

Besides, Supreme Commander for Allied Powers' (SCAP's) officials were confronted with practical difficulties in the implementation of the deconcentration programme. The Zaibatsu system was a complex institution built over the years by competent business brains in Japan. Officials in General Headquarters in Tokyo did not possess thorough knowledge of the working of the Zaibatsu and therefore had to depend on the information supplied to them by the combines themselves. Inflation and poverty created difficulties for prospective buyers of the securities. Only two percent of the securities held by the government had been resold by the end of 1947.[104] Moreover, the top Japanese bureaucrats who actually executed the programme were hostile to the objectives of the occupation and did not hide their displeasure over the directives that flowed from General Headquarters day after day.[105]

The result was that the deconcentration programme became one of the most controversial reforms both in Japan and the United States and was the first reform to be abandoned.

In April 1948 the Japanese Diet revised the law on excessive concentration of economic power. Early in 1948 the Holding Company Liquidation Commission had listed 325 companies as falling under the deconcentration law; of these two hundred, ninety-five were quickly disposed of as not being excessive according to law. Eleven were ordered to be divided into independent companies, seven were directed to divest themselves of certain properties, ten had not received any orders by 1950, and two were dissolved not under deconcentration law but under other legislation.[106] To cap all this, in the summer of 1949, MacAurthur officially announced that Zaibatsu reform had been completed.

The deconcentration programme like other socio-economic

reforms became a casualty of the cold war. The question that arises from this brief survey of the attempts at the dissolution of the Zaibatsu is what did they actually accomplish ? The scope of the book does not permit a detailed analysis of the ramification of the companies involved in the programme. However, certain net results of it should be noted. The deconcentration law affected some twenty-five of the biggest operating companies, distribution of shares covered holding companies and a large number of their subsidiaries and the capital levy imposed on the wealth of the shareholders in the Zaibatsu froze the assets of fifty-six members of the financial houses for ten years. Finally, several thousand officials were barred from holding top positions in one hundred and eighty-seven companies.[107] Thus, seen in summary the programme was quite extensive in scope. Nevertheless, according to one of the authors of the reform "the net effect was far less drastic than would appear".[108]

In 1953 the conservative government further revised the deconcentration law and enacted other legislation facilitating the emergence of new cartels.[109] These new financial centers have come to wield extensive influence over the political and economic structure of the country.[110]

LAND REFORMS

Since the beginning of its modern history, Japan had been ruled by an oligarchy consisting of five groups : (1) The military and naval officers, (2) The Zaibatsu, (3) The top bureaucrats, (4) The leaders of the conservative political parties and (5) The big landlords.[111] These groups worked in co-operation with each other, suppressed liberal thought and democracy, and ruled the country with an iron hand in the name of the emperor. Rural Japan constituted the backbone of this oligarchy. In terms of capital investment and net value of output, agriculture was by far the country's leading industry. Further, the agricultural population, more than any other group in the country, showed the 'spirit and habit of feudalism'.[112] The peasant owed an unquestioned loyalty to the emperor, the symbol of the oligarchy, and through him to his representatives.

The landlords and the local bureaucrats controlled the peasants in the name of the state symbol. Farm families lived in abject poverty and were chained to the land by crushing debts inherited from their forefathers.

Three per cent of the farm owners possessed thirty per cent of the cultivated land one-half of the tenanted land. Tenants and part tenants constituted seventy percent of the 5,700,000 Japanese farm families.[113] Fifty per cent of the tenants rented, on an average, one-half acre of land. Intense competition among the tenants for land had kept the rentals high—fifty percent of the rice crop and only slightly less of other crops.[114] As farm families grew bigger, and unemployment increased, young people of the rural community were forced to move to urban areas, providing cheap labour for industry and tough men for the army.

The allied powers recognized the undemocratic and reactionary influence of the landlords on the country's politics and also saw the misery of the tenants. In pursuance of the initial United States Post-Surrender Policy of "wide distribution of income and ownership," on 9 December 1945, SCAP issued a directive which called for the extermination of "those pernicious ills which have so long blighted the agrarian structure of a land where almost half the total population is engaged in husbandry".[115] It directed the Japanese Government "to take measures to incure that those who till the soil of Japan shall have a more equal opportunity to enjoy the fruits of their labour," not as an end in itself but in order to "remove economic obstacles to the revival and strengthening of democratic tendencies, establish respect for the dignity of man, and destroy the economic bondage which has enslaved the Japanese farmer to centuries of feudal oppression".[116]

In order to pacify the occupation authorities, the Diet passed a land reform bill in December 1945, and submitted it to SCAP for its perusal. Supreme Commander for Allied Powers' (SCAP's) officials expressed sharp dissatisfaction with the programme, but forwarded the Japanese proposals to the Allied Council for discussion. The British Commonwealth member in the Council made a number of suggestions on the agrarian reform which were accepted by the American officers.[117]

After persistent pressure from SCAP the Diet enacted two bills, the special measure for the Establishment of Owner-Farmer, and Agricultural Land Adjustment Law in October 1946. The first bill defined the land available for transfer to new owners and the methods to effect the transfer. The law required the absentee landlords to sell off all their lands. It put a ceiling on land holding for cultivators and non-cultivators in Honshu, Kyushu and Shikoku, at the rate of seven and one-half and two and one-half acres respectively, while in Hokkaido the ceiling was thirty and ten acres respectively.[118] Tenant cultivators received first option on the purchase of the land and could buy it outright or pay for it in thirty annual installments at three and two tenths percent interest. The government was to act as both the purchasing and the selling agent. The price of the land to be acquired by the government for distribution was fixed at the rate of 757.60 per tan (.245 acres) for paddy fields and 464.98 per tan for upland farms. The landlords were to be paid in the form of bonds spread over thirty years. The second law a revision of the Land Adjustment Law of 1938, prohibited rentals above twenty-five percent of the value of the crop in the case of paddy field, and fifteen per cent in the case of upland farm.[119] In order to prevent the arbitrary eviction of tenants by landlords, the law required all future leases to be written agreements.

The land reform law also provided for the establishment of a land commission in each village, town, and city for the supervision of the actual purchase and sale of lands. These commissions would consist of equal numbers of landlords and tenants, to be elected, and additional members to be selected by agreement of these elected. In an effort to invalidate improper transfer, the reform was made retroactive from November 1945.

While welcoming the new reforms, General MacArthur said in a statement that :

> It marks the beginning of the end of an outmoded agricultural system that has persisted from time immemorial. If its letter and spirit are faithfully carried out, Japanese

farmers will find in it their long awaited Bill of Rights.[120]

The agriculture reforms cut at the very root of oligarchic control of the rural population. Therefore, from the beginning, landlords and their friends in the government steadily refused to make any changes in the rural structure. As it has already been observed, under pressure from SCAP the Japanese Government adopted in December 1945 a mild land reform bill which was finally rejected by the occupation authorities. Even those minor modifications in the land system proposed in the bill met with stern resistance of the landlords and their representatives in the Diet at that time.[121] The fight was so important that the legislators were pressed into it even when most of them were so frightened by the political purge that they were willing to obey SCAP's orders promptly on other matters.

When evasion and half-hearted attempts did not work, the old guard accepted the Allied Council's proposals on land reform under the special circumstances prevailing in the country at that time.[122] Nineteen forty-six was a dangerous year in Japanese politics. Urban workers, pressed by economic hardships, were becoming more and more militant under the new freedom given to them by SCAP. There was an acute shortage of food in the country. The labour unions organized a Food May Day parade on the 19th of May 1946. On that day workers in hundreds of thousands gathered on the grounds of the Imperial Palace waving red flags and shouting revolutionary slogans. Some of them entered the Imperial Palace and demanded an audience with the emperor. Conservative leaders were frightened by the revolutionary fervor of the working class movement. The guardians of the old order calculated that if the peasants in the countryside joined hands with their brothers in the cities, the consequence would be disastrous. This would happen should the rural discontent be aroused by the working class movement.[123] Therefore, in order to prevent a possible socio-economic revolution of the workers and peasants, the ruling group yielded to SCAP's pressures.

The landlords criticised the reforms as "penalizing the thrifty, the efficient and the mentally better endowed."[124] They predicted that the reforms would bring economic and cultural deterioration in the countryside. The land owners argued that transfer of ownership of land to the tenants was a poor exchange for the security the farmer provided to the latter. Perhaps 'security' in the vocabulary of the landlords was synonymous with debts, since in times of distress the peasants could always borrow money from the lords. An interesting comment was added to this criticism of the agrarian reforms by the chief of the Hommas, a well-known landowning family in Japan. He said that "without their land the Hommas will be the most lone-some men in the world".[125] The landlords also complained that their land was being bought at a mere fraction of its value because of inflated currency. Japanese Communists criticised the land reforms as mild and regarded the compensation to be paid to the landlords as excessive.[126]

According to an American official the Japanese Government's attitude toward the agrarian reform was lukewarm. This was reflected in the appointment of Kozen Hirokawa as Minister of Agriculture in January 1949. Hirokawa all along opposed the agricultural reorganization and made his views known during the parliamentary debates on the issue.[127] Japanese sources indicated that Prime Minister Yoshida's intention in the appointment was to strengthen his position in the Liberal Party.[128] However, the Minister made use of his office to limit the scope of the reforms.[129] In 1949 he tried to halt the land registration programme ostensibly for economic reasons. The real intention was to delay the programme. Then he proposed to merge the land commissions with the Agricultural Adjustment Commission, on which the tenants had no representation. Again in October 1949 he attempted to remove or transfer those officials in the ministry who lent their enthusiastic support to the reform and tried to push forward the implementation of it. As a result the matters in the Ministry of Agriculture came to a head.[130] General MacArthur, in his message to the Japanese on the occasion of the anniversary of the land reform bill, warned the subverters of the reform.[131]

While the Minister for Agriculture was trying his best to circumvent the reforms, the landlords were exercising considerable influence on the Land Commission, and thus helped slow down the programme. Taking advantage of the low level of political consciousness and social conservatism of the farmers, rural chiefs attempted to intimidate them.[132] Out of fear and apathy the tenants did not exercise their newly-won rights in the beginning. Many of the seats on the Land Commission could not be filled because a large number of tenants failed to vote. Others showed reluctance to desert the past for a gamble on invested freedom. When SCAP, through its education programme, sought to explain the significance of the agriculture reform to the general mass of the people, the fears of the tenants slowly melted away. Rural communities began to show some interest in the program.[133]

By 1951 approximately three million cultivator-tenants or part tenants acquired in ownership a total area of four to five million acres of land. Nearly eighty-nine per cent of all arable land in Japan came to be controlled by the farming families who lived on it.[134] Another aspect of the agriculture programme was the law on co-operative farming enacted by the Diet in December 1947. Under this law the government-managed pre-war co-operative farming system was dissolved and co-operative farming on a voluntary basis was encouraged. By mid 1949 there were 32,000 such co-operatives.[135]

The agriculture reform marked a peaceful revolution in the social and economic pattern of Japanese agriculture. "It broke the power of the landlords who far so many years had controlled the social life of Japanese farm villages and brought a new period of development to Japanese agriculture".[136] In other words it transformed the Japanese peasant into a *petit bougeoisie* who had a small investment in the total life of the nation, and, therefore, had a stake in the existing order. From the political point of view it set into motion a process of great importance which might ultimately bring a momentous change in the power structure of the country. This process was already visible in 1947. The pre-war Farmers' Union, which was revived after the occupation, had an officially-estimated membership of 1,300,000 with 5500 local chapters by the end of 1947.[137]

Soon the right wing in the union walked out and formed a rival National Farmer's Union. Together these unions had 85 members in the Diet and they formed a significant voting block in the nation's parliament. It was an indication of the beginning of a shift in the political power of rural Japan. Conservative leaders quickly noticed the organized strength of the peasants. In an attempt to weaken the Farmers' Union and draw the peasants into conservative politics, the ruling party sponsored a third farmers' forum called the "All-Japan Farmer's Union."

As the occupation approached its end, the fate of the agriculture reform, like all other measures introduced by SCAP, remained uncertain. Whether the establishment would reverse the whole process of reform time alone could tell. But the conservatives by their utterances and actions made it very clear that they did not like the changes. For the time being the battle was postponed for another try another day.[138]

EDUCATIONAL REFORMS

In the pre-war days, the Japanese militarist used education as a tool to indoctrinate the younger generation. When the army ruled the country, the Ministry of Education was headed by a high-ranking general and the education department tightly controlled the nation's schools and colleges. "Pre-war education tried to distort that basic human spirit which gives importance to individual's life, liberty and pursuit of happiness. The goal of education was to pluck out any awareness one had of human rights and prevent the development of individual consciousness and insight. To accomplish these goals, educations' role was to make man believe that the individual in Japanese society is completely without rights and he has to give himself up wholly to the state which transcends the individual. It taught that man's role was to give his life to the divine Emperor".[139] This concept of education was embodied in the Imperial Rescript on Education promulgated on 30 October 1890.[140] To the Japanese ruling oligarchy, education meant acquisition of knowledge rather than development of mind, the teaching of what to think rather than how to think.[141] Japanese accorded the student and the college graduate a high social position and made a college degree a badge of honour. At the same time they perpetuated a social system which frowned upon any questioning of the authority sanctioned by mythology and age. Supreme Commander for Allied Powers (SCAP) regarded educational reform as fundamental to its programme of democratization of the country. The Potsdam Declaration provided that obstacles to the revival and strengthening of democratic tendencies among the Japanese people should be removed. Accordingly, on 22 October 1945 SCAP issued a directive on the "administration of the Educational System of Japan." The directive stated that the content of education should be examined entirely and that instruction in schools and colleges should be "in harmony with representative government, international peace, the dignity of the individual and such fundamental human rights as the freedom of assembly, speech, and religion ..." It ordered the expulsion of teachers who were exponents of militarism and ultranationalism. Further it directed the Japanese government that persons who were previously dismissed for reasons of liberal or antimilitaristic opinions be made eligible for reappointment.[142]

In March 1946 the United States sent a mission of educators to Japan. After a three-week study of that country's educational problems, the mission made a series of recommendations on the re-organization of the system. It called for a basic alteration of the content and methods of instruction and recommended decentralization of the educational system. On 27 March 1947 the United States, State Department issued a policy statement on Japanese education based on the recommendations of the Education Commission. Thereupon the Diet passed a law on school education in March 1947. It emphasized individual initiative and inquiry, guaranteed academic freedom, and accorded equal educational opportunities for all. In addition, the law provided for a uniform system of education, six years of lower secondary school, three years of higher secondary school, and four years of university. The upper range for compulsory education was extended to nine years and co-education was permitted even after the primary school.[143] It sought another basic change, the decentralization of the control of education, through the formation of local elective school boards responsible to the community. The once-powerful Ministry of Education was reduced to the status of a co-ordinating body.

Supreme Commander for Allied Powers' (SCAP's) officials also broadened the academic curricula, revised the textbooks, and introduced new teaching methods. As has been observed pictures of the emperor and the empress were removed from the schools and enforced visits of children to Shinto Shrines were stopped. The American officers introduced social studies in place of courses on Japanese morals and history which were used by the militarist for nationalistic indoctrination. Great emphasis was placed on vocational education. In an effort to re-educate the Japanese people, SCAP established night schools and libraries, and parent-teacher associations were organized. The Civil Information and Education Section in General Headquarters tried to implant the American system of boards of trustees for Japanese universities. The educational circles in the country resisted the trusteeship concepts, and, therefore, SCAP finally dropped it.[144]

Japanese teachers unaccustomed to American Educational practice, on which the new system was modeled, were baffled and confused. The older teachers were unfriendly to the new system and doubted its usefulness. The younger instructors enthusiastically welcomed the reforms and co-operated with SCAP's officials. These two opposing groups of teachers distrusted each other and questioned one another's motives.[145] Dearth of text-books, shortage of trained teachers, and lack of classroom facilities presented difficulties in the implementation of the programme. A great number of teachers were hastely and poorly trained and, as a result of this, academic standards fell.

The Japanese government argued that the country, in view of its impoverished condition, could not afford a nine-year compulsory education. Then the Prime Minister Ashida was reported to have told the prefectural authorities that there was "no need of adopting the costly new system, because the Americans soon will be gone anyway".[146] Conservative leaders criticised the new system as lacking in content and aim.[147] Further, it was urged that reforms undermined parental discipline, national loyalty, and personal morals. The top bureaucrats, products of the old system, did not like the changes and resisted them. The old guard, alarmed by the popularity of progressive teachers on campus, accused them of being Communists. The Japan teacher's union became a special target of conservative attack.[148] Critics of the new system pointed out that the country's educational system was mistakenly subjected to Americanization because the American model was not always the best.[149]

In the fall of 1949, when the CISE officials began to pressure Universities to dismiss alleged Communists and leftists on their faculties, education reforms suffered a great set-back. High-ranking members of SCAP toured the nation's schools and universities preaching anti-Communist philosophy. These methods of American occupation authorities did not differ greatly from the techniques used by the Japanese army during the war.[150] The anti-Communist campaign hardly impressed the Japanese intellectuals in favour of freedom. In fact, it weakened the influence of democratic elements in Japanese society. The difference between the preaching and practice of SCAP's officials on democracy and freedom became obvious. In 1949 the Ministry of Education, by giving new interpretation to the Education Standard Law of 1947, prohibited teachers from exerting political influence on students during school hours, and on and off campus.[151] In addition, the revised National Public Service Law deprived teachers of the right to organize and strike. The cumulative effect of these reverses was that many university teachers withdrew their manuscripts from publishers and declined speaking invitations for the fear of being branded as Communists.

Emboldened by SCAP's anti-Communist philosophy, in 1950, Minister of Education, Dr. Teiyu Amano proposed "An outline of Ethical Practice for the People" and advocated that courses on moral education similar to those of the pre-war period be revived in the school system. In 1951, during a parliamentary discussion the Minister reasserted the old philosophy of education by saying that "one is not conscious that the state is the mother, the basic body of the individual".[152] At the same time the Ministry of Education began to reverse the decentralization of education.[153]

EMANCIPATION OF WOMEN

One of the most popular features of the occupation reforms was perhaps the emancipation of Japanese women. The family institution was the base of the old order in the country. Customs, traditions and the civil code recognized the superiority of men over women. "The Confucian social order imposed three types of obedience upon women : obedience when young to parents, obedience when married to husband, and obedience when aged to children".[154] Under the old civil code, the head of the family enjoyed wide powers. He made the choice of spouse and chose the occupation of his children and minors.

The new constitution recognized the equality of sexes; Article Thirteen stated that "All of the people are equal under the law and there shall be no discrimination in political, economic or social relations because of race, creed, sex, social status or family origin".[155] The fundamental law of the land gave women the right to vote and receive the same education as men. The Diet amended laws concerning marriage, divorce, and inheritance in accordance with the provisions of the constitution.

Japanese women were quick in taking advantage of their new position. They participated actively in politics and labour unions. During the occupation period two thousand women enlisted in the police force.[156] In the first general election after the war, held in April 1946, women won no fewer than thirty-nine seats in the Diet. By 1950 one and a half million women joined labour unions. In addition, the Labour department estimated more than ten million membership in women's organizations in 1951.[157] The economic recovery programme initiated by SCAP created demand for women workers in business, industry and banks.

Articulate Japanese regarded the emancipation of women as one of the outstanding achievements of the occupation. On the contrary traditional elements in the country held that it destroyed the old family system.

In a survey conducted by the Mainichi Shimbun in 1947 on the issue of the revision of the old civil code, sixty per cent of those questioned favoured the abolition of the family system, while thirty-seven per cent opposed it. Sixty-five percent supported the equality of the sexes and thirty-two per cent opposed it.[158] One of the frequently-stated criticisms in Japan, as elsewhere, was that women, being unduly influenced by their fathers, brothers and husbands, seldom voted independently. Nevertheless, the liberation of women had a solid effect on the democratizing process set in motion in the country.

HEALTH AND OTHER WELFARE

The Japanese militarists claimed the superiority of the Yamato race but took very little care of the health and welfare of the nation. In fact MacArthur claimed that at the end of the war, there were only two sanitary engineers in the country.[159] Supreme Commander for Allied Powers' (SCAP's) Health and Welfare Section reorganized the Ministry of Health to integrate the four fundamental aspects of health and welfare : (1) preventive medicine, (2) medical care, (3) welfare, and (4) social security. The occupation's health programme aimed at immunization of the Japanese population against disease, efficiency in hospitals, and lowered cost to individuals. It touched almost every branch of the medical profession. The Japanese government opened health and welfare departments in all prefectural governments and inaugurated 800 health centers throughout the country.[160] American medical graduates in General Headquarters inoculated almost the entire population in the country in order to immunize it against standard ailments. Supreme Commander for Allied Powers' (SCAP's) officials also tried to control tuberculosis, which was widely prevalent in Japan. The Health and Welfare Section in General Headquarters organized six-man sanitary teams for a population unit of 135,000.[161] These units went around the country teaching preventive medicine, checking water supply, and demonstrating modern methods of medicine. The occupation authorities also supervised the establishment of a factory for the manufacture of penicillin.

Supreme Commander for Allied Powers' (SCAP's) health programme against communicable diseases reduced the over-all incidence of disease to a great extent. The Table 2.4 shows the effect of the programme on the Japanese populace.[162] Supreme Commander for Allied Powers (SCAP) also reorganised medical education in the country. In order to elevate the standards of medical care, the government passed the Medical Service Law, which prescribed minimum hospital standards. The Nurse's Law passed by the Diet in 1948 set forth standards and qualifications for the licentiate, the pre-war Veterinary Law was amended to provide adequate protection to the livestock industry. The government also established a nation-wide food inspection service. The immediate effect of all these measures showed itself in the reduction of death rates from twenty-nine and two-tenths per thousand in 1945 to eleven and six-tenths in 1949.[163]

TABLE 2.4 : **Effects of SCAP's health programme on Japanese**

Diseases	1945	1949	% reduction
Diptheria	122.8	18.0	85.3
Dysentery	138.0	29.2	78.8
Typhoid fever	82.9	7.9	90.5
Smallpox	2.3	0.2	91.3
Tuberculosis	280.0	168.8	39.7

Supreme Commander for Allied Powers (SCAP) initiated a child welfare programme and organized a community chest to finance private relief and welfare activities. Under SCAP's supervision the Japanese government undertook to simplify and unify various laws concerning the social security system. Soon welfare became an occupation for some people. Many prefectures devoted as much as eighty percent of their budget to welfare activities despite the fact that they were short of funds for normal operations. There were 1,090 private welfare organizations in one prefecture alone.[164] Neighbourhood associations were turned into civil welfare commissions with a hierarchy of officials appointed by prefectural governors. These commissions collected a forty yen membership fee and 200 yen annual dues from each member. Military government officials estimated that a large amount of the fund thus collected went into political campaigns and officers' pockets.[165]

REFERENCES

1. SCAP, n. 10 in Chapter 1, p 429-39.
2. *Ibid.*, p. 742.
3. *Ibid.*, p. 413.
4. *Ibid.*, p. 671.
5. Public Information Office : General Headquarters, Supreme Commander for Allied Powers and Far Eastern Command, *Two years of Occupation* (Washington, 1947), GS-4.
6. SCAP, n. 10 in Chapter 1, p. 16.
7. Quoted by Nobufumi Ito, *New Japan : Six years of Democratization* (Tokyo, 1951) p. 27.
8. SCAP, n. 10 in Chapter 1, p. 58.
9. *Ibid.*, p. 31.
10. Brines, n. 34 in Chapter 1, p. 75.
11. Yoshida, n. 9 in Chapter 1, p. 160.
12. Kazuo Kawai, *Japan's American Interlude* (Chicago, 1960) p. 93.
13. Yoshida, n. 9 in Chapter 1, p. 15.
14. Mark Grayn, *Japan Diary* (New York, 1948) p. 124.
15. Kawai, op. cit., p. 94.
16. Yoshida, n. 9 in Chapter 1, p. 151.
17. Kawai, op. cit., p. 97.
18. Grayn, op. cit., p. 42-43.
19. Yoshida, n. 9 in Chapter 1, p. 162.
20. Hans H. Baerwald, *The Purge of Japanese Leaders under the Occupation* (San Franciasco, 1959) p. 98.
21. SCAP, n. 10 in Chapter 1, p. 413.
22. Yoshida, n. 9 in Chapter 1, p. 129.
23. *Ibid.*, p. 130.
24. *Ibid.*, p. 129-30.
25. Yoshida, n. 9 in Chapter 1, p. 132.
26. SCAP, n. 10 in Chapter 1, p. 98.
27. *Ibid.*, p. 95-96.
28. *Ibid.*, p. 97.
29. *Ibid.*,
30. *Ibid.*, p. 101.
31. *Ibid.*, p. 109.
32. *Ibid.*, p. 102-5.
33. *Ibid.*, p. 106.
34. Yoshida, n. 9 in Chapter 1, p. 133.
35. SCAP, n. 10 in Chapter 1, p. 649.
36. *Ibid.*, p. 650.
37. *Ibid.*, p. 649.
38. *Ibid.*, p. 654.
39. Yoshida, n. 9 in Chapter 1, p. 143, also see Naoki Kobayashi, "The establishment of the constitution. An analysis," *Journal of Social*

and Political Ideas in Japan, I (August 1963) 14-5, in the same issue, see Kentaro Hayashi, "Some Comments on Current Constitutional Debates," p. 17-18.

40. MacArthur, n. 33 in Chapter 1, p. 303.
41. Yasuo Tatsuki, *General Trends of Japanese opinion following the end of war* (Tokyo, 1948) p. 19-21.
42. *Ibid.*, p. 22-23.
43. *Ibid.*, p. 23-24.
44. SCAP, n. 10 in Chapter 1, p. 460.
45. *Ibid.*, p. 461.
46. Kawai, op. cit., p. 214.
47. *Ibid.*
48. *Ibid.*, p. 215.
49. *Ibid.*
50. Ball, n. 30 in Chapter 1, p. 18.
51. Jones *et al*, n. 4 in Chapter 1, p. 415.
52. *Ibid.*
53. A.K. Reischauer, 'Religion' in Hugh Borton, ed., *Japan* (New York, 1950) 188.
54. *Ibid.*, p. 190.
55. SCAP, n. 10 in Chapter 1, p. 467-69
56. SCAP, n. 19 in Chapter 1, p. 26.
57. *Ibid.*
58. U.S. Department of State, *Occupation of Japan, Policy and Progress* (Washington, 1946) p. 135.
59. MacArthur, n. 33 in Chapter 1, p. 310-11.
60. *Ibid.*
61. SCAP, n. 19 in Chapter 1, p. 26.
62. Jones, *et al*, n. 4 in Chapter 1, p. 395-400.
63. SCAP, n. 10 in Chapter 1, p. 435.
64. Jones, *et al*, n. 4 in Chapter 1, p. 365-400.
65. *Ibid.*
66. *Ibid.*, also see Fuko Noda, "The Japanese Labour Movement, Notes by the Editor," *Journal of Social and Political Ideas in Japan* n. 39, p. 51.
67. *Ibid.*
68. Robert A. Fearey, *The Occupation of Japan, Second Phase : 1948-50* (New York, 1950) p. 85.
69. Yoshida, n. 9 in Chapter 1, p. 217.
70. *Ibid.*, p. 224.
71. Brines, n. 34 in Chapter 1, p. 165.
72. SCAP, n. 10 in Chapter 1, p. 762.
73. Yoshida, n. 9 in Chapter 1, p. 230-31.
74. Ball, n. 30 in Chapter 1, p. 157-58.
75. Secretary General, *Report, activities of the Far Eastern Commission, February 26, 1946—July 10, 1947* (Washington, D.C., 1947) p. 92.

76. Quoted in Robert B. Textor, *Failure in Japan with keynotes for a Positive Policy*, (New York 1959) p. 130.
77. SCAP, n. 10 in Chapter 1, p. 581-3.
78. American Federation of Labour, *Report of Proceedings of the Sixty-seventh Convention, November 15 to 22, 1948* (Cincinnati, Ohio) p. 338.
79. *Ibid.*, p. 339.
80. Textor, n. 76, p. 139.
81. American Federation of Labour, n, 78, p. 489.
82. *Nippon Times* (Tokyo), 8 February 1949, p. 1.
83. *Yoshida*, n. 9 in Chapter 1, p. 218.
84. Textor, n. 76, p. 144.
85. Secretary General of the FEC, n. 75, p. 93.
86. Borton, n. 53, p. 109.
87. *Ibid.*, p. 108.
88. MacArthur, n. 33 in Chapter 1, p. 308.
89. Masao Maruyama, *Thought and Behaviour in Modern Japanese Politics*, (London, 1963) p. 45.
90. U.S. Department of State, *Report on the Mission on Japanese Combines* (Washington, 1946) VII.
91. Edwin W. Pauley, *Report on Japanese Reparations to the President of the U.S., November 1945 to April 1946* (Washington, 1946) p. 39.
92. Reischaurer, n. 32 in Chapter 1, 273, Hugh Borton, *Japan's Modern Century* (New York, 1955) 417, see also Akira Irie, "The Legacy of Modern Japanese Diplomacy" *JSPIJ* 3 (August 1965) p. 28.
93. SCAP, n. 10 in Chapter 1, p. 425.
94. *Ibid.*, p. 565.
95. *Ibid.*, p. 201-6.
96. Jones *et al*, n. 4 in Chapter 1, p. 407.
97. *Newsweek* 1 December 1947, p. 34-8.
98. Walter Millis, (Ed.), *The Forrestal Diaries* (New York, 1951) p. 328.
99. Yoshida, n. 9 in Chapter 1, p. 152.
100. *Ibid.*, p. 156.
101. William Costello, *Democracy vs Feudalism* (Tokyo, 1948) p. 97.
102. T.A. Bisson, *Prospects for Democracy in Japan* (New York, 1949) p. 88.
103. *Ibid.*
104. *Ito*, n. 7, p. 121.
105. Ball, n. 30 in Chapter 1, p. 127.
106. SCAP, n. 19 in Chapter 1, p. 70.
107. T.A. Bisson, *Zaibatsu Dissolution in Japan* (Berkeley, 1954) p. 201-2.
108. *Ibid.*
109. Takeshi Ishida, "The Direction of Japanese Political Reorganization," *JSPIJ*, n. 40 in Chapter 1, p. 27.
110. Akira Sakaguchi, "The Power of the Financial World in Politics," *Ibid.*, p. 118-9.

111. Bisson, n. 102, 3. also see Yoshido, n. 9 in Chapter 1, p. 197.
112. Ball, n. 30 in Chapter 1, p. 132.
113. William M. Gilmartin and W. I. Ladejinsky, "The Promise of Agrarian Reform in Japan" *Foreign Affairs*, 26 (2 January 1948) p. 312.
114. *Ibid.*
115. SCAP, n. 10 in Chapter 1, p. 575.
116. *Ibid.*
117. Ball, n. 30 in Chapter 1, p. 114-9.
118. SCAP, *Summation of Non-Military Activities in Japan* 13 (October 1946) p. 67-8.
119. *Ibid.*
120. SCAP, n. 10 in Chapter 1, p. 760.
121. Yoshida, n. 9 in Chapter 1, p. 198.
122. *Ibid.*, p. 200.
123. *Ibid.*
124. Gilmartin and Ladejinsky, n. 113, p. 318.
125. *Ibid.*
126. Brines, n. 34 in Chapter 1, p. 221.
127. Fearey, n. 68, p. 94.
128. Fukuji Taguchi, "Conservative Political Parties : A Preliminary Study," *JSPIJ*, n. 92, p. 38.
129. Fearey, n. 68, p. 94.
130. *Ibid.*, p. 95.
131. *Ibid.*
132. Shirokuro Yamaguchi, *Some Aspects of Agrarian Reform in Japan* (Tokyo, 1948) 14. also see SCAP, n. 10 in Chapter 1, p. 577.
133. Brines, n. 34 in Chapter 1, p. 221.
134. W.I. Ladejinsky, "Agriculture," in Borton, n, 53, p. 59.
135. *Ibid.*, p. 60.
136. Tadaski Fukutake, "The Revolution in Japanese Agriculture, Fact or Illusion," *JSPIJ*, 3 (December 1965) p. 16.
137. Brines, n. 34 in Chapter 1, p. 229.
138. *Ibid.*, 223. It is interesting to note that in 1963 some of the ex-landlords contested the legality of SCAP sponsored land reforms in the Japanese supreme court. However, the court upheld the Allied Power's right in the matter. See Nobutake, Ike, "Japan Twenty Years after Surrender" *Asian Survey*, I (January 1966) p. 20.
139. Seiya Munakata, "The Fundamental Law of Education," *JSPIJ*, I (December 1963) p. 55.
140. Herbert Passin, *Society and Education in Japan* (New York, 1965) p. 151-3.
141. *The Times* (London) 27 October, 1965, 10. See also Taro Ogawa, "Reflection on Postwar Education" *JSPIJ* op. cit., p. 24.
142. General Headquarters Supreme Commander for Allied Powers, *Education in New Japan* (Tokyo, 1948) p. 26-8.
143. Japan Ministry of Education, *Progress of Education Reform* (Tokyo,

1950) p. 122.

144. Fearey, n. 68, p. 37.
145. Kawai, n. 17, p. 200.
146. Brines, n. 34 in Chapter 1, p. 241.
147. Yoshida, n. 9 in Chapter 1, p. 170.
148. *Ibid.*, see also Seiichi Miyahara, "The Japan Teacher's Union and Its Code of Ethics." *JSPIJ* n. 139, p. 103.
149. Kawai, n. 12, 194. see also Tokiomi Kaigo, "A Short History of Postwar Japanese Education," *Ibid.*, p. 17.
150. *Ibid.*, p. 206.
151. Fearey, n. 68, p. 43.
152. Japan, *Debates of the House of Councillors, The Official Gazette Extra*, 12th session 3 (13 October 1951) p. 8-9.
153. Yoshida, n. 9 in Chapter 1, p. 173, and Kaigo, n. 151, 21-2. The Japanese education system had become in some ways more thoroughly dominated by the government today than it was before the war." See Reischauer, n. 32 in Chapter 1, p. 268.
154. Shio Sakanishi, "Women's Position and the Family System," *The Annals of the American Academy of Political and Social Sciences* 308 (Philadelphia November 1956) p. 131.
155. SCAP, n. 10 in Chapter 1, p. 644.
156. MacArthur, n. 33 in Chapter 1, p. 305.
157. John M. Maki, *Government and Politics in Japan : The Road to Democracy* (New York, 1964) p. 128.
158. Tatsuki, op. cit., 43-7. According to the old Civil Code the house consists of members of a family controlled by the head of the house, who exercised various legal rights including those of designating the place of residence, marriage, adoption of son or daughter, entry or exit of members of the house. It is a legal unit in official family registers.

     Some of the reasons given by those who favoured abolition of the family system were as follows : (1) the head of the house will no longer exercise absolute rights over the question of marriage, property rights of sons. (2) All children will be able to share the inherited property equally. (3) Marriages will take place on the basis of consent. (4) Concepts such as family honour or family's social standing will be cast aside and as a result national life will become more cheerful.

     Persons opposing change in the old System gave the following reasons : (1) old traditions will disappear. (2) younger members in families will not feel responsible for parents and grand-parents. (3) preservation of ancestor's memories, family lineage and family name will be forgotten.
159. MacArthur, n. 33 in Chapter 1, p. 312.
160. SCAP, n. 19 in Chapter 1, p. 31-5.
161. *Ibid.*

162. *Ibid.*
163. *Ibid.*
164. Brines, n. 34, in Chapter 1, p. 194.
165. *Ibid.*

3

JAPANESE RESPONSE TO SUPREME COMMANDER FOR ALLIED POWERS' MEASURES AND EVALUATION OF THE REFORMS

THE restoration of basic freedoms and the purge of pre-war leaders created a great political fermentation in Japan. A number of political parties and groups emerged out of this convulsion. But only five major parties, (i) The Liberal Party, (ii) The Progressive Party, (iii) The Social Democratic Party, (iv) The Communist Party, and (v) The Co-operative Party, had political following throughout the country.[1]

The Liberals and the Progressives represented the conservative and traditional elements in the country, and the Socialist, Communists, and Co-operatives represented the progressive and leftist forces. For the sake of convenience these five parties could be categorized into two groups, the conservatives and the socialists.

The leaders who took over the reigns of government after the surrender were those who either actively supported the militarists or themselves were parties to the ultranationalist movement. It was clearly reflected in the number of conservative leaders who were purged under SCAP's directive in January 1946.[2] Out of the hundred and seventy-four Diet members of the Progressive Party only twenty-seven were eligible for re-election. The Liberal Party had twenty of its fifty parliament members eliminated, and three members of the Shidehara cabinet were exempted from purge until after the election in April 1946.[3]

The conservative group consisted of elder statesmen, corrupt politicians, old time bureaucrats, wealthy landlords and rich merchants [4] The names of the conservative parties were rather misleading, because they were basically the pre-war political parties reorganized under new names. In the matter of policies, the Liberals were as illiberal at the Progressives were unprogressive.

The ruling oligarchs remained unrepentant and determined to preserve the old order. As one Japanese diplomat has put it "Defeat has brought about entirely new conditions but I could not discern any trace of a corresponding change in mental outlook of the leaders".[5] According to certain writers, in the early hours of the defeat, when the Emperor was recording his message to the people, the patriarchs of the conservative groups kept themselves busy in pondering and preparing a basic strategy for a final future victory and laid down careful plans to circumvent the occupation.[6]

In a top secret document entitled Toa Renmei or the East Asian Federation, the authors wrote that the defeat of the nation was divinely ordained, "for the purpose of causing the people to reflect upon themselves to repent, to steel their faith in the nation, and to mobilize their entire strength in preparation for the final war".[7] The master plan contained both a long-range strategy and an immediate programme. The architects advocated external obedience to the will of the conquerors, which would help in getting a mild peace treaty and an underground movement for the final war. The conspirators advised their followers, who were to administer the country, (i) to study the causes of the defeat (ii) to enforce a simple standard of living throughout the country, and (iii) to disperse cities.[8]

Whether or not this blue print had the approval of the entire ruling oligarchy is difficult to say. The authenticity of the document itself could be questioned. However, certain pronouncements of the conservative leaders in the early weeks of the occupation and the exposure of the scandal regarding the hoarded goods in 1947 gave some substance to the existence of such a plan. The old guard made good use of the two week interval between the announcement of the surrender and the arrival of the first allied troops in Japan. During this period the militarists burnt all incriminating documents.[9] The Suzuki cabinet met on 14 August 1945 and decided to issue secret orders for the disposal of all war goods possessed by the Army and Navy Ministries. The goods, which were worth y100,000,000,000 included precious metals, light and heavy oils, drugs, storage batteries, aluminium, zinc, mercury, wire rope, uniforms, blankets, sugar and paper.[10] Approximately eighty percent of the goods fell into the hands of the *Zaibatsu* and affiliated companies. The Government also paid out nine and nine-tenths million yen as extraordinary military budget funds. In September 1945 an additional twenty-four billion yen was disposed of in a similar fashion.[11] "The accomplishment of these physical operations was the result of co-operative action by virtually the entire ruling oligarchy including the military, the Emperor, the Zaibatsu and the bank of Japan officials."[12] In the words of another author "the accumulated loot of an empire was at stake".[13] It should be remembered that the Japanese government wilfully misinterpreted Allied instructions. The Potsdam Declaration had stipulated that the Japanese government would surrender all arms and war material to the Allied powers on the effectuation of the cease fire. The Suzuki cabinet chose to understand that only arms would be handed over to the Allies.[14] It may be recalled that on the eve of impending surrender Prince Konoye made a revealing report to the Emperor. In that report the prince pleaded for a cessation of hostilities in the interest of preserving the traditional order in the country.[15] On 24 November 1945 the Shidehara cabinet appointed a War Enquiry Council ostensibly with the purpose of "investigating the causes of war and preventing future wars."[16] Meanwhile, the Allied Council for Japan became inquisitive about the War Council and demanded more information. Knowing that the game was up, Prime Minister Yoshida, who had succeeded Shidehara, dissolved the council with the explanation that its abolition was "advisable in order to free Japan from world suspicion".[17] Whether the Liberals and Progressives believed in the final victory or not we do not know. Further, it is difficult to say whether the utterances and actions of the conservative government were based on a pre-plan. However, the declared policies of the two conservative parties were as follows ; (i) supression of communist ideology, (ii) preservation of national policy (Kokutaigoji), which actually meant the retention of the Emperor system and the traditional order of society, (iii) establishment of democracy, the concept of democracy was to be defined in accordance with Japanese polity, (iv) free economy, (v) an undeclared objective of the conservative parties was to obtain an early and favourable peace treaty from the allied powers.[18] The old guard favoured only minor alteration in the Meiji constitution, and gave mere lip sympathy to the democratic concept. In a final show down between itself and SCAP, the ruling party accepted the new constitution reluctantly. The bureaucratic element in the group held the view that the mass of the people were too ignorant to judge the best course for themselves ; that the bureaucracy alone was capable of directing the government; and that people's representatives were incompetent.[19]

When Supreme Commander for Allied Powers (SCAP) through its first directive abolished the weapons of the totalitarian system introduced by the pre-war Japanese Government, the then Prime Minister Higashi Kuni was reported to have said that he could not govern the country without thought-control and secret police.[20] As far as the economic policy was concerned all groups in the ruling oligarchy collectively agreed to safeguard the Zaibatsu interest. With this goal in mind the Suzuki government had tried to strengthen the business clique with war goods worth more than 100 billion yen, and Shidehara's successors used various means to water down the deconcentration programme. In order to shift the war responsibility of the militarists on the people, the conservative group issued a call to the nation to repent for the war. They also attempted to emphasize the continuity of the war regime by uttering catchy phrases like the pre-war *Kokutaigoji.*[21] This phrase was used as a substitute for the old mythical symbols of *Tenno* and *Kokutai*. In short, the oligarchic group "conspired in a thousand ways to preserve the ruling authority for a hereditary class".[22]

Being confident in their knowledge of the secrets of government, the top bureaucrats and leaders set out to circumvent the occupation. They would bend when convenient and resist when necessary. For example, when SCAP ordered Prime Minister Yoshida to introduce a measure in the Diet which he disliked he obeyed by flaunting a white rose in the tradition of the rebel in medieval Japan.[23] However, in a few weeks SCAP proved more than a match for the old guard. In the face of strong public pressure for reform and the steady flow of SCAP directives, the ruling group felt helpless. It had neither power nor necessary mental and moral resources to offer any effective resistance. Its policy of delay and maneuvering was quickly detected by SCAP's officials. For example, in the early stage of the occupation, the militarists endeavored to retain the prewar organization of the army and navy under the guise of demobilization bureaus, which had been set up for the purpose of demobilization of Japanese defence forces immediately after the surrender. On 1 July 1946 the demobilization departments were combined to form a single Demobilization Board. The Japanese government retained several military officers in the bureaus in order to save them from being purged. When SCAP came to know the design, it ordered an investigation of the demobilization machinery, and in October 1947 ordered the dissolution of the Demobilization Board.[24]

Alarmed by the growing strength of the labour movement and frustrated by the failure of its moves to keep the changes at a minimum, the Japanese traditional elements resorted to dubious methods to discredit the occupation. In an attempt to enlist the support of some influential officials in General Headquarters, certain conservative leaders arranged lavish dinner parties in honour of the American officials, offered them costly presents, and made their mansions available to the dignitaries.[25]

In the first two years of the occupation, the conservative government offered hardly any constructive proposal for the future well-being of the nation. Administrators and politicians simply waited for the directives and sat on their hands when the flood of directives stopped.

The conservative group was reluctant to part away with power even in the face of strong popular demand for its resignation. As one of the Japanese conservative newspapers commented:

"The Shidehara cabinet is attempting to remain in office in

spite of the unfavourable public opinion. It is universally admitted that such an attempt is very undemocratic, unconstitutional and reactionary".[26] In 1946 the four main opposition parties in the Diet started a nation-wide movement to bring down the Shidehara government. Both Shidehara and Yoshida followed policies which aggravated the economic problems of the country. The government did not take any effective measures to control inflation and relieve the shortage of food.[27] When they could not win the election because of the disgust in which they were held by the people and becuase of organizational weaknesses, the conservative government tried to change the election laws. For example, in 1947 the Yoshida government, with the assistance of the Progressives, succeeded in gerrymandering. The large constituencies in which the socialists had greater appeal and could easily win, were reduced to medium-size constituencies.[28] In spite of this reorganization the result of the May 1947 elections was that the Japanese people voted the Socialist Party to power because the conservatives failed to meet the pressing needs of the country.

The bureaucracy being one of the constituent elements of the ruling oligarchy resisted changes in its setup.[29] It held the view that the old "system of government and its rules were absolute and had unlimited applicability".[30] When SCAP demanded the reorganization of the country's bureaucratic setup in February 1946, the Cabinet Bureau of Legislation, which was responsible for personnel, submitted to the government section in General Headquarters for approval a plan for the reform of the civil service. It included some simplication of the hopelessly complicated pay and allowance scales, and modification of the elaborate system of personal ranks.[31] The plan did not touch the heart of the problem and obviously was an attempt to soften the impact of SCAP's interest in the reform of the civil service. Distrusting the common people as they did, the bureaucrats did not believe in decentralization of governmental power and thwarted efforts toward that effect. It could be seen in the functioning of local autonomy established under the new constitution in the prefectures. Out of forty-eight vice-governors appointed between 1947-50, twenty-five were ex-officials of the defunct Ministry of Home Affairs and four had served in the office of the overseas governor generals before World War II. These vice-governors being in actual control of the local administration attempted to perpetuate the pre-war system of centralized bureaucracy.[32] According to a Japanese scholar "The bureaucracy with its authoritarian methods has curbed the spontaneous development of the will of the people".[33]

To sum up, "The Japanese oligarchy, confronted with the necessity of military surrender, marshaled its forces for a post-war struggle to preserve the political and economic bases of its power".[34] For the conservatives, SCAP was a necessary evil to be tolerated. Their aim was to bring an early end to the occupation of the country. The spokesmen of the group were convinced that it would come about only as a result of disunity among the allied powers. They were sceptical about the durability of the friendship between the United States and the Soviet Union and hoped that these two great war-time allies would fall apart soon. Meanwhile, their efforts would be to help create disunity in the ranks of the allies and build Japan as a bulwark against Communism. For the Japanese oligarchs, the capitulation of the country was not necessarily the end of Japan as a great power, but merely the beginning of a new chapter in the country's long history.[35]

In the wake of defeat and the breakdown of the old order, intellectuals, students, industrial workers, small businessmen, and Communists hailed the GIs as an army of liberation.[36] In the past, the Japanese police had described this group as "dangerous people" and had watched them closely. A distinction should be made here between the Communists and other leftist groups. The Communists stood for proletarian revolution abolition of the emperor system, and the establishment of a Communist state.[37] On the other hand, the Socialists and other leftist intellectuals advocated a constitutional monarchy and democratic Socialism.[38] Despite the fundamental differences, both the Communists and other leftist groups had certain immediate common goals which could be described as follows:

(i) elimination of militarism and militant nationalism,
(ii) implementation of the Potsdam Declaration, and
(iii) opposition to the ruling conservative group.[39]

Both the Socialists and Communists acclaimed and supported the political and socio-economic measures sponsored by SCAP. The fact of the matter was that the reforms which had long been cherished by the leftist groups were being accomplished with the aid of a foreign power.[40] Taking advantage of the basic freedoms restored by SCAP this group plunged itself into activity. They organized and led the labour unions, launched a country-wide movement to eradicate militarism, and held street demonstrations against the hoarders of food and other essential commodities. The intellectuals discussed and debated the concept of democracy endlessly and tried to explain it to the people.

The common people of Japan were pleasantly surprised by the friendly attitude of the American troops. The militarists had endeavored to instill in the minds of their countrymen that the allied soldiers were monsters and the defeat of the nation would result in killing of innocent men, women, and children, rape and looting of property by the allied troops.[41] Similarly, the willing co-operation and enthusiasm of the common people came as a surprise to many Americans. The western impression of Japanese as fanatical fighters ready to sacrifice all for the glory of the emperor gave place to sympathy and friendship for the Japanese.

Rapid changes in the country's political and socio-economic setup first brought confusion to the masses. They understood little and hoped much. They were bewildered and did not know whether to believe in them or not. However, ordinary workers, peasants, and others obeyed the orders of the authorities as they had always done, when gradually they came to understand the significance of the socio-economic upheaval, they enthusiastically supported it.[42] The period of confusion was followed by an era of gratitude, hope and despair. The general mass of the people were grateful to the occupation for the food it supplied, had hope in the realization that an effort was being made to improve their living conditions, felt disappointed because the reforms failed to bring immediate relief. The hope lived in the understanding that once the masses enjoyed the democratic rights bestowed upon them, they would be reluctant to part with these rights.

AN EVALUATION OF THE REFORMS

A general question is often asked by historians and political scientists as to what the overall effect of the occupation reforms on Japanese society was. It is difficult to provide a definite answer to this question. However, in this section an attempt will be made to analyze the issue and assess the accomplishment of SCAP in the occupied country.

The occupation had three main objectives: (i) demilitarization (ii) democratization, and (iii) deconcentration of the country's economic system. These aims were based on the assumptions that democracy could be taught and that conquerors could reform a defeated nation.[43] With these goals and suppositions, the occupation set upon its course. It may be appropriate to raise certain questions here.

(1) Did SCAP achieve its objectives in full measure? If the answer is in the negative, then

(2) Why couldn't it fulfill the aims?

(3) Did the democratic institutions introduced by SCAP take root in the country?

(4) Were the assumptions right? In the following pages an attempt will be made to answer these questions.

Perhaps for the first time in modern history of military occupation, a conquered nation made a serious attempt to reform its former enemy. A cartload of papers flowed from General Headquarters carrying hundreds of major and minor directives and orders for the reform and regulation of virtually every aspect of Japanese life, from imperial house to village shrines and temples.

Supreme Commander for Allied Powers (SCAP) abolished the absolutist theory of the emperor system. The Bourbons stood discredited. The top militarists were tried as war criminals by an international tribunal. The bureaucrats were made to realize that they were servants of the people. The common mass of the Japanese breathed the fresh air of freedom for the first time, and their energy and initiative, released from imprisonment, has opportunity for growth. New status for women, better health conditions, concern for welfare, land reform, and more democratic educational system, were the things which contributed to the general welfare of the Japanese people and should be put on the credit side.

This attempt was a success to the extent that the Japanese accepted the reforms as permanent features of their society. Natural co-operations of the Japanese with SCAP made it difficult to determine to just what degree they accepted the changes out of conviction and to what degree just to please their conquerors. Certain groups in Japanese society who undoubtedly benefited by the reform measures such as labour, women and peasants, would probably resist any attempt on the part of the Japanese government to reverse the course of the reforms. On the other hand, the foregoing account of the various reforms in Chapter II made it clear that the original purposes were only partially realized. As occupation tumbled along, the initial vigor and enthusiasm of the American officials faded away. Efficiency gave place to complacency, and to a great extent the original purpose of the reforms underwent modification. For example, toward the end of 1948, SCAP abandoned the deconcentration programme, began to depurge the purgees, and initiated a reverse course in labour legislation. The Japanese government, no longer prodded by SCAP's officials, quickly reverted to its old habits of dodging and indifference to public opinion.

Reforms had not been successful largely because of the rivalry between the United States and the Soviet Union. In other words the occupation measures became a victim of the cold war. Secondly, according to an American author, the United States "failed to achieve the announced aims of its initial post-surrender policy toward Japan, primarily because these aims could not be achieved through the instrumentality of Japan's old guard. It was virtually inevitable that once given the chance to control the application of SCAP's directives, the representatives of the old regime would be able to defeat or at least water down every measure designed to curtail their power".[44]

The occupation wrote a constitution for the country and created institutional forms of democracy. But the spirit of democracy was absent. In other words, the Japanese pursued shadowy formalisms and ignored the substance of democracy. The President of Keio University, Koji Ushioda, put it this way :

> even those who are seeminly most active in pushing the campaign of democratization in this country attach too much importance to form, not enough to substance. They cannot think of democracy except in terms of complete set of democratic system.[45]

The concept of democracy was a novelty to a large number of Japanese people. In many cases democracy was taken as a license for personal freedom, such as demanding a seat in an over-crowded train as a democratic right.[46] According to a Japanese labour leader, democracy did not catch the imagination of the people because "it was a present of foreign origin".[47] For the same reason the press in the country described the experiment as 'rationed democracy.'[48] Another Japanese scholar wrote:

> In Japan democracy and tradition are even now basically contradictory. For this reason a universalist democracy has not been successful in working through Japan's nationalism and cultural inheritance which constitute Japan's particularist ideology.[49]

The Oyabun-Kobun, that is, reciprocal obligation between landlord and vassal, between labour boss and worker, and between patron and protégé pervaded almost all aspects of Japanese life and did not change with the introduction of democracy. The habits of centuries were not easily obliterated. Intra-family relations, based on a patriarchal system, continued unhampered. "Kaoyaku or bossim constituted a feudal supra legal force completely at odds with the essential nature of democracy".[50] The social structure of the country had its own inner laws and dynamics, too deep-seated to be changed by a statute or a set of police measures alone. SCAP could not legislate feudalism out of Japan. This point was well illustrated in the famous Ozu case involving a notorious gangster named Ozu in 1947. This gangster was arrested for illegal seizure of property and intimidation of its rightful owners. One of the attorneys defending the accused said that the Oyabun-Kobun

System, on which the accused gangster operated, was good. Further, "even the Emperor System, in my opinion, is similar to the Oyabun-Kobun System!"[51] This experiment in democracy proved that revolution from without or from above has fundamental limitations.

Another thing which should be mentioned in this connection was the military nature of the occupation. The military officers of SCAP who were trained to obey orders from their superiors, were perhaps not well equipped to teach democracy to a vanquished nation. Moreover, SCAP did not practice what it often taught. It copied pre-war Japanese methods, such as the employment of secret police to keep an eye on occupation personnel, censorship, dictation to the Diet, orders to the courts, discrimination against the lower ranks, and finally reservation of the best residences, of compartments in the trains, and other facilities, for American officials. These undemocratic things were practiced in the name of freedom, equality and democracy.

However, SCAP's experiment in Japan had been described variously as an induced revolution, a bloodless revolution, a moral rearmament of Japan and finally as an age of enlightenment.[52] Another opinion was that no revolution occurred in Japan. The people of the islands experienced a highly successful renaissance.[53] According to a well-known Japanese political scientist, "the defeat and the subsequent occupation of Japan accomplished one thing that is that the Japanese people awoke from their deep despondency and determined to build a new Japan".[54] On the other hand conservative opinion in the country regarded the occupation as a seven year period of national humiliation and a continuation of the war. Further, the condemnation and the subsequent reorganization of the Japanese society was not all for good. Because "relentless severing of all ties between the old Japanese empire and postwar Japan caused the Japanese people to lose their national consciousness which had been fostered since the Meiji Restoration in 1868".[55] Yet another assessment of the occupation was that it contributed to an intellectual resurgence among the youth of the nation. "At least in part, the present support of democracy by the youth of Japan, their antagonism against belligerent policies, their seeking of a more wholesome and cultural life and their demand for freedom of thought are all an outcome of"[56] *the occupation of the country.*

A highly respected American authority on Japan had characterized the occupation measures as an attempt to aid peaceful and democratic tendencies in Japanese society, so as to make them a dominant force in the country.[57] In the initial stage of the occupation, perhaps this was the intention of the allied powers. The United States' Initial Post-Surrender Policy toward Japan was probably written with that purpose in mind. But the directions issued to the Japanese government in 1948 to curtail the basic right of the Labour union to strike and bargain collectively, and the abandonment of the deconcentration programme in the same year, were by no means helpful in strengthening the peaceful and democratic elements in Japan. On the contrary, these measures reversed the democratic trend in the country. Therefore, in this sense, and in this sense alone, the democratization process probably was not a success.

The significance of the reforms lies in the fact that they were instituted by an alien power not by force but largely through persuasion and open discussion. The conquerors could not alter the ancient social mores of the Japanese completely; perhaps no foreign power could accomplish such a feat in a conquered territory. "History tells of no case in which an occupation of one country by another produced within a short span of years a sincere conversion to the beliefs of the conquered".[58]

To sum up, "the Japanese have been shaken up, stimulated, forced to come out of their shell and learn some of the facts of life which will be useful for future reference. They have gained some elementary knowledge of the theory and practice of democracy".[59]

PEACE PROPOSALS BY THE UNITED STATES IN 1947

By the spring of 1947 the corrective and reformative measures of the occupation had largely been completed. The absolutist theory of the Emperor system and the political influence of the military clique had been removed. Institutions of democracy had been set up. The structure of the Zaibatsu and the feudalistic agrarian system had been likewise radically reformed. Now it was for the Japanese themselves to adjust the new rules to Japanese realities through assimilation and adoption. The time had come for the occupation forces to withdraw in accordance with the Potsdam Declaration, which stated that "the occupying forces of the Allies shall be withdrawn from Japan as soon as these objectives have been accomplished and there has been established in accordance with the freely expressed will of the Japanese people a peacefully inclined and responsible government." Keeping this point in mind, the State Department had been working on the draft of a peace treaty since early 1947.[60] As early as September 1946, on the occasion of the first anniversary of the Allied occupation of Japan, MacArthur publicly favoured an immediate conclusion of a peace treaty with Japan. The Supreme Commander believed that a speedy peace settlement would strengthen Japan's newly acquired democracy. To this end MacArthur sent George Atcheson, Jr., the deplomatic adviser to SCAP, to Washington, but his trip was unsuccessful. On 19 March 1947 MacArthur again made a statement, before the press club in Tokyo, emphasizing the need for an early peace settlement with Japan. MacArthur's view on the peace treaty and the differences between the views of the various agencies of the United States Government on the peace settlement will be dealt with in detail in subsequent chapters. It will suffice to say here that in July 1947, the United States Government proposed to the other ten member governments of the Far Eastern Commission that a peace conference be held on 14 August 1947 to discuss a peace treaty for Japan. In the face of Soviet objections to the procedure to be adopted for the proposed peace conference, the idea of an early peace settlement for Japan was abandoned.

The unsuccessful attempt of the United States to call an early peace conference indicated that basic changes in policy towards Japan might be imminent.

REFERENCES

1. SCAP, n. 10 in Chapter 1, 343-4. See also Robert A. Scalapino and

Junnosuko Masumi, *Parties and Politics in Contemporary Japan* (Berkeley and Los Angeles, California, (1962) p. 28.

2. SCAP, n. 10 in Chapter 1, pp. 16-7.
3. *Ibid.*, p. 25.
4. Yoshisato Oka, "Political Parties and Party Government," *Journal of Social and Political Ideas in Japan* n. 40 in Chapter 1, p. 16. See also Hirohide Ishida, "The Vision of the Conservative Party," *JSPIJ* (2 August 1964) p. 55.
5. Mamoru Shigemitsu, *Japan and Her Destiny*: *My Struggle for Peace* (New York, 1958) p. 380.
6. William Costello, *Democracy Vs. Feudalism* (Tokyo, 1948) pp. 97-101, Bisson, n. *Prospects for Democracy in Japan*, (New York, 1949), pp. 11-4., Brines, n. 34, 78, Ball, n. 30 in Chapter 1, p. 59.
7. *Ibid.*, p. 99.
8. *Ibid.*, p. 100.
9. Brines, n. 34 in Chapter 1, p. 182.
10. SCAP, in 10, n Chapter 1, pp. 307-13.
11. *Ibid.* See also Jerome B. Cohen, *Japan's Economy in War and Reconstruction* (Minneapolis, 1949) p. 418.
12. Bisson, op. cit., p. 13.
13. William Costello, *Democracy Vs. Feudalism* (Tokyo, 1948) p. 149.
14. SCAP, n. 10 in Chapter 1, pp. 307-308.
15. See footnote n. 9 in Chapter 1.
16. Costello, op. cit., p. 101.
17. *Ibid.*
18. Oka, op. cit., 15, Scalapino and Masumi, n. op. cit., 30-1, Mr. Ichiro Hatayama's statement in *Nippon Times* (Tokyo), 11 November 1945, p. 2.
19. *Nippon Times* (Tokyo) 13 October 1945, 4. SCAP, n. 10 in Chapter 1, p. 137.
20. SCAP, n. 10 in Chapter 1, p. 342.
21. Jun-ichi Kyogoku and Junnosuke Masumi, *Japanese Politics* : *Is it Democratised*? 10. (Twelfth Conference, Institute of Pacific Relations, Kyoto, 1954) p. 10.
22. Costello, op. cit., p. 144.
23. Wildes, n. 42 in Chapter 1, p. 132.
24. SCAP, n. 10 in Chapter 1, p. 139.
25. Wildes, n. 42 in Chapter 1, p. 35.
26. *Nihon Keizai* (Tokyo), 21 April 1946. in Supreme Commander for Allied Powers, *Press Translations* 4, (Editorial Series 588) p. 2.
27. Jones *et. al.*, n. 4 in Chapter 1, p. 362.
28. Oka, op. cit., p. 17.
29. Kiyoaki Tsuji, "The Bureaucracy Preserved and Strengthened," *JSPIJ*, n. 40 in Chapter 1, p. 88.
30. Maso Maruyama, "Japanese Thought" *JSPIJ* 2 (April 1964) pp. 45-6.

31. SCAP, n. 10i n Chapter 1, p. 137.
32. Kiyoaki Tsuji, n. 29, p. 88.
33. Yasuo Watanabe, "The Function of High Ranking Civil Servants," *JSPIJ*, n. 40 in Chapter 1, p. 92.
34. Bisson, op. cit., p. 14.
35. Kase, n. 2 in chapter 1, p. 230.
36. Kentaro Hayashi, "How to Approach Postwar Japanese History," *JSPIJ*, n. 92 in chapter 2, p. 68. See also Rokuro Hidaka, "Intellectuals and Masses," *JSPIJ*, op. cit , 106. The author also formed this impression from his talks with professors in Tokyo University, labour leaders and students in Tokyo during 1961-62.
37. Rodger Swearningen and Paul Langer, *Red Flag in Japan, International Communism in Action* (Cambridge, Mass., 1952) p. 125.
38. SCAP, n. 10 in chapter 1, p. 97.
39. *Ibid.*
40. *Nippon Times*, (Tokyo), 24 November 1945, p. 4.
41. Mrs. Ai Kume, *The Reminiscences* (Oral History Research Office, Columbia University, New York, 1962) p. 39.
42. Tsuneo Baba, "Japanese Response to the Peace Treaty" *Contemporary Japan.* (Tokyo), 20 (July/September 1951) pp. 293-300. See also Yoshihiko Seki, Introduction : Japan in Transition, *JSPIJ*, op. cit., p. 4.
43. Robert A. Fearey, *The Occupation of Japan*, Second phase: 1948-50 (New York, 1950) p. 100.
44. T.A. Bisson, Prospects for Democracy in Japan (New York, 1949) p. 130.
45. Costello, n. 101 in chapter 2, p. 211.
46. *Ibid.*, 5, Tokyo Shimbun, 6 May 1946, in General Headquarters Supreme Commander for Allied Powers, *Press Translations* 16 (editorial series-730) 1. See also Hajime Shinohara, "Postwar Democracy and Parliamentary Politics," *JSPIJ*, n. 39 in chapter 2, p. 37.
47. Shigeru Hara, "Who Will Promote Reforms," *JSPIJ* n. 39 in chapter 2, p. 58. See also Yoshihiko Seki, op. cit., p. 5.
48. See Introduction entitled "Education in Japan," in *JSPIJ*, n. 139 in chapter 2, p. 5.
49. Joshikazu Sakamoto, "Japan in a World of Tension," *JSPIJ* Ist (April 1963) p. 44.
50. William Costello, *Democracy Vs. Feudalism* (Tokyo, 1948) p. 131.
51. *Ibid.*, pp. 137-47.
52. *Nippon Times* (Tokyo) 18 November 1945, p. 4; Yoshida, n. 9 in chapter 1, p. 159. See also the editorial entitled "Japanese Intellectuals : Their Role and Responsibility," in *JSPIJ*, n. op. cit., p. 76.
53. *Nippon Times*, (Tokyo), 24 November 1945, p. 4.
54. Quoted by Jun Eto in his article "The Bankruptcy of our Idealistic Intellectuals," *JSPIJ* n. op. cit., p. 102.
55. Nobuyukia Okum, "The Japanese People" *JSPIJ* n. op. cit., 29.

In the same issue of the Journal see Kai Ōi, "Toward the Formation of a New Japanese Nationalism," p. 18.

56. Roburo Hidaka, "The Role and Aims of Social Studies in Education," *JSPIJ*, n. 139 in chapter 2, p. 81. Emphasis by the author.
57. Reischauer, n. 32 in chapter, 1, p. 51.
58. *Ibid.*
59. George Sansom, "Can Japan be Reformed," *Far Eastern Survey* 18 (2 November 1949, New York) p. 259.
60. Jones *et al.*, n. 4 in chapter 1, p. 423.

4

TURNING POINT IN JAPANESE-AMERICAN RELATIONS

THIS chapter deals with the second and third phases of the occupation, namely the periods of rehabilitation and revision. The second phase began in the spring of 1947 with the declaration by Under-Secretary of State Dean Acheson that, "the United States should push ahead with reconstruction of those two great workshops of Europe and Asia—Germany and Japan upon which the ultimate recovery of the two continents so largely depends".[1] This policy became clearer as 1948 wore on and concluded with the outbreak of the Korean War in June 1950. The Korean War accelerated the third and the final phase which ended with the conclusion of the San Francisco Peace Treaty in September 1951. The first aim of this chapter is to analyze the various factors which influenced the United States to adopt a policy of economic rehabilitation of Japan; the second is to show how the economic recovery program resulted either in the revision or abandonment of some of Supreme Commander for Allied Powers' (SCAP's) earlier reform measures. The third aim is to indicate the significance of these policies to a peace settlement with Japan.

An indefinite postponement of a peace treaty for Japan in early 1948, because of Soviet and Chinese opposition, marked the beginning of a major shift in the American attitude toward its former enemy. The emphasis in the occupation shifted from the reform of the Japanese society in the direction of Western democracy to its economic recovery and social stability. There also developed a tendency to look upon Japan as a potential ally rather than an enemy.[2] The United States provisionally decided to utilize Japan's geographical position, man-power, and industrial potential in its global effort to check alleged Soviet expansion. Policy-makers in Washington did not seem to be sure whether the United States should commit itself to the defense of Japan in case of aggression by Communist powers, until the fall of China to Communism. In January 1950 the United States fully committed itself to defend Japan. Meanwhile SCAP would focus its attention on the rehabilitation of Japanese industry. The policy of economic recovery found its formal expression in United States Representative General McCoy's statement to the Far Eastern Commission on 21 January 1948. He stated :

> It is the view of the United States government that if the fundamental objectives of the occupation are to be achieved and if there are to be established the conditions necessary to enable Japan to make its proper contribution to the economic rehabilitation of world economy and to take its place in the community of nations, a much greater effort must be made to bring about the attainment of a self-supporting Japan with a reasonable standard of living. To this end my government believes that the Japanese government and people, the Far Eastern Commission and its members states and the Supreme Commander, recognizing the conditions which now require that more emphasis be placed on such a programme, should take all possible and necessary steps, consistent with the basic policies of the occupation, to bring about the early revival of the Japanese economy on a peaceful, self supporting basis.[3]

Three factors seemed to have brought a change in the United States policy toward Japan : (i) The decision to reduce the economic burden of Japan on the American tax-payer (ii) the United States re-evaluation of the world situation and Japan's relationship to it, and (iii) the completion of the reforms introduced by SCAP and the realization that the reorganization of the Japanese society without economic stability would have little meaning.[4] These factors were inter-related and influenced each other. However, the most important variable was the international situation which over-shadowed the other factors.

The disagreement among the Allied powers in 1948 on how to begin a peace treaty highlighted the importance of Japan in the struggle for power between the United States and the Soviet Union. The procedural wrangle was only a symptom and not the cause of the conflict. The Japanese problem, therefore, could be understood better in the broader context of the post-war tension between the East and the West.

COLD WAR AND ITS EFFECTS

The defeat of Germany and Japan in World War II initiated profound changes in international politics. Among other things, it created military and economic vacuums in Europe and Asia.[5] The European colonial powers stood exhausted in terms of military and economic resources and were faced with the liberation movements in their colonial areas. The United States and the Soviet Union emerged out of the turmoil as the two most important great nations. Utilizing the situation created by the war, the two powers either wished to occupy as much of the vacuum as possible or at least prevent hostile states from occupying it.[6] In other words, the United States and the Soviet Union engaged themselves in a contest for power and influence in the world. The bond of unity that existed among the allies during the war evaporated with the disappearance of common enemies. The war time agreements became inconsistent with the post-war political, economic and military interest of the great powers. There soon developed distrust and suspicion between them. This phase of the post-war history of the world has come to be known as the cold war. When, where, and how the cold war began is an interesting question to ask, but very difficult to answer. A detailed investigation of the cold war issue is rather irrelevent to the subject matter in this chapter. However, certain broad facts of the situation should be noted.

At the Yalta conference in the winter of 1945, President Roosevelt, Winston Churchill, and Joseph Stalin made a military settlement which fixed the boundaries where the Allied armies were to meet. It was a provisional arrangement and the Allied armies were to be withdrawn after the government of the areas concerned negotiated the terms of peace.[7] As the Russian armed forces marched westward they established, in the liberated areas in Eastern Europe, governments which were friendly toward the Soviet Union. During and after the war the Soviet Union consolidated its position in Eastern Europe and strengthened it by concluding political and economic agreements of the countries concerned.

The Soviet Union was accused of taking unilateral action in the liberated territories in Eastern Europe, which was contrary to the agreement reached at Yalta between Roosevelt and Stalin.[8] In this connection it should be noted that the Soviet Union had been excluded from effective participation in the Italian occupation during 1944-45. Under the Moscow Declaration of 1943, the Russians had the right to have an equal share in the Italian occupation. Nevertheless, the Allied control of Italy was strictly a British-American show.[9] The Russians seemed to justify their domination of the Allied control commissions in Rumania, Bulgaria, and Hungary in the light of their experience in Italy. It is equally important to remember in this context that in October, 1944 the United Kingdom and the Soviet Union had signed a secret treaty under which the British accepted Soviet interest in the three former Axis satellite states in exchange for Russian recognition of British predominance in Greece. Under the same agreement both powers agreed to have an equal division of influence in Yugoslavia.[10] In view of these agreements, the Soviet Union felt that her interest in Eastern Europe had been recognized by western powers during the war and in the Armistice agreement. According to an American authority :

> The charge that Russia controlled Eastern Europe was without strong foundation. She was there because the pre-war Allied effort to turn Hitler to the east had backfired. Far from wanting to prevent her entry into Eastern Europe

> we had been keenly afraid Russia might stop on her own borders, but myriads of Americans would forget their history and bristle at the idea of appeasing the Reds".[11]

In November 1945 the then British Foreign Secretary Anthony Eden, discussing Russian motives in Europe, said that Soviet arrangements in that area were directed against a German resurgence and therefore were defensive in character.[12]

Germany, under four-power occupation, was rapidly becoming a battle ground in the cold war rather than the symbol of Allied unity. In theory, all three great powers had abandoned their war-time schemes for the dismemberment of Germany. In fact, the boundary dividing the Russian from the British and American zones had already severed the country. Berlin, an enclave in the Russian zone, was divided, like Germany as a whole, into four zones.

Another important controversy between the United States and the Soviet Union was related to the control of atomic energy. In 1946 the United States presented to the United Nations Security Council a proposal for the outlawing of the atomic bomb and for plac ing the manufacture of atomic energy under international control and inspection, whereas the USSR proposed to outlaw and destroy the bomb first and create an international control for the manufacture of atomic energy next.[13] The Soviets did not agree on inspection. The USSR also rejected the United States proposal to disarm Germany for twenty-five or forty years.

In the Far East the antagonism between the United States and the Soviet Union assumed such forms as the division of Korea, the Soviet seizure of Japanese assets in the Manchuria, and the Russian refusal of an American offer to negotiate a pact for the permanent disarmament of Japan.

In short, the unconditional surrender of Germany and Japan did not bring peace and security to the war-torn world. The conflict between the United States and the United Kingdom on the one side, and the Soviet Union and her satellites on the other, was growing wider and deeper. Each side accused the other of ruthlessness and of reaction. In American eyes, the Soviet Union was the greatest offender.[14] Hostility of most

Americans to Communist ideology coloured their evaluation of the Soviet Union and its policies to a great extent. Toward the end of 1945, anti-Communist and anti-Soviet feeling in the United States reached its high point. Angry and emotional speeches against the Soviet Union poured out of the halls of the United States Congress. For example, in December 1945, Senator James O. Eastland of Mississippi said that the American people "must realize that Russia is a predatory, aggressive nation, and that today she follows the same fateful road of conquest and aggression with which Adolph Hitler set the world on fire". Speaking about alleged Russian atrocities in Czechoslovakia, the Senator from Mississippi stated, "we find in Czechoslovakia savage barbarian Mongolian hordes stalking the streets of western civilization as conquerors."[15]

In March 1946, Winston Churchill, in his famous speech at Westminster College at Fulton, Missouri, gave expression in his inimitable prose to the image of the Soviet Union held by the western powers. He said that:

> from Stettin in the Baltic to Trieste in the Adriatic an iron curtain has descended across the continent. Behind that line lie all the capitals of the ancient states of central and eastern Europe, Warsaw, Berlin, Prague, Vienna, Budapest, Belgrade, Bucharest, and Sofia, all these famous cities and populations around them lie in what I might call the Soviet sphere, and all are subject, in one form or another, not only to Soviet influence but to a very high and in some cases increasing measure of control from Moscow.[16]

The message of Churchill's speech was that only an alliance of English-speaking people could prevent a future war and ensure the successful operation of the United Nations. Churchill's speech had the full support of Washington, and, in fact, it was prepared after consulting President Truman.[17] Therefore, Churchill's Fulton speech is regarded as the beginning of cold war diplomacy between the Western powers and the Soviet Union. It "launched the United States openly upon a policy of dealing with Russia as an incorrigible menace."[18]

In the middle of 1946, United States policy-makers seemed

to have concluded that the Soviet Union wanted "to expel the American influence from the Eurasian land mass generally, and wished to replace it by that of its own".[19] In order to upset the alleged Soviet design, the United States took a series of military and economic steps during the year 1947-48.

The first step was taken in Greece in 1947 when the United States agreed to give military and economic aid to that country to resist the Communist guerrilas. It may be recalled that in February 1947 Britain decided to pull out its forces from Greece and Turkey and told the United States that His Majesty's government could no longer meet its traditional responbilities in those two countries. At this time the Governments of Greece and Turkey were on the verge of collapse as a result of pressure from the Communists. The United States felt an immediate need to sustain the position the British had been supporting on the Eastern Mediterranean against Soviet influence.[20] President Truman asked the Congress for emergency aid to Greece and Turkey. Presenting his proposals to the Congress on 12 March 1947, the President made the following remarks.

> One of the primary objectives of the foreign policy of the United States is the creation of conditions in which we and other nations will be able to work out a way of life free from coercion. . . . We shall not realize our objective, however, unless we are willing to help free peoples to maintain their free institutions and their national integrity against aggressive movements that seek to impose upon them totalitarian regimes. This is no more than a frank recognition that totalitarian regimes imposed on free people, by direct or indirect aggression, undermine the foundations of international peace and hence the security of the United States. Further, he said that "it must be the policy of the United States to support free peoples who are resisting attempted subjugation by armed minorities or by outside pressure.[21]

This statement of the President of the United States has since then come to be known as the Truman Doctrine of Containment of Communism.

The policy of containment was based on the assumptions that (1) the Soviet Union was an expansive power whose policies could not be explained in rational terms. The only way to check Soviet ambition was a firm resistance at each point that aggression was threatened. In the words of George F. Kennan, "the Soviet pressure against the free institutions of the westren world is something that can be contained by the adroit and vigilant application of counter force at a series of constantly shifting geographical and political points, corresponding to the shifts and maneuvers of Soviet policy but which can not be charmed or talked out of existence."[22]

(2) The line to be held against the Soviet Union was the existing boundary of the USSR, because further Soviet expansion would whether appetite.

(3) The appeal of the Russian Communist Movement was likely to be strong in those countries in which political and socio-economic conditions were unstable. Therefore, it was necessary to strengthen non-Communist governments which had potentially strong Communist opposition.[23]

(4) The military and economic resources of the United States being limited, it could not by itself resist Soviet encroachment. Hence, it was essential to build a system of alliances with other non-Communist nations having a common interest in containing the aggressive tendencies of the Soviet Union.[24] In short, the containment strategy was a declaration of ideological and economic war against the Soviet Union.[25] The Soviets denounced this policy as imperialistic and charged that the Truman Administration was following the "path of Hitler in seeking world domination".[26]

The next step was in the form of the European Recovery Programme or the Marshal Plan. It was a programme of economic aid designed to assist European countries to reconstruct their economics. Western Europe, exhausted by the war, and scourged by the severe winter of 1946-47, was not making the necessary economic recovery. Strikes were frequent and the communist parties of Italy and France were gaining strength. The policy makers in Washington calculated that if the economic chaos was left unchecked, the Communists in

Italy and France would probably come to power.[27] The containment doctrine was evolved to prevent such a situation. Therefore, a massive economic recovery programme was formulated under the leadership of the Secretary of State George C. Marshal in time to influence the Italian elections scheduled to be held in April 1948.

Meanwhile, in February 1948, Communists seized power in Czechoslovakia. Memories of Hitler's march into that country, and the Munich Conference heightened feelings of tension in the West and created an atmosphere of crisis in the United States.[28] Russians were believed to be behind the communist capture of the government of Czechoslovakia. On the other hand, as has been pointed out, the Kremlin saw in the containment policy and in the European Recovery Plan, a western design to encircle the Soviet Union. The Russian resentment of Western policies found its outlet in the Berlin Blockade. In the spring of 1948, the Soviet Union began to tighten traffic control between the western sector of Berlin and Western Zone of Germany. The United States and the United Kingdom answered the Soviet action by inaugurating the Berlin airlift. In April 1949, in an amendment to the Economic Co-operation Act of 1948, the Congress declared that it was the policy of the United States to encourage the unification of Europe.[29] Under this act, the United States, along with other West European countries, established the North Atlantic Security Pact, the forerunner of the North Atlantic Treaty Organization (NATO). These moves and counter moves on the part of the United States and the Soviet Union precipitated the division of Europe and in a way the division of the world into Eastern and Western blocs.[30] The division rested on the assumption of a bipolar world, one part of which was organized and led by the Soviet Union, and the other part of which was formed under the leadership of the United States.[31]

The purpose of this brief survey of major events in Europe is to indicate that immediately after World War II Western Europe, more than any part of the globe, loomed large in the minds of policy makers in the United States. Secondly, containment of Communism became the dominating feature of United States foreign policy both in the West as well as in the East.

Economic conditions in Japan after the surrender and SCAP's economic recovery programme

In losing the war, Japan lost fifty-two per cent of its land and the dream of carving an Asian empire.[32] The Allied air attack had destroyed thirty per cent of its industries, eighty per cent of its shipping, and thirty per cent of the country's thermal power.[33] As has been observed, there was an acute shortage of food and other essentials of life. The Japanese overseas administrators, colonists, and soldiers poured in, adding to the mouths to be fed. In over two years, five million soldiers were repatriated. Inflation was rampant and unemployment was widespread. In the past the country had lived on foreign trade which amounted to five per cent of total world trade. After the war, its share dropped to a fraction of one per cent.[34] Moreover, Supreme Commander for Allied Powers (SCAP) put restrictions on Japan's access to food and raw material and prohibited the reconstruction of industries conceived to be of strategic value. The first three years of the occupation saw confusion and chaos in the country's economic life.

The reforms introduced by the occupation corrected the political ills of the country but made no immediate contribution to economic recovery. With the passage of years things did not improve. In fact, the economic situation became more chaotic. Owing to shortage of food, inflation, and low production, the living conditions of wage earners steadily deteriorated throughout 1946. In the summer of 1947, mass starvation appeared very real. Large scale supply of food by the United States alleviated the food problem. What did the successive conservative governments do to improve the living conditions of the people? The two successive conservative Prime Ministers, Shidehara and Yoshida, stubbornly resisted popular demand for control on prices. Instead, they blamed the working class for the economic ills of the country. According to an American observer big business encouraged and exploited the situation for their own ends.[35] They would not work for a socio-economic order as envisioned by the Initial Post-Surrender Policy for Japan, in which the former ruling class would no longer exercise domination. The oligarchs told the people that nothing could be done until the country became free. In March 1947,

MacArthur wrote a letter to Prime Minister Yoshida criticising his half-hearted measures to arrest inflation. He warned the Japanese Government that future food supply from the United States would be minimum and advised Yoshida to put control on wages and prices, and ration commodities.[36] Yoshida's government did little to carry out SCAP's instructions. In contrast to the poor conservative performance, the Socialist government of Katayama, which came to power in June 1947, took an active interest in inaugurating effective controls. It activated the Economic Stabilization Board under Hiroo Wada's chairmanship, and tried to improve the living conditions of the working classes.[37] The Socialist government also proposed to regulate the country's coal mining industry. Sensing a threat to their economic interest in the socialist programme, the oligarchs manuevered to overthrow the Katayama cabinet.[38]

In accordance with the instructions contained in the United States Basic Initial Post-Surrender Policy that "you will not assume any responsibility for the economic rehabilitation of Japan or the strengthening of the Japanese economy. You will make it clear to the Japanese people that you assume no obligation to maintain, any particular standard of living in Japan," SCAP did not take any interest in the economic rehabilitation of the country in the first three years of the occupation.[39] The occupation authorities left the Japanese Government free to tackle its economic problems and devoted themselves to the demilitarization and reform of the country. However, a deteriorating Japanese economic situation and the increasing inability of the conservative leaders to put their house in order forced SCAP to reverse its policy of nonresponsibility in the economic sphere. Moreover, in January 1947, the Far Eastern Commission, in its policy statement on the Japanese economy, declared that "the peaceful needs of the Japanese people should be defined as being substantially the standard of living prevailing in Japan during the period 1930-34".[40] The Far Eastern Commission's policy was vague, for it did not clarify whether or not SCAP should take positive steps to raise the Japanese economy to its 1930-34 level. According to one well-known authority on Japanese affairs, what the policy meant was that, since at that time the Japanese economy was operating far below the prescribed level, "the industrialists could triple their current industrial production until goods and services became available for the payment of reparations".[41] It should be noted that Far Eastern Commission's policy statements had very little influence on SCAP's programme in Japan. Major decisions were made the State and Defence Departments.

Washington had its own reasons for wanting the economic recovery of Japan. The occupation was costing the United States a good deal of money and material. For instance, in 1947 alone American aid to Japan amounted to $400 million dollars. In addition, the United States had supplied 1,652,276 tons of food to the country during the same year.[42] Economic and military assistance to Greece and Turkey and Europe put a heavy burden on American tax payers. Japan added to the cost. The economy-minded congressmen, being weary of foreign aid, urged the administration that steps be taken to make Japan self-sufficient.[43]

Economic rehabilitation of Japan was also imperative for containing Communist influence in that country. A weak and hungry Japan would fall an easy prey to Communism, for democratic institutions would not flourish in an economy which did not furnish sufficient food and provide opportunities for employment.[44] Moreover, the various reform measures introduced by SCAP would have little meaning if they did not result in the economic well-being of the country. Should the deteriorating economic conditions remain unchecked, the Japanese would blame the occupation for their suffering and would resent the presence of United States armed forces in that country. On the other hand, a prosperous Japan would not only take care of its own needs, but also contribute immeasurably to the rehabilitation and reconstruction of the rest of Asia. Despite the destruction brought by the war, Japan was still the only leading industrial nation in Asia. It possessed an industrial base, technical know-how, and a dynamic population of over ninety million people. With these assets and with the United States assistance, Japan could quickly build her industries and provide needed machinery and technical knowledge to the developing nations in Asia.[45]

The Defense Department played a major role in shifting

United States policy toward Japan. This seemed to be in keeping with the general trend in United States foreign policy during this period. The military had considerable influence in foreign policy matters in the early years of the post-war period. In some cases the Pentagon rather than the State Department appeared to be the real force behind the formulation of foreign policy.[46] Japan is an excellent case in point. As the differences between the Western Powers and the Soviet bloc became sharper, United States Army officers began to think of Japan as an active partner in the cold war and within the American sphere of power in the Far East. This thinking in the Pentagon was reflected in the military measures undertaken by the army in Japan. In 1948 army engineers embarked on the construction of a huge air base in Misawa, which was located at the northern tip of Honshu and was within easy range of the Russian installation at Vladivostok. It was followed by an extensive expansion of facilities in airfields and ports in the country for modern use.[47] At the same time, the army gave top priority to Japanese economic rehabilitation. Between February 1947 and March 1948, the Defense Department despatched three important economic missions to Japan. In February 1947, the United States War Department sent Clifford Strike to Japan to study the country's economic situation and the reparation programme. Then after a year, a group of engineers who called themselves "overseas consultants" visited Japan and reported on their industrial reparation survey of the country to the Army Department. In March 1948, a delegation of American businessmen headed by Percy Johnson accompanied the Under Secretary of the Army William Draper to Japan and Korea and submitted a report on the economic positions of those countries. The objective of these various commissions ostensibly was to study the economic situation in Japan. But in reality they were animated by other than economic considerations. The purpose of the Army in sending these delegations was to build up a case for putting an end to the reparation programme and prepare the ground for massive economic aid to Japan[48] The missions dutifully accomplished the task assigned to them. For example, each successive report recommended considerable reduction in the level of reparations to be exacted from Japan. The Johnson Committee report made the following statement on the removal of machinery as reparations. "Plants which are needed in bringing about the recovery of Japan should be retained and only excessive capacity removed".[49] The Johnson mission also recommended that the army proposal pending before Congress for the appropriation of 144 million dollars for Japanese recovery be approved.[50] This amount was in addition to 424 million dollars requested for the expenses of government and relief in that country for the fiscal year 1948-49.

In January 1948, the United States Secretary of the Army, Kenneth C. Royal, in a speech in San Francisco, further revealed the thinking of the Defense Department toward Japan. He admitted that the demilitarization of Japan was a mistake; the deconcentration programme hampered Japanese economic rehabilitation and the purge of former military leaders was unwise.[51] In March of the same year the Under Secretary of the Army, William Draper, announced in Tokyo that the United States was not bound by the Far Eastern Commission's resolution on the peaceful needs of Japan. He gave his own interpretation to the Commission's policy statement by saying that the "proposal to return Japan to the pre-war levels referred only to the basis for reparation removals and not to the production levels to which the Japanese would be permitted to extend their economy".[52] Secretary Draper told press correspondents that the policy of his department was to make Japan self-sufficient by 1952 or 1953 at a cost of 480-580 million dollars to the American treasury.[53]

Perhaps the military chiefs in the Pentagon were themselves greatly influenced by intelligence reports received from the head of the G2 section in General Headquarters, General Charles Widloughby. Wiiloughby was one of the trusted persons in General MacArthur's inner circle and was known for his rabid anti-Communist views.[54] He was a great admirer of Generalismo Franco of Spain. Willoughby was opposed to a thorough reform of Japanese society and headed a group of like-minded persons in the General Head-quarters. This group questioned the zeal of the Government section in General Headquarters for the alteration of the Japanese political and social system. The feud between Willoughby and the head of the Government section, General Whitney, was well known in Tokyo.[55]

As early as 19 August 1945 Willoughby was believed to have told Japanese military officers in Manila, who had gone there to learn the details of the surrender, that the occupation would like to have their co-operation as intelligent agents.[56] Accordingly, SCAP exempted a dozen Japanese top army and navy officers from the purge and kept them on the occupation pay roll. The list included among others Torashiro Kawabe, who was the Japanese military attache in Germany during the Hitler regime and later headed the surrender mission to Manila, the Intelligence Chief of the Army, Seizo Ansue, and Tojo's Military Secretary, Colonel Takashiro Hattori.[57] These high-ranking officers were ostensibly working in the historical division of G2 section on the Japanese history of the war. In reality they were believed to have been co-ordinating Japanese and American intelligence reports concerning the activities of the Soviet Union in the Far East.[58] Impressed by the anti-Soviet feelings and fighting spirit of the Japanese officers, General Willoughby and his followers advocated that Japan should be made a bulwark against Communist expansion in Asia. According to Willoughby's group, Japan could fulfill this role only when its economy was strengthened and the country was permitted to build an army.[59]

American businessmen, being aware of the importance of Japan as a trading country, took great interest in the occupation of the former enemy. Some of the best talent in SCAP Headquarters came from business concerns in the United States. Companies had lent these hands to the occupation so they could watch out for their companies' future. When SCAP took steps to curb the power of the Zaibatsu and purged its leaders, United States captains of industry loudly protested these measures as un-American and said that reforms stood in the way of Japanese economic recovery. As has already been pointed out, a prominent New York lawyer visited Japan on behalf of his business clients to observe the operation of the deconcentration programme and after his return denounced the dissolution of the Zaibatsu.[60] In 1947 the former head of

SCAPs' Economic Section advocated that American businessmen invest capital in Japan and make use of the country's cheap labour.[61] In short, economic rehabilitation of the country would facilitate American investment in Japan, increase opportunities for trade, and bring profits. Therefore, business interests in the United States advocated restoration of Japan to its economic health. The cumulative effect of all these pressure groups on policy makers in Washington was great indeed.

In accordance with the policy of rehabilitation, SCAP took a number of steps to boost the Japanese economy during 1948. In order to stimulate foreign trade, MacArthur lifted restrictions on the visits of foreign business representatives to Japan. He also permitted Japanese technicians, traders, and educators to go abroad. In May 1948 the United States appropriated $150,000,000 for economic recovery of all occupied areas including Japan.[62] At the same time private business circles in the United States along with the Export-Import Bank granted $60,000,000 loan for the improvement of the national textile industry.[63] As a result of these measures, industrial production increased considerably and foreign trade expanded. But the Japanese economy as a whole remained in a distressed state. Moreover, despite all the encouragement given by SCAP, the Japanese government and the people evinced little enthusiasm in the recovery programme. For one thing, the country lacked political stability. The Socialist government of Katayama was forced to resign in February 1948. Ashida, who succeeded Katayama, headed a weak and divided coalition government. In October 1948 a series of political scandals involving the Prime Minister and other officials brought the demise of the Ashida cabinet. Thereafter Yoshida formed a caretaker minority government. The political groups which succeeded one another were preoccupied with internal dissensions and partisan politics, and relied on American economic aid. The general mass of the people were war weary and were not prepared for further sacrifice. This state of affairs prompted Washington to use compulsion. On 10 December 1948, the United States issued an interim directive to SCAP, authorizing MacArthur to order the Japanese government to adopt immediately "whatever measures might be required to achieve fiscal, monetary, price, and wage stability in Japan and to maximize production for export."[64] The directive contained nine measures, such as achievement of a balanced budget, an effective system of tax control, limitation of credit facilities, an effective wage programme. MacArthur transmitted the directive to the Japanese government. President Truman appointed Joseph M. Dodge to supervise the programme; therefore, the nine-point measure has come to be known as the Dodge Plan. Since the plan called on the Japanese to pull their belts in and work harder and longer, it was greeted with almost universal public hostility.[65] The farmers resented the Supreme Commander for Allied Powers—sponsored measures reducing their black market income. Labour felt that it was being arbitrarily prevented from demanding and securing legitimate wage increases. Industrialists were opposed to a progressive devaluation of the currency as well as greatly increased difficulty in securing new credits and the renewal of outstanding loans. The policy designed to effect promotion of exports was opposed on the ground that it would result in keeping the domestic standard down.

In January 1949, shortly after the announcement of the Dodge Plan, Japan went to the polls. The Liberal Party won an absolute majority in the Diet. The leader of the party, Yoshida, was called upon to form the government. Inspired by the anti-Communist policies of Supreme Commander for Allied Powers and dismayed by the growing strength of the Japanese Communist Party, Yoshida set out to implement the Dodge plan effectively.

Growing Strength of the Japanese Communist Party

In the January 1949 election, the Communist Party won thirty-five seats in the Diet, polling ten per cent of the total votes cast in the country.[66] In view of the small registered membership of the party, it was a significant gain for the Communists and a disturbing development for the occupation and the Japanese government. According to some writers, a large number of the Japanese voted for the Communist Party as a protest against the reverse policy of Supreme Commander for Allied Powers and its instrument—the Japanese old guard.[67]

This argument only partially explained the growing strength of the CPJ, a full explanation of the Communist gains in the 1949 elections lies in the growth of the party after the inauguration of the occupation.

In accordance with the 4 October 1945 directive which required restoration of freedom and release of all political prisoners, the Communist Party was granted legal status for the first time in Japanese history. Communist leaders came out of their prison cells hailing the occupation forces as liberators.[68] As has been pointed out, during 1945-48 the party actively supported the reforms sponsored by SCAP and tried to rally the support of all progressive elements in the country. Since it was the only political party in the country which had consistently and uncompromisingly opposed the militarists and had suffered in their hands, a large number of people showed sympathy toward the Communist leaders. SCAP also tolerated them because the Communist leaders provided useful information on the activities of the militarists and also the party identified itself with the objectives of the allied powers in Japan. In the first two years of the occupation, the Communists organized labour unions and came to have dominant influence in the Congress of Industrial Union. In short, the party attempted to build its image in the country as a 'lovable Communist Party' engaged in a 'peaceful revolution'.[69]

As the tension of the cold war between the Western bloc and the Soviet bloc increased, however, the party began to change its emphasis from peaceful revolution to an anti-imperialist policy. The Communists concentrated their attack on the occupation policy of economic rehabilitation of Japan. They denounced the Dodge plan as a "measure aimed at subjecting Japan to the complete domination by foreign monopolistic capital," and accused the conservative government of selling out the country to foreign imperialists.[70] Matters came to a head in the summer of 1949 with the government's decision to dismiss a large number of railway workers in accordance with its recent policy of retrenchment. The workers naturally opposed such a course on the part of the government but could not air their grievance through the weapon of a general strike. The recently revised national service law prohibited strikes by government employees. Therefore the railway unions resorted to direct action. A number of incidents occurred during the summer. In June the Communists in Taira, northeast Japan, were reported to have seized the police station of the city and to have held it for a day. In July a train ran away at Mitaka near Tokyo killing six people and injuring one hundred and thirty others. During the same month the president of the National Railway Corporation, Sadanori Shimoyama, was found dead on a railway embankment. The Communists were accused of having a hand in all these incidents.[71] But the CPJ denied the charges. Apart from these violent incidents it should be noted here that the Party's earlier policy of peaceful revolution was only a tactic and not an accepted policy in Communist ideology. Early in January 1950 the tactic of peaceful revolution came under attack. The official organ of Cominform criticised the Japanese Communist leader Nozaka for attempting "the naturalization of Marxism and Leninism in Japanese conditions," and described peaceful revolution as "alien to the working class."[72] Under pressure from International Communism, Nozaka confessed his error and the CPJ reaffirmed its firm belief in violent revolution.

Two days before the murder of the president of the NRC, in a message to the Japanese people MacArthur hinted for the first time that it might be necessary to outlaw the Communist Party of Japan. He said that the CPJ was "an avowed satellite of an international predatory force and a Japanese pawn of alien power policy, imperialistic in purpose and subversive in propaganda." The nature of the Party's subversive acts, he added, created "doubt as to whether it should any longer be regarded as a constitutionally recognized political movement."[73]

The ruling conservative party, which regarded the Communists as their enemy number one, wildly applauded MacArthur's statement. The conservative government saw in SCAP's stiffened attitude towards the Communists an opportunity to suppress all leftist elements in the country. As had been pointed out, it found a convenient excuse in the austerity measures required by the Dodge Plan to get rid of a large number of workers in the railway union, which was supposed to be under Communist domination. After the July incidents, the government openly used the retrenchment policy for discharging Communists and other leftist labour leaders.[74] Left wing groups in the country were forced to register with Competent authorities and were subjected to official control. During 1949-50 the government dismissed 11,000 civil servants and an equal number of school teachers, charging them with being Communists.[75] In August 1949 the police raided the office of the Communist Party newspaper, *Red Flag*, on charges of illegal sales of rationed newsprint. A similar raid was made on Communist headquarters at Kobe. The government also took the opportunity to dissolve the League of Korean Residents, alleged to be a Communist-dominated organization. To cap all these repressive measures the conservative party in the Diet activised the Examination Committee of the lower house, which was a counterpart of the House Un-American Activities Committee of the United States Congress. The actions of the government against those who did not agree with it posed a serious threat to the newly won freedom of the Japanese people and reinforced the opposition's charge that the ruling party's belief in democracy was only skin deep.[76]

Victory of Communism in China and its implications for Japan

While Japan was making a slow recovery under the Dodge Plan, and while the CPJ was gaining strength, Washington was confronted with an explosive situation in the Far East, which caused a major upheaval in United States foreign policy in Asia. In October 1949 the Chinese Communist Party won a decisive victory on the mainland and established the People's Republic of China. It was an event of far-reaching consequence in international politics. Communist China, being a natural ally of the Soviet Union, added to the strength and prestige of the Communist bloc and tipped the world's balance of power. And Communist gains on the mainland were a great set-back to the United States position in Asia.[77] Not only did American business lose China's markets, but the United States faced a potential rival in that part of the world. The Chinese Communist victory also posed a threat to Japanese security. Occupation authorities realized that the Communist bloc would try to minimize American influence in Japan through the Japanese Communist Party.

China occupied a prominent place in United States post-war foreign policy. Washington made several attempts during and immediately after the war to help build China as a strong democratic nation closely allied with the United States and exercising a stabilizing influence in Asia.[78] As late as June 1948 Secretary of State George C. Marshal said before the House Committee on Foreign Affairs:

> It is the desire of the State Department and the government on the executive side to see a stable China and one that has a form of government sympathetic to our form of government.[79]

In order to achieve this objective it was essential to put an end to Japan's hegemony in Eastern Asia. Therefore, the United States stripped Japan of its territorial conquest and attempted to remove militaristic strains in its social structure. At the same time Washington encouraged the political, socio-economic, and military development of China and other nations of the Far East whose pre-war weakness had been largely the measure of Japan's strength.

Policy-makers in Washington found themselves mentally unprepared for this confrontation. The Democratic Administration came under strong Republican criticism in the Congress for its alleged failure in China.[80] That the United States lacked a clear cut and integrated policy for the Far East was a commonplace American political comment at that time.[81] Popular and Congressional pressure was forcing policy-makers to revise the United States attitude toward Asia. The United States dilemma was whether or not it should assume the responsibility of defending non-Communist countries in the Far East, and, if the answer was in the affirmative, what should be the role of Japan in the United States Far Eastern policy.

There existed two schools of thought on the problem. One school, whose views were perhaps shared by the administration, believed in giving first priority to the defense of Western Europe over Asia.[82] This controversy over priorities was not a new development. It had its origin in World War II. At that time the United States faced two enemies—Germany in Europe and Japan in the Far East. Military strategists in Washington gave the European threat their main attention in the belief that Germany's defeat would facilitate Japan's downfall. Concentration of efforts on Japan would give Germany time to consolidate her gain and increase her strength.[83] After the end of the war, we have already seen, Washington again chose Western Europe as the main area to be defended against Soviet expansion. The United States initiated the Marshal Plan and organized the North Atlantic Treaty Organization for the defense of the area.

The spokesmen of this school were of the opinion that the real contest between the Western bloc and the Communist bloc was over the possession of Western Europe. This area possessed preponderance of world's developed wealth, scientific and technical knowledge, transportation network, and, what's more, it was the custodian of the Western liberal humanitarian outlook. In this sense it held the key to the world's balance of power and therefore ought to be defended under all circumstances.[84] This school also believed that neither of the areas would have to be surrendered, but if a choice were imperative, then the Far East rather than Western Europe should be sacrificed.[85] Further, given the limits of American economic and military resources, it would be unwise to make extensive commitments in the world. Moreover, the spokesmen of the school held the view that Communist control of China made the defense of Japan unfeasible. For example, in 1948 the Secretary of State, General George C. Marshal, in his reply to a question in the House Committee on Foreign Affairs as to whether or not Japan could ever become self sufficient or long remain secure if the continent of East Asia north of the Yangtse was controlled by the Communists—said that "that would present a great problem for Japan to take care of herself without help from the outside".[86] Secretary of the Army K. C. Royall was reported to have made the following remarks in Tokyo in February, 1949 :

> I tend to the opinion that it [Japan] is valueless in the case of war with Russia. I don't know what our troops here could do in the event of war. I am not certain we could

> hold Japan nor am I certain it would be worthwhile as long as we have Okinawa and the Philippines.

He added :

> I think it might be better to pull out before the war started—in any event, our west coast is not endangered. Our east coast is, so all priority should be given to hold Western Europe.[87]

According to this school, Japan could be helped to develop its industries, provided the Japanese themselves showed sufficient interest in the economic reconstruction of their country. This would be the best way to save Japan from Communism.

The opposite school pointed out that the Soviet Union had primary interest in Asia and Africa and it was on the defensive in Europe.[88] It advocated that the United States adopt a firm attitude against Soviet expansion in Asia. The spokesmen of this school regarded Japan as an indispensable bastion of democracy and a great military bulwark against Communism in the Far East. The advocates of this school argued that Japan, being close to the centers of Communism, occupied a strategic position and it lay athwart the American defense line in the Pacific. Also, Japan, because of her military and industrial traditions, occupied a key position in East Asia like that of Germany in Western Europe and represented a major obstacle to the spread of Communism. In view of these advantages, this school of thought demanded that Japan be made an integral part of American defensive perimeter in the Far East.[89]

On the Europe versus Asia controversy, the sponsors of this school pleaded that Europe and Asia should be given equal importance in United States policy of containing Communism. To consider the problems of one sector while being oblivious to those of another was to court disaster for the whole. Emphasising the importance of Asia, they pointed out that half of the population of the world lived on the Asian continent and that it held sixty per cent of the world's natural resources. General MacArthur, in his letter dated 20 March 1951 to Congressman Joseph Martin, Minority Leader of the House of Representatives, wrote:

> It seems strangely difficult for some to realize that here in Asia is where the Communist conspirators have elected to make their play for global conquest, here we fight Europe's war with arms while the diplomats there still fight with words, that if we lose the war to Communism in Asia, the fall of Europe is inevitable; win it and Europe most probably would avoid war and yet preserve freedom.[90]

John Foster Dulles also held similar views on the Europe versus Asia problem and expressed them strongly in many of his speeches. In his address over the Columbia Broadcasting System on 1 March 1951, Dulles said:

> Many seem to think that our safety is linked only to the West, meaning Europe, and that the East can be ignored. Of course Europe is important. But just as the United States would be in peril if Europe were overrun, so also we and Europe would be in peril if the East were overrun. Stalin long ago laid down as basic Communist strategy that the road to victory over the west lies through the East.[91].

Thus in the period ending in 1948-49, the United States was of two minds as far as Asia in general and Japan in particular were concerned. It was not apparently certain of the policy best suited to its global objectives.

While a debate on the lines mentioned above was going on and while the fall of China was imminent in the summer of 1949, the United States made a decision to halt any further extension of Communist domination on the continent of Asia. Secretary of State Dean Acheson in his instructions to Ambassador Philip C. Jessup, dated 18 July 1949, said:

> You will please take as your assumption that it is a fundamental decision of American policy that the United States does not intend to permit further extension of Communist domination on the continent of Asia or in the Southeast Asia area.[92]

The cardinal principle of protecting Japan against aggression was fully established by the end of 1949. It was publicly stated by Secretary of State Dean Acheson in his important speech before the National Press Club in Washington on 12 January 1950.

He said :

> The defeat and the disarmament of Japan has placed upon the United States the necessity of assuming the military defense of Japan so long as that is required, both in the interests of the security of the entire Pacific area, and in all honor, in the interest of Japanese security—I can assure you that there is no intention of any sort of abandoning or weakening the defenses of Japan and that whatever arrangements are to be made either through permanent settlement or otherwise that defense must and shall be maintained. The defense perimeter runs along the Aleutians to Japan and then goes to the Ryukyus—they are essential posts of the defense perimeter of the Pacific, and they must and will be held.[93]

Korean War : On 24 June 1950, North Korea invaded South Korea. The day after the invasion, the Security Council of the United Nations by a vote of nine to nothing, the Soviet Union being absent, adopted a resolution declaring that a breach of peace had been committed by the North Korean action, and ordered an immediate ceasefire and withdrawal of North Korean forces. In the autumn of 1950, Communist China intervened in the Korean War, which emphasised the Communist threat to Japanese security and accelerated the United States policy of revision in that country.[94] In addition, the Korean War had the following consequences for United States policy towards Japan :

1. Japan became an indispensable military base and source of military supply for the United Nation's forces in Korea. It also brought an economic boom to Japan.
2. Japanese-American economic co-operation became the slogan of the day; until then the United States policy had been to make Japan a self-sufficient economic unit.

From then on it was to be an economic partner with American business against Communism.

3. Japan, Korea, Okinawa, Formosa, and the Philippines were to form a defense ring against Communist expansion.
4. Japan was authorized to organize a police reserve force which was to form a nucleus for Japanese rearmament.
5. It also became necessary to restore self-government to Japan and to accelerate the efforts to obtain a Japanese peace settlement.
6. Anti-Communist movements all over Asia were to be supported and incorporated into the United States defense organization. Japan was given a major economic role in that organization.[95]

Thus Japan became a potentially active factor in the policies of Asia and by a strange stroke of luck it regained a position to be reckoned with in the future politics of that continent.

Results of the policy of rehabilitation and revision on the internal conditions in Japan and Japanese reaction

The economic rehabilitation of the country came in direct conflict with attempted reforms at various levels. As has been observed in the second chapter, during 1948 MacArthur authorized the Japanese Government to revise the antimonopoly law. At the same time SCAP advised the Japanese Government to amend existing labour laws, which in practice meant putting more and more restriction on organized labour. A large number of former leaders were released from the purge, thereby facilitating their return to political influence. In the summer of 1948, MacArthur suggested to Prime Minister Ashida that the new constitution be examined in the light of experience. On 12 May 1949, the United States announced to the Far Eastern Commission its decision to suspend interim reparations.[96]

One of the three major occupation reforms, demilitarization (the other two being democratization and deconcentration), was openly abandoned with the outbreak of the Korean War. In July 1950 MacArthur authorized the Japanese Government to form the so-called National Police Reserve of 100,000 men.[97]

This was to be the embryo of the new Japanese army and was so treated by Supreme Commander for Allied Powers' officials. It is interesting to note here that as early as 1949 General R. L. Eichelberger, Commander of the Eighth Army, advocated that Japan have a 150,000 man well-equipped army.[98] The establishment of the National Police Reserve was alleged to be counter to Article Nine of the constitution which stated that:

> The Japanese people forever renounce war as a sovereign right of the nation and the threat or use of force as means of settling international disputes.
> In order to accomplish the aim of the preceeding paragraph, land, sea, and air forces, as well as other war potential, will never be maintained. The right of belligerency of the state will not be recognized.[99]

Supreme Commander for Allied Powers (SCAP) maintained, however, the fiction that the National Police Reserve was merely a police force created to supplement the existing police units which were rather ineffective. Further, occupation officials pointed out that since the National Police Reserve had no artillery, no engineers, no communications, and other paraphernalia of a military organization, it would be wrong to call it an army.[100] This argument was invented to give a facade of constitutionality to the military project. According to a reliable authority, plans were being contemplated for equipping the National Police Reserve with machine guns, mortars, light tanks, aviation facilities, and so on.[101] It was a far cry from the proposal of a 40-year treaty to ensure the demilitarization of Japan made by the war-time Secretary of State James F. Byrnes in 1946.[102]

The so called national police reserve was organized into five divisions and was equipped with the arms supplied to it by the United States. In the words of the American diplomatic adviser to SCAP who had inside knowledge of the Japanese government at that time "The new Japanese army, in fact, looked as though it had been made in the United States." Indeed MacArthur advocated the formation of ten divisions and in a letter dated 11 August 1950 and addressed to the head of the American Veteran organization stated that "should the course of world events require that all mankind stand in arms in defense of human liberty and Japan came within the orbit of immediately threatened attack, then the Japanese should mount the maximum defensive power which their resources permit."[104] After his relief as the Supreme Commander for Allied Powers, MacArthur proudly proclaimed that National Police Reserve became an excellent ground force under his guidance. Later in 1951 the Japanese government admitted 405 depurged majors, lieutenant colonels and colonels of the former imperial armed forces for training the National Police Reserve.[105]

Thus, from 1948 the occupation in practice reversed its policies in many important fields one by one. Finally, in May 1951, General Ridgeway authorized the Japanese Government to review and if necessary revise occupation-sponsored legislation. The circle was almost complete and in case any doubts remained in the minds of Japanese observers, they were effectively dispelled by Vice President Nixon, when on his visit to Japan in 1953, he admitted that the United States had been mistaken in insisting on the 'no war' clause in the constitution.[106] These steps on the part of SCAP were hardly consistent with the previous trends in the occupation. The original objectives gave place to expediency and opportunism.[107] The five years since the inception of the occupation had been in some respects a history of doing and then undoing. The fact of the matter was that for the American policy-makers the danger of Communism had come to outweigh all other dangers. If in fighting this danger it should prove necessary to encourage the former discredited leaders to stage a comeback, to curb the rights of labour, and arm the country, these were to be regarded as unfortunate necessities of the cold war.

Japanese reactions to the latest policies of SCAP were a combination of relief, disillusionment and cynicism.[108] It came as a relief to the Japanese conservatives. With the turn of events the Japanese old guards found themselves in the fortunate position of being able to implement policies which they previously could not for fear of being branded as feudalistic and undemocratic. They were hitherto on the defensive, now once more they came into their own and began to co-operate whole-heartedly with the spirit and letter of the new occupation policies. A gradual friendship and alliance began to take shape between American policy-makers and the Japanese conservative leaders.[109] Anti-Communism was the mutual bond between them. It should be noted here that during 1950 the United States was under the grip of McCarthyism. In February 1950, Senator Joseph McCarthy initiated an anti-Communist crusade in America by accusing high officials in the United States Government and others of being Communists.[110] After the outbreak of the Korean War, and under pressure from critics of its Far East foreign policy, the United States had come to associate with Syngman Rhee, Chiang Kai-Shek, and other dictators and undemocratic elements in Asia. In Japan the occupation encouraged the regrouping of the very power-patterns that it had originally tried to destroy. United States policy-makers were also convinced that the Japanese canservative leadership would be more than the progressives amenable to the retention of American forces in and around Japan and would willingly co-operate with the Western powers against the Soviet Union.

The Japanese Socialists and other leftist groups who had earlier enthusiastically supported the SCAPs' reforms, became disillusioned with the reverse course and described it as a 'roll back operation'.[111] They felt deeply betrayed. America's reactionary 'reverse course' as they termed it, was forcing them to defend the American reforms not only against the conservatives, but against the Americans themselves".[112] The Socialists strongly opposed the rearmament of the country and tried to bloc the measure by taking it to the court on the plea that it violated the constitution. The court rejected the contention and stated that the issue was unprecedented, abstract, and theoretical.[113] A thin layer of intellectuals turned cynical toward Supreme Commander for Allied Powers and expressed sympathy with the Communist stand concerning American policies in Japan.

Meanwhile, the economic situation of the country showed marked improvement. The Korean War brought an economic boom to Japan. Japanese manufacturers received special procurement orders from the United Nations forces in Korea. As a result, in 1951, the industrial production of the country exceeded the pre-war volume for the first time since 1944.[114] At the same time, the Japanese were becoming restive under the occupation and demanded its termination. In order to pacify Japanese feelings and get their full co-operation with its military strategy in the Far East, the United States decided to restore Japan to the formal status of an independent state. If a peace treaty meant complete independence for the country, the United States would oppose it. It would also oppose a peace treaty which would put restrictions on Japanese Government and industry. Any peace settlement for Japan that might be agreed upon was to be permanently tied with American political and business interest in that part of the world. This brings us to the story of the peace settlement which was concluded in San Francisco in September, 1951.

REFERENCES

1. United States Department of State, *Bulletin* 26 (18 May 1947) p. 991.
2. *The New York Times*, 22 June 1948, p. 10.
3. *Ibid.*, 22 January 1948, p. 10.
4. John C. Campbell, *The United States in World Affairs : 1947-1948* (New York, 1948) pp. 138-9.
5. John C. Campbell, *The United States in World Affairs : 1945-1947* (New York, 1947) p. 4.
6. *Ibid.*, p. 6.
7. Department of State, *A Decade of American Foreign Policy : Basic Documents, 1941-9* (Washington, 1950) 27-34, Walter Lippman, *The Cold War : A Study in United States Foreign Policy* (New York, 1947) p. 35.
8. The Yalta Agreement stated that "the three governments will jointly assist the people in any European liberated state of former Axis satellite state in Europe where in their judgement conditions require (a) to establish conditions of internal peace; (b) to carry out emergency measures for the relief of distressed peoples, (c) to form interim governmental authorities broadly representative of all democratic elements in the population and pledged to the earliest possible establishment through free elections of governments responsive to the will of the people; and (d) to facilitate where necessary the holding of such elections." *ibid.*, 29, Campbell, op. cit., pp. 6-7.
9. Campbell, op. cit., pp. 49-50.
10. *Ibid.*, p. 59.

11. D.F. Fleming, "American Responsibility for the Cold War" in Daniel M. Smith, (ed.), *Major Problems in American Diplomatic History : Documents and Readings* (Boston, 1964) p. 595.
12. *Ibid.*, p. 596.
13. Campbell, op. cit., pp. 391-400.
14. *Ibid.*, p. 10.
15. Smith, op. cit., p. 595.
16. *The New York Times*, 6 March 1946, p. 4.
17. Smith, op. cit., pp. 597-9.
18. *Ibid.*, p. 600.
19. George F. Kenan, *Russia and the West under Lenin and Stalin* (New York, 1962) p. 361.
20. Campbell, op. cit., pp. 31-2.
21. Harry S. Truman, *Public Papers of the Presidents' of the United States* (Washington, D.C., 1963) p. 178.
22. George F. Kennan, *American Diplomacy 1900-1950* (New York, 1963) p. 99.
23. Truman, op. cit., p. 180.
24. Kennan, op. cit., p. 105.
25. Campbell, op. cit., p. 33.
26. *Ibid.*, p. 38.
27. *Ibid.*, p. 56.
28. *Ibid.*, p. 492.
29. William Reitzel, *et al.*, *United States Foreign Policy 1945-55* (Wisconsin, 1956) pp. 121-2.
30. John C. Campbell, *The United States in World Affairs, 1948-1949* (New York, 1949) p. 1.
31. Reitzel *et al.*, op. cit., p. 113.
32. Jerome B. Cohen, *Economic Problems of Japan* (Princeton, 1952) 2, according to Shigeru Yoshida Japan lost forty-five per cent of its entire land. See United States Department of State, *Conference for the conclusion and signature of the Treaty of Peace with Japan, San Francisco, September 4-8, 1951* (Washington, 1951) p. 278.
33. *Ibid.*
34. Jerome B. Cohen, "International Aspects of Japan's Economic Situations," in Ernest A. Gross, (ed.) *Japan between East and West* (New York, 1957), p. 110.
35. T.A. Bisson, *Prospects for Democracy in Japan* (New York, 1949) pp. 51-2.
36. Campbell, op. cit., p. 157.
37. Jones, *et al.*, n. 4 in Chapter 1, p. 391.
38. *William Costello, Democracy vs. Feudalism*, (Tokyo, 1948) p. 120.
39. SCAP, n. 10, in Chapter 1, pp. 433-4.
40. Secretary General of the Far Eastern Commission, n. 75 in Chapter 2, p. 85.
41. Jones *et al.*, n. 4 in Chapter 1, p. 390.

42. Campbell, op. cit., p. 151.
43. *Ibid.*, p. 159.
44. President Truman said that "the needs of totalitarian regimes are nurtured by misery and want. They spread and grow in the evil soil of poverty and strife" see Truman, op. cit., p. 180.
45. Lindesay Parnot, "Japan Still Worships at Shinto Shrines" *The New York Times Magazine* (10 August 1947) p. 11.
46. William O. Douglas, General of the Army Omar N. Bradley, "The Influence of Military Men in Policy Making" in Gordon B. Turner, *A History of Military Affairs* (New York, 1956) pp. 681-4.
47. *Ibid.*, Burton Sapin, "The Role of the Military in Formulating the Japanese Peace Treaty" p. 724.
48. *Ibid.*, p. 715.
49. United States, Army Department, *Report on Economic Position and Prospects of Japan and Korea and the measures required to improve them.* (Washington, 1948) pp. 14-5.
50. *Ibid.*, p. 14 and 19.
51. Japan, Foreign Office, *Documents concerning the allied occupation of Japan* 2 (Tokyo, 1949) pp. 8-9.
52. *The New York Times*, 27 March 1948, p. 6.
53. *Ibid.*
54. Wildes, n. 42 in Chapter 2, 72. Also see Textor, n. 122, pp. 190-1.
55. Mark Grayn, *Japan Diary* (New York, 1948) p. 341.
56. Wildes, n. 42 in Chapter 1, p. 72.
57. *Ibid.*, 307-8, Robert Guillian, "The Resurgence of Military in Japan" *Pacific Affairs* XXV (September 1952) p. 214.
58. Wildes, n. 42 in Chapter 1, pp. 307-8.
59. General Robert L. Eichelberger, former commander of the Eighth Army was reported to have said in Washington the "I regret that Japan ever was disarmed to an extent that she cannot protect herself from internal disorder." *Nippon Times* 7 February 1949, p. 2.
60. Zaibatsu, n. 95 in Chapter 2.
61. R.C. Kramer, "Japan must compete" *Fortune* 35 (June 1947) p. 179.
62. Campbell, op. cit., p. 293
63. *Ibid.*
64. Peter Calvocaressi, *Survey of International Affairs 1947-48* (London, 1952) p. 344.
65. *Ibid.*, 345, Kawai, n. 12 in Chapter 2, p. 178.
66. Fearey, n. 68 in Chapter 2, p. 112.
67. Reischauer, n. 32 in Chapter 1, p. 325.
68. Swearingen *et al.*, n. 37 in Chapter 2, p. 89.
69. *Ibid.*, 134. See also Munemutsu Yamada, "The Development of Left-wing Intellectuality," *JSPIJ*, n. 30 in Chapter 3, p. 62.
70. *Ibid.*, p. 138.
71. *Ibid.*, p. 210.

72. *Ibid.*, p. 199,
73. Courtney Whitney, *MacArthur : His Rendezvous with History* (New York, 1956) p. 308.
74. Fearey, n. 68 in Chapter 2, p. 84.
75. Ivan Morris, *Nationalism and Right Wing in Japan* (London, 1960) p. 110.
76. See Masao Maruyama, 'A Letter to a Liberal' in the editorial notes entitled "Japanese Intellectuals : Their Thought" *JSPIJ*, n. 30 in Chapter 3, p. 35.
77. Nathaniel Peffer, "The China Crisis is a Crisis for US." *The New York Times Magazine* (14 November 1948), 75-6. See also A. Doak Barnett, *Communist China and Asia* (London, 1960) p. 1.
78. Robert E. Sherwood, *Roosevelt and Hopkins, an Intimate History* (New York, 1948) p. 709.
79. United States Congress, *House Committee on foreign affairs, hearings* 12 (Washington, 1948) p. 1562.
80. Campbell, op. cit., p. 420.
81. Richard P. Stebbins, *The United States in World affairs, 1949* (New York, 1950) p. 425.
82. *The New York Times*, 9 February 1966, p. 38.
83. Andrew Roth, "Asia is Just as Important" *The Nation*, 172 (24 March 1951) pp. 274-6.
84. Truman, n. 39 in Chapter 1, p. 380.
85. Kenneth Scott Latourette, *American Record in the Far East* (New York, 1953) p. 37.
86. United States Congress, op. cit., 1566.
87. *The New York Times*, 14 February 1949, p. 149.
88. Smith, n. op. cit., 618, *The New York Times*, 9 February 1966, p. 38.
89. United States Congress, *Senate Committee on Foreign Relations, Hearings* 20 (Washington, 1952) 6, Richard P. Stebbins, *The United States in World Affairs, 1950* (New York, 1951) p. 181.
90. MacArthur, n. 33 in Chapter 1, p. 386.
91. United States Department of State, *Bulletin* 24 (1951) p. 403.
92. McGeorge Bundy, (ed.), *The Pattern of Responsibility* (Boston, 1952) p. 180.
93. United States State Department *Bulletin*, 22 (1950) pp. 115-6.
94. Reischauer, n. 1 in Chapter 1, p. 217.
95. See the State and Defense Departments recommendations to President Truman, n. 39 in Chapter 1, pp. 400-1, Stebbins, op. cit, 202, 207 and 331-3.
96. Stebbins, op. cit., p. 450.
97. MacArthur, n. 33 in Chapter 1, p. 337.
98. *The New York Times*, 13 February 1949, p. 1.
99. Reischauer, n. 32 in Chapter 1, p. 351. See also Kentaro Hayashi, *JSPIJ*, 39 in Chapter 2, pp. 19-20. In the same issue see also Yoshimi Takeuchi, "Peace and Self-defense," pp. 21-2.

100. Wildes, n. 42 in Chapter 1, p. 49.
101. *Ibid.*
102. Byrnes, n. 23 in Chapter 1, p. 311.
103. Ambassador William Sebald and Russel Brines, *with MacArthur in Japan* (New York, 1965) p. 198.
104. MacArthur, n. 33 in Chapter 1, p. 304.
105. *The New York Herald Tribune*, 21 October 1951, p. 14.
106. Richard M. Nixon, "To the Japanese People" *Contemporary Japan* 22 (Tokyo, 1953) pp. 370-1.
107. Sir George Sansom, "Conflicting purposes in Japan," *Foreign Affairs* 26 (January 1948) p. 309.
108. Richard Storry, *A History of Modern Japan* (London, 1960) p. 245.
109. Textor, n. 76 in Chapter 2, p. 144, Yoshida, n. 9 in Chapter 1, p. 287.
110. Stebbins, op. cit., p. 56.
111. Yoshikazu Sakamoto, "Neutralism and Democracy in Japan" *Far Eastern Survey* 29 (October, 1960) p. 155.
112. Herbert Passin, "The Stratigraphy of Protest in Japan" in Morton A. Kaplan, (ed.) *The Revolution in World Politics* (New York, 1962) p. 106.
113. Wildes, n. 42 in Chapter 1, p. 50.
114. G.C. Allen, *A Short Economic History of Modern Japan* (London, 1962) p. 172.

5

AMERICAN VIEWS ON THE PROBLEM OF A PEACE TREATY AND SECURITY PACT, 1947-51

MACARTHUR'S VIEWS: The making of the Treaty of Peace with Japan, which terminated the allied occupation of that country in September 1951, was a long drawn-out process. It may be recalled that on 17 March 1947, General MacArthur brought the problem of peace with Japan as an inter-allied issue to the attention of the world. Speaking to a gathering of foreign press correspondents in Tokyo on that day, MacArthur stated that the occupation of Japan fell into three phases: military, political, and economic. Supreme Commander for Allied Powers (SCAP) completed the military phase of the occupation by disarming the former enemy and by purging the pre-war leaders responsible for the war. In its political phase, the occupation provided a legal framework in the new constitution for the Japanese people to work out their problems in a democratic way. The occupation forces could do nothing more than watch, control, and guide.[1]

MacArthur had his own concept of the occupation. He was of the opinion that the occupation of the country should not last too long. Prolongation of the occupation would give rise to a colonial psychology both on the part of the occupier and the occupied.[2] He also believed that an early peace treaty would relieve American soldiers from their unfamiliar jobs in Japan and would also further the interests of United States businessmen in that country. He maintained that the economic blockade of Japan at that moment was as severe as it had been during the war. If the blockade were kept up, the choice before the allies lay between supporting Japan or allowing the Japanese to die by millions. He advocated normal trade between Japan and other countries. Finally he concluded that the best solution would be to sign an early peace treaty with Japan which would place that country under the general supervision of the United Nations.[3] In other words, MacArthur favoured withdrawal of American forces from Japan after the signing of a peace treaty.

In April 1947, General MacArthur elaborated further his point of view in an interview with Hugh Borton.[4] According to Borton, MacAthur said that he desired an early peace settlement for Japan because he believed that the occupation had outlived its usefulness. He stated that a settlement with Japan would facilitate a settlement of outstanding differences in Europe between the Western powers and the Soviet Union. He suggested that the peace conference should be held in Tokyo in the summer of 1947, under his general supervision. MacArthur emphasized that the treaty should be non-punitive and that the allies should avoid the mistakes of the Versailles Treaty. He maintained there should be a gap of six months between the formal signing of the treaty and the conference, so that occupation forces could be withdrawn in an orderly fashion. He suggested that the Japanese should be allowed to express their opinion and even be given a vote at the conference. The United States should persuade other countries to sign an early peace with Japan with or without the Soviet Union. As a last resort, the United States and her friends might make a separate treaty with Japan.

Officials in both the state and defense departments seemed to have been displeased with MacArthur's public announcement for a peace treaty with Japan, for they did not share MacArthur's views on the peace settlement.[5] Knowing the prevailing opinion in Washington as he did, MacArthur used the press conference in March 1947, to force the hands of the American authorities.

The views of the war and navy departments.

The views of the War and Navy Departments on the Japanese

peace settlement were diametrically opposed to that of General MacArthur. The military departments were mainly concerned with the alleged Communist threat to Japan. The admirals and generals in the Pentagon believed that an unarmed Japan would fall easy prey to any aggressor from the north. They doubted the ability of the United Nations to defend Japan. Desiring the rearmament of Japan, the military officers regarded the incorporation of the anti-war clause in the Japanese constitution as a mistake. As has been observed, the army did not attach much importance to the reforms introduced by MacArthur, and were willing to reverse some of them in the interest of stability. The fact was that army personnel were reluctant to relinquish their favourable position in the occupied country.

They would not give their consent to a peace settlement which would deny the United States military bases and free movement of troops in the Japanese Islands. Enjoyment of these facilities by the United States was, in their view, a non-negotiable requisite for any peace treaty.[6] The Navy showed great interest in a base at Yokosuka. It also wished to continue its control of the Japanese Mandated Islands and Ryukyu Islands indefinitely. The Navy Department suggested that these islands should be administered by the United States as strategic areas rather than as trust territories, which would be subject to the supervision of the United Nations Trusteeship Council. The army wanted to annex Okinawa and other territories having strategic importance.[7]

Division in the State Department

In the State Department itself, there were divergent views regarding the peace settlement with Japan in 1947. Mainly, there were two groups advocating two different points of view on the issue.[8] One group was headed by High Borton, who was entrusted with the task of preparing a peace treaty for Japan at that time. The general approach of this group was that Japan was capable of reviving its militaristic policy in the Pacific and Asia. Therefore, every precaution should be taken through the treaty to prevent a possible emergence of Japanese military power. The draft treaty prepared by Borton in March 1947, and the revised draft of August 1947, and January 1948, reflected the general thinking of this group. The 1947 draft treaty proposed several restrictions on future actions of Japan. Japan was to have no military forces. It was to engage in no military research, including research on fissionable materials; the building and use of military or civil aircraft were prohibited, as was the stockpiling of strategic raw materials. The draft favoured twenty-five years of surveillance of the country. It provided for a council of ambassadors composed of the representatives of the Far Eastern Commission to maintain overall supervision of Japan. Beneath this group, a Commission of Inspection was to be created to report on any violation of the demilitarization provisions contained in the treaty. The rights and freedom of the Japanese were to be guaranteed by the Allied Powers. Japan was to continue Supreme Commander for Allied Powers-instituted reforms. The draft treaty barred Japanese groups associated with pre-war military activities from holding public office.[9]

The other important group in the State Department concerned with the Japanese Peace Treaty was Policy Planning Staff (PPS), created in April 1947. It was headed by George F. Kennan and its function was to centralize the planning activities of the various organs of the State Department. The thinking of this group on the problem of peace reflected the views of its chairman, who was widely known in the United States as one of the best exponents of the doctrine of containment of Communism.

To begin with, the Policy Planning Staff thought that the draft treaty prepared by Hugh Borton did not take into account the Cold War situation that was developing in 1947.[10] The members of this group did not favour an early peace treaty for Japan for the following reasons. They regarded the political, economic, and social conditions of Japan as unstable and doubted that country's ability to stand on its own feet so soon. The Policy Planning Staff felt that SCAP had weakened the pre-war fabric of Japan by depriving the nation of its experienced leaders and by re-organizing the country's economic structure.

Taking a dim view of Japan's economic prospects, the members of the group expressed the possibility of a national upsurge in that country after the signing of a peace treaty. In the unstable conditions of the country, only extreme groups—the old clique or the Communists—would have a chance to capture power in Japan. The weak and decentralized police would not be able to cope with internal disturbance and subversion. In view of these possibilities it would be unrealistic to think that Japan would be friendly toward the United States after the peace settlement. The Policy Planning Staff recommended, therefore, that the United States should not emphasize an early peace treaty for Japan. Instead, the United States should utilize time by prolonging the occupation to strengthen Japan economically and politically.

Regarding security matters, the members of the group felt that the immediate threat to Japan did not come from external aggression but from internal Communist subversion. In order to meet this challenge, the Policy Planning Staff suggested that the United States negotiate a security pact with Japan after the conclusion of a peace treaty. It is interesting to note that this group did not favour the idea of making the two treaties inseparable. It was felt that the linking of the two treaties would give the impression of dictation by the United States.[11] It is clear from the foregoing account that the Policy Planning Staff shared neither the views of the Borton group nor those of General MacArthur.

While the experts in the State Department were struggling to evolve a policy for Japan, economy-minded Congressmen came forward in favour of an early peace treaty. As has been pointed out earlier, Japan was costing the United States a million dollars per day. During the years 1945-57, the United States had already spent 759 million dollars on Japan, excluding army expenses in that country.[12] In 1947, when the War Department requested the Appropriation Committee to sanction 725 million dollars for relief in Germany, Japan, and Korea, the chairman of the Appropriation Committee sought the advice of Herbert Hoover. Ex-president Hoover recommended an immediate peace treaty with Germany and Japan on the ground that these countries, it freed from allied occupation, would be able to contribute to the free economy of the world and would no longer be dependent on the United States. American business interests also advocated an early peace treaty for Japan. Financial circles in the United States believed that a peace settlement would facilitate trade investment in Japan and hasten Japanese reconstruction.[13]

At the same time the British Commonwealth countries were also showing active interest in an early peace treaty with Japan. They had called a conference of foreign ministers of the Commonwealth, which was to be held on 26 August 1947, in Canberra. The Australian Secretary of External Affairs, Hebert Evatt, took a personal interest in the Japanese peace settlement.[14]

MacArthur's advocacy of an early peace, the concern of the Congressmen over the cost of the occupation, and the interest of the British Commonwealth members in the Japanese Peace Settlement created pressure on the United States. Policy-makers in Washington were of two minds with regard to an early peace settlement for Japan. However, in order to pacify the various pressure groups, the United States decided to call an early peace conference.

The United States proposal for a peace treaty in 1947

The Council of Foreign Ministers was making very slow progress on the German Peace Treaty. It appeared that it might be years before the Council could consider a peace treaty for Japan. It was handicapped by its procedure, which gave each member a veto. Any United States proposal on Japan contrary to the Soviet interest in the Far East would be vetoed. In view of these difficulties, the United States sought some other approach to the peace settlement in the Far East. The Far Eastern Commission, with its broad representation, seemed to be a proper forum for drafting a peace treaty with Japan. Moreover, the United States could be sure of substantial support in the Far Eastern Commission on any proposal she might make.

In July 1947, the United States Government proposed to the governments of the other ten countries serving on the Far Eastern Commission that a conference of governments represented on the Far Eastern Commission be held on 19 August 1947 to consider a peace treaty for Japan.[15] It was suggested that, in the initial stage, the conference be composed of the deputies of the foreign ministers and that it tackle problems of substance in the treaty. The United States made an attempt to avoid the veto problem by suggesting that decisions at the conference be made by a simple two-thirds majority. All the countries except the Soviet Union and China agreed to the proposal. Countries attending the Canberra conference, which was scheduled for 26 August 1947, asked for a postponement of the peace conference until September. The Soviet Union was of the opinion that the Council of Foreign Ministers was the proper forum to discuss a peace treaty for Japan. This procedural wrangle, and other differences between the United States, the Soviet Union, and other countries will be discussed in the next chapter.

The big question that emerges from the foregoing account is, did the United States really want the peace conference to materialize ? If the answer is in the affirmative, then why did the State Department schedule the conference on 17 August, knowing that the foreign ministers of the Commonwealth were going to meet at Canberra on 26 August. Authorities in the States Department should have known that it would be physically impossible for the British Commonwealth countries to give attention to two conferences which were scheduled to take place within a week's time. It is possible that the State Department did not intend that the conference meet, therefore, it chose an inconvenient date. Further United States policy-makers proposed a procedure which they probably knew would be rejected by the Soviet Union, and as a result a deadlock would occur. The United States peace proposal seemed to be an adroit diplomatic move made to silence critics and pacify peacemakers. Policy-makers in the United States could cite the proposals as an evidence to Congressmen and the public that steps were being taken for a peace settlement with Japan. If the peace proposals failed, the United States could still say that it was not because of any lack of concern on the part of Washington, but because of Soviet objections. What did the United States gain by its Machiavellian diplomacy ? According to an American author :

> If any Machiavellianism at all is to be imputed to the State Department at this time, it should perhaps be nothing more than the minor Machiavellianism of thinking up a desire for gaining time."[16]

The United States needed time to settle interdepartmental differences and also to consolidate its position in Japan. In addition, the then Under Secretary of State Dean Atcheson was of the opinion that progress on European peace treaties would be necessary before the allied powers could consider a peace treaty for Japan.[17]

The real reasons behind the Machiavellian diplomacy were that, first of all, a peace treaty in 1947 would have assigned Japan to no particular sphere of influence. Secondly, a treaty at that time would have sanctioned Russian membership on the allied supervisory commission to observe Japan's adherence to the terms of the peace treaty. As we have already seen, United States military authorities were firmly opposed to such an arrangement. In view of these unpleasant possibilities, a peace settlement was to be avoided. Therefore, in January 1948, the United States, after exchanging copious notes with the Soviet Union and other concerned governments quietly dropped the subject and got on to the business of economic reconstruction of Japan.

In the latter part of 1947 and throughout 1948, pressure was exerted on the United States from various quarters for a peace treaty with Japan. On 16 August 1947, *The New York Times*, in an editorial, called for an early peace settlement with the former enemy, with or without Soviet participation.[18] On 28 September 1948, Senator Taft from Ohio, a prominent Republican leader, suggested in his Seven Point Foreign Policy Programme that negotiation for a peace settlement be initiated as rapidly as possible.[19] In November 1948, the House Sub-committee on Armed Forces expressed its concern over the great cost of continuation of the occupation and recommended that the occupation be ended by signing a peace treaty with or without Soviet consent. On 3 November 1948, the General

Assembly of the United Nations, in a resolution, urged the great powers to reconcile their differences and make peace with Germany and Japan.[20] In spite of all these pressures, the United States did not make any fresh diplomatic move to break the deadlock in 1948.

Second attempt at peace settlement—1949

In September 1949, the United States made another attempt to reach a settlement on the Japanese peace treaty. The situation had changed in at least two important ways since the first attempt made to sign a peace treaty, two years earlier. First the United State policy toward Japan had changed from reform to economic reconstruction. Secondly, dramatic events had occurred in the world since 1947. A coup d'etat had taken place in Czechoslovakia. The Marshal Plan for Europe was in operation. NATO had just held its first meeting in Washington. The Chinese Communist Party had won a decisive victory on the mainland of China, and the Soviet Union had exploded its first atomic bomb. All these developments, and especially the communist control of China, had introduced new elements in the security problems of the United States in the Pacific.[21]

There was considerable disagreement among the different agencies of the United States Government on the mode of defending a disarmed Japan after a peace settlement.

Lt. General J. Lawton Collins, Vice Chief of Staff of the Army, stated in February 1949 that American forces in Japan should be strengthened greatly, especially in view of the Chinese Communist success on the mainland.[22] Few days later, in March 1949, MacArthur said in a newspaper interview that he did not believe that the Soviet Union would attack Japan. However, in case of attack the United States should certainly defend her. With regard to the future security of Japan, MacArthur said that:

> Japan should be the Switzerland of the Far East and neutral for the same reasons Switzerland is neutral———no matter which side she might join, she would be inevitably destroyed.[23]

He further stated that the United States never intended to use Japan as an ally. The Supreme Commander was of the opinion that despite the Chinese Communist victory on the mainland, American interests in the Pacific were quite secure. On the problem of the rearmament of Japan, MacArthur held the opinion that the question could be decided only after the signing of a peace treaty. It may be recalled here, that MacArthur apparently changed his views on the issue and openly advocated the rearmament of Japan after the outbreak of the Korean War.

According to a report from Manila on 4 November 1949, MacArthur was again reported to have made three alternative suggestions on security arrangements for Japan.[24] He proposed: (i) entrance of Japan into the United Nations and a guarantee of her territorial integrity by that organization; (ii) establishment of United States millitary bases in Japan as a long-term arrangement, and (iii) protection of Japan by joint United States-Commonwealth forces. At the same time MacArthur pressed for an early settlement with Japan.

Before we deal with the differences of opinion between the State Department and the Defense Department, on the question of security in the Pacific, the immediate cause which brought these differences to the fore should be mentioned. In the middle of 1949 the demand for a Japanese peace settlement grew greater. In May 1949, at the meeting of the Council of Foreign Ministers in Paris, the Soviet Foreign Secretary proposed that the members of the council should meet at an early date to consider a peace treaty for Japan. The Pacific nations, especially Australia, continued to be critical of the American policy of granting piece-meal peace to the Japanese and suggested that the matter be dealt with in a peace treaty.[25] The British government, under pressure from her Commonwealth partners, urged the United States to move toward a quick settlement in the Far East. In the middle of September 1949, British Foreign Secretary Bevin, and the Under-Secretary for the Far East, Sir Easter Denning, journeyed to Washington and held a series of meeting with their American counterparts. The officials of both countries recognized the urgency of the Japanese peace problem. They also agreed on the fundamentals of a peace treaty: that it should be a non-punitive treaty and that the United States should have military bases in post-treaty Japan to protect that country. The British officials expressed their willingness to go along with the United States on matters of procedure, that is, that the treaty be considered by the member-governments of the Far Eastern Commission. To make sure that the United States had sufficient votes in the proposed conference to carry its proposals, the American officials requested the British Foreign Secretary to have a prior understanding among the members of the Commonwealth on the American proposals concerning a Japanese peace treaty. Bevin agreed to act as an intermediary between the United States and the Commonwealth at its forthcoming meeting at Canberra in November 1949. He requested a statement of American requirements to be presented to Commonwealth members at the meeting. At the conclusion of these parleys, Secretary of State Dean Acheson annouced to the press that the United States and Britain had agreed on the urgent need for a Japanese peace treaty.[26] However, a date for a peace conference was still to be decided. At this moment the scene again shifted to the inter-departmental tug of war in Washington.

In order to comply with the request of the British Foreign Secretary, Dean Acheson instructed the officials in charge of Japanese affairs in the State Department to prepare a draft peace treaty. Knowing that the Pentagon had strong reservations regarding the Japanese peace settlement, Acheson requested Defense Secretary Johnson to assign an official to work with the State Department, and provide a statement on the military needs of the United States in the Pacific.

The State Department completed a draft treaty on 13 October 1949. This draft will be discussed later in the chapter. The Defense Department had fundamental differences on the need for an early peace treaty, and on more important matters, namely, security arrengements in the Pacific.[27] Because of this, the United States could not provide a complete statement of American demands in time either for the Canberra meeting in November 1949, or the conference of Commonwealth Foreign Ministers in Colombo in January 1950.

Differences between the state department and the defense department on the problem of peace and security

By the middle of 1949 a firm impasse had arisen between the Department of State and the Defense Department. The Joint Chiefs of Staff, with the backing of Defense Secretary Johnson and Army Under Secretary Tracy S. Voorhees, were reported to be of the opinion that a peace treaty with Japan at that time, even if it could be negotiated, would be detrimental to the interests of all nations, including Japan, which feared Soviet agression.[28] The underlying idea was that no post-treaty security arrangement could be as advantageous militarily to the United States as the situation during occupation, and therefore, it was claimed that the treaty was premature. Military authorities argued that if a contractual arrangement were made with Japan for the use of particular bases in that country, American ability to defend the Japanese islands would be limited. Under that kind of arrangement, American forces in particular bases would be vulnerable to pin-point attack. In other words, the military leaders desired the conversion of all of Japan into an American military base and wanted no interference from the Japanese Government on the movement of troops in that country and to other parts of Asia. As one author has put it :

> American military strategists were thinking only in terms of another Spain in the Far East, ... to make a fortress of Japan, and while certain American business circles were aiming to supply with the raw products from which the material of war can be produced . . .[29]

According to the military chiefs in the Pentagon one of the greatest deterrents to Soviet aggression in Europe or in the Middle East was the realization that the Soviet Union would have to fight a two-front war, in both Europe and in Asia. So long as Japan was protected by United States' troops, Soviet Communism could not dominate the Far East, nor could the Soviet Union risk a war in which it might be attacked from the Japanese Islands.[30]

The Defense Department was also concerned with the military consequences of a treaty to which the Soviet Union was not a signatory. In that case the Soviet Union would still be technically at war with Japan and, in accordance with the Moscow Agreement of 1945, might legally be allowed to continue the occupation.[31]

The officials in the State Department did not disagree with the analysis of the importance of Japan, but felt that a reliable association between Japan and the Western powers could be negotiated only by restoring a large measure of independence to the Japanese Government in a peace treaty.

It was felt by officials of the State Department that the United States occupation of Japan was becoming increasingly unpopular with the Japanese people. The longer a peace treaty was delayed, the more difficult it would become to keep Japan on the side of Western powers. The Communists and other leftist groups in Japan were doing everything they could to inflame Japanese public opinion against the occupation authorities. As time passed, it was felt that the authority and prestige of the occupation troops would deteriorate and might reach a point where the Japanese might not agree to any treaty in which the Western powers retained security bases in Japanese Islands. Considering the time-factor, the State Department felt that the United States should go ahead with a peace treaty without the participation of the Soviet Union and Communist China.

State Department officials contended that it was for the Joint Chiefs of Staff to define the kind of arrangements they thought were necessary in Japan for the security of the United States, and it was the function of the State Department to negotiate those arrangements.[32] Merely to prolong the occupation of Japan indefinitely because the Japanese islands provided base of operation against a Soviet attack, was regarded by the officials at the State Department as short-sighted and probably in the end a dangerous policy. State Department officials maintained, also, that a secure base in Japan over a long period of time could be obtained with the approval and support of the Japanese people.

The Army's real intentions were revealed in the proposals made by the then Under Secretary of the Army, Tracy Voorhees, in March 1950. In December 1949 Under Secretary Voorhees led a delegation of top military officials to Japan and after his return made the proposal that the United States should grant a half-treaty to Japan. Under this ingenious treaty, Japan was to enjoy internal autonomy, with defesce matters and foreign relations of the country to be looked after by the United States through Supreme Commander for Allied Powers.[33] The essence of the half-treaty was that Japan should be reduced to the status of a protectorate of the United States. This device would also solve the legal right of the Soviet Union to send troops to Japan. Since Supreme Commander for Allied Powers would continue its existence, it would exercise its legal authority to control the number of Soviet soldiers entering the country. This suggestion was made on the assumption that the Soviet Union would not be a party to such a treaty and, therefore, still would be technically at war with Japan, possessing the legal right to station her troops in that country. This proposal, though rejected at the moment it was made, was ultimately accepted by the State Department by making the security treaty a part of the peace settlement.

The 13 October 1949 Draft Treaty of Peace

The 13 October 1949 Draft Treaty of Peace, to which reference has been made, further explained the difference that existed between the State Department and the Defence Department.[34] Unlike the 1947-48 draft, the 13 October 1949 draft contained very few restrictions on Japanese sovereignty. The draft prescribed no control commission to supervise its observance by the Japanese. Under this draft, the Far Eastern Commission, the Allied Council for Japan, and Supreme Commander for Allied Powers were to be abolished. Japan was required to preserve a democratic form of government, including freedom of speech, religion, and so forth. The draft did not mention agricultural, labour, and deconcentration reforms; instead it left them to the discretion of the Japanese themselves. Japan was to pay reparations, but the draft made no reference to the stock of gold in Japan or to gold owned by Japan in neutral countries. It thereby exempted Japan from making indemnification from the stock. Japan was to pay GARIOA and EROA grants from the United States and the payment of these was to have priority over all reparations.[35] The draft also gave the United States control over the volume of reparations to be extracted from Japan by the other allied nations. The draft treaty contained security provisions, as they were to be incorporated after collaboration with the Defense Department.

A commentary on intentions and motivations accompanied the draft treaty. The primary motive was to make Japan a close ally of the United States. The farmers of the draft calculated that this objective could be achieved by offering a non-restrictive and liberal treaty. It was mentioned that insistence on the retention of the occupation reforms would be considered humiliating by the Japanese, but, at the same time, omission of reference to these measures did not mean a repudiation of them. Economic pressure and other means could be used to influence the Japanese to continue them.

The commentary also anticipated the legal problem that would arise if the Soviet Union did not sign the treaty. In that case the abolition of the Far Eastern Commission and the ACJ could be considered to be in violation of the Moscow Agreement of December 1945. It was suggested that if this issue should arise, it could be referred to the International Court of Justice. These differences between two very important agencies of the United States Government, the State Department and the Defense Department, continued until the outbreak of the Korean War.

At this juncture John Foster Dulles entered the picture. On 6 April 1950 Dulles was appointed foreign policy advisor to the Secretary of State. He was assigned the task of preparing a peace treaty for Japan. An unusual combination of domestic circumstances brought Dulles to this undertaking. It has been observed, in 1950 the Democratic Administration was under fire in the Congress for the alleged failure of its policy in China. President Truman, in order to restore bipartisanship in foreign policy, brought Dulles, who enjoyed the confidence of both the Republican and Democratic parties, to the State Department as an advisor. Dulles had a certain concept of a peace treaty which was based partly on his moral conviction and partly on his long experience in foreign affairs.[36]

He advocated a liberal treaty for Japan and maintained that Japan should not be treated like a venquished nation. Harsh terms, he thought, would necessarily inspire Japan with a desire for vengeance. The allies should be just and magnanimous and should avoid the mistakes of the Versailles Treaty. Further, it should be a treaty of trust and opportunity explaining why Japan should be trusted, Dulles observed that it was "not because the past justified trust, but because the act of extending trust usually evokes an effort to merit trust."[37]

Dulles believed that the greatest threat to world peace was the international Communist movement, which promoted world revolution.[38] In his view, Communism was immoral, and at times he appeared to advocate dubious means to fight the advancement of Communism. For example, in his memorandum on the Japanese peace treaty issued on 6 June 1950, Dulles said that it was possible to capitalize on the Japanese feeling of racial superiority to Chinese, Koreans, and Russians, and to convince the Japanese that as a part of the free world they would be in equal fellowship with the Western group, which was superior to the members of the Communist world[39] Dulles suggested also that a security treaty, independent of the peace treaty, should be concluded. This should involve all the nations participating in the preliminary conference. At the same time Dulles insisted on the rearmament of Japan. To solve the question of Chinese representation in the peace conference, Dulles suggested that both the Nationalist and the Communist governments be invited to send delegates and each should be allowed one vote on issues on which they disagreed. On matters on which they agreed, however, there would be only one vote for both of them. There should not be any reparations and there should not be any restriction on the Japanese economy.

With these convictions Dulles set to work on a peace treaty for Japan. He made several trips to Japan and visited other countries which were interested in the Japanese peace settlement.

The first problem that confronted Dulles was the deadlock between the States and Defense Department regarding security matters in the Pacific. This dilemma had to be resolved before any meaningful negotiation for a peace treaty could be initiated. On 17 June 1950, the two departments sent their top men to Tokyo to enlist the support of General MacArthur to their respective points of view on the Japanese issue. One party was led by Dulles. The second party consisted of the Secretary of Defense, Louis Johnson, and General Omar Bradley, the Chairman of the Joint Chiefs of Staff. The two delegations arrived separately in Tokyo within a few hours of each other. This demonstrated the acuteness of the differences between the two departments. According to an American diplomat, Secretary Johnson openly denounced the attitude of the "State Department crowd" and Dulles in "shocking terms."[40] The Defense Secretary described Dulles as an impractical man. The spokesmen for the military again insisted that the occupation be continued indefinitely. MacArthur's sympathies were with the State Department. He set his familiar views on the peace settlement in a memorandum and made it available to the visiting dignitaries. Regarding the security of Japan, the memorandum stated that the United States forces should continue to occupy 'points in Japanese territory' until irresponsible militarism is driven from the world...[41] In a three cornered discussion between Dulles, General Omar Bradley, and General MacArthur, "The groundwork was laid for an agreement based on the practical logic of the time."[42] The Defense Department's condition that the American forces should enjoy unrestricted rights in Japan was accepted, as was evidenced by the Security Treaty and the Administrative Agreement, which was signed after the peace settlement. The agreement amounted to a half treaty. Leaders of the Japanese government also played a significant role in this agreement. The Japanese role in the making of the peace treaty will be dealt with in a later chapter.

The agreement reached at Tokyo was formalized several months later in a joint memorandum prepared by the Departments of State and Defense. On 8 September 1950 the President approved the memorandum.[43]

The outbreak of the Korean War on 25 June 1950, as we have already seen, accelerated the process of peace-making. Dulles saw in the attack an attempt by the Soviet Union to check United States' efforts to conclude a peace treaty. For a few weeks, the treaty had to wait while the United States took stock of the situation. The assessment of the new situation convinced many hitherto reluctant people of the need for a rapid peace settlement with Japan if she were to be brought into an anti-Communist orbit in the Pacific. The Korean War also strengthened the position of the Defense Department on the problem of Japanese security.[44]

Challenges to the occupation from the forces of right and left in Japan

Dulles had met a number of Japanese leaders of both the ruling party and the opposition parties while he was in Tokyo in June 1950 and had observed the growing impatience of the Japanese for the end of the occupation. The Communist Party and other leftist groups in Japan were exploiting the national feelings of Japanese workers againt foreign occupation.[45] As we have already seen, during 1949-50 the occupation had stiffened its attitude toward labour unions. The result of these actions and reactions was an explosive incident on 30 May 1950, the American Memorial Day. On that day, during a labour demonstration in front of the Imperial Palace, some workers and students clashed openly with the American G. I.'s. The industrialists of the Kansai area, desiring to resume trade with Communist China, were eagerly looking toward a peace settlement. In 1950 the local tax reform bill was for the first time in the history of the occupation defeated in the House of Councillors, despite the fact that the bill had the backing of Supreme Commander for Allied Powers. This was the first open challenge to occupation authorities on the part of the Japanese Diet. These were all unmistakable signs that the Japanese people wanted independence. In the Korean War the Japanese saw a threat to their security and became acutely aware of their unarmed position.

Dulles contended that the growing desire for independence and the threat of Communist expansion made the Japanese more anxious than ever before to regain their sovereignty under the terms offered by the Western powers.[46] He said that the opportunity should be utilized by the western powers.

On 14 September 1950, President Truman announced in a press conference that the State Department was authorized to initiate further discussion with the member-nations of the Far

Eastern Commission in regard to a peace treaty with Japan.[47] This announcement was followed in November 1950 by the circulation of a seven-point memorandum to the members of the Far Eastern Commission on the suggested contents of the treaty.[48] The first of the seven points left little doubt that the United States was by that time quite prepared to make peace without the Soviet Union if the Soviets should prove uncompromising.

The Seven-Point Memorandum

The Seven Point Memorandum may be summarized as follows:

(1) *Parties* to the treaty would be any or all nations at war with Japan which were willing to make peace on the basis proposed or as might be agreed;

(2) *UN* membership by Japan was to be comtemplated;

(3) *Territory*: Japan was to recognize the independence of Korea, agree to UN trusteeship of the Ryukyu and Bonin Islands, with the United States as administering authority, accept the further decision of the UK, USSR, China and United States with reference to the status of Formosa, the Pescadores, South Sakhalin and the Kuriles. In the event of no decision within a year after the treaty came into effect, the UN General Assembly was to decide. Special rights and interests in China were to be renounced by Japan.

(4) *Security*: Pending a satisfactory alternative security arrangement, such as a UN assumption of effective responsibility, there was to be continuing co-operative responsibility between Japan and the United States, and perhaps other forces, for the maintenance of international peace and security in the Japanese area.

(5) *Political and Commercial Agreements*: Japan was to agree to multilateral treaties dealing with narcotics and fishing. Pre-war bilateral treaties were to be revived by mutual agreements. Pending the conclusion of new commercial treaties, Japan was to extend most-favoured-nation treatment, subject to normal exceptions.

(6) *Claims*: All parties were to waive claims arising out of war acts prior to 2, September 1945, except that

(a) the allied powers were to hold Japanese property within their territories, and

(b) Japan was to restore allied property or, if the property was not restorable, Japan was to provide yen to compensate for an agreed percentage of lost value.

(7) *Disputes* : Claims-disputes were to be settled by a special neutral tribunal to be set up by the President of the International Court of Justice. Other disputes were to be referred, either to diplomatic settlement, or to the International Court of Justice.

The memorandum made it clear that the statement was only suggestive and tentative and did not commit the United States Government to the detailed content or wording of any future draft. The memorandum further stated that after the members of the Far Eastern Commission had had an opportunity to study the statement, a series of informal conferences would be held to make clarifications and elaborations of other points.

On 10 January 1951, the President approved a joint recommendation of the Secretary of State and the Secretary of Defense that a presidential mission headed by John Foster Dulles be sent to Japan and to other capitals of the Allied powers to explore their views regarding collective security in particular, and the peace treaty in general.[49] The mission was to explore especially Japanese views regarding collective security arrangements.

The Pacific Security Arrangements

The outbreak of the Korean War had made the problem of security in the Pacific more complex. When Dulles undertook his mission in June 1950, he had been instructed to negotiate a regional security pact for the Pacific. But a Pacific Pact did not materialize for the following reasons. During his trip to Australia, New Zealand, and the Philippines, Dulles learned that the leaders of these countries looked upon the problem of security in the Pacific from a different angle. For them security meant safeguards against the revival of Japanese aggression. They feared Japanese aggression, which they had experienced, more than the threat of Chinese or Russian Communist expansion. Therefore, they refused to join a security arrangement which included Japan.[50] The differences among the allied powers on the question of security and other matters concerning the peace treaty will be discussed in the next chapter.

Secondly, it was felt by some that there was a danger in drawing a line of defense in the Pacific. It would have a bad effect on the other countries in that area which were left out. It would also look like an invitation to the Communists to extend their influence over the excluded areas. The implication was that the United States would not go to the assistance of the areas outside the defense line in case of attack.

On the other hand, for various reasons it was not practicable at that time to define a line which would bring all the free people of the Pacific and Asia into a formal security arrangement.

First of all, Australia, New Zealand, and the Philippines would not be a party to such a treaty for the reasons already described. Second, the future of Korea was still uncertain in 1951. Third, newly independent nations such as Indonesia and Burma which had the bitter experience of Japanese aggression and the exploitation of Western colonial powers, would not enter into a security relationship either with Japan or with the Western powers. Fourth, in Malaya and Indo-China, military help had to be given through Britain and France, a procedure which many in Asia would look upon as perpetuating colonialism. Fifth, other countries in Asia were unwilling to qualifying for definite security arrangements under the Vandenberg Formula of continuous and effective self-help and mutual aid.[51]

Lastly, military authorities of the United States did not look favourably upon any arrangement which obliged the United States to extend its protection to all of the Southeast Asian countries. Such an arrangement might compel it to spread its strength so widely that it would have no reserves and would be vulnerable at every point; and it would weaken the defense of Europe.

In the end it was decided to have three interlocking pacts. First, there would be a bilateral pact between the United States and Japan which would provide for Japanese security through the presence of American troops on the invitation of the

Japanese Government. Second, there would be a bilateral pact between the United States and the Philippines which would recognize existing obligations and put them on a mutual basis. And third, there would be a three-power pact, including the United States, Australia, and New Zealand, which would assure those countries of American assistance in the event of renewed aggression from Japan.[62]

The foregoing account indicates that the pentagon played a primary role in making the peace settlement with Japan. In this connection it should be remembered that the occupation of Japan was a military set-up. As we have already seen in previous chapters, military officers and civilian personnel in the Army and Defense Departments played a major role in evolving a policy for Japan and also in the day-to-day operation of the occupation. They were responsible to a large extent for reversal of the occupation policy toward Japan in 1947 and in rearming that country after the Korean War. Within the military establishment there were two groups with divergent views on the Japanese peace settlement. One group consisted of the civilian and military personnel in General Head-quarters, Supreme Commander for Allied Powers in Japan. The other group was made up of those military and civilian officials within the Army and Defense Departments in Washington with policy-making responsibility for the occupied areas. MacArthur and other Supreme Commander for Allied Powers' officials sided with the State Department in its controversy with the Defense Department over the peace settlement. Secondly, security desiderata were at the very heart of the Japanese peace treaty problem. In fact, policy makers did not seem to be so much concerned with peace-making as they were with the security arrangement. After 1947, the United States increasingly viewed the Japanese peace settlement as a cold war issue. Washington wanted to establish a peace settlement which would act as a deterrent against Communist expansion. The three interlocking military pacts described above constituted the deterrent in the Far East. Japan was a vital link in this arrangement. Also the Army, Navy, and the Air Force had been using, and in some cases expanding and building, new air and naval bases in Japan since the end of the war. They were reluctant to give up their command position and, therefore, had a stake in the peace treaty. The security problem further involved such delicate matters as the stationing of American forces in post-treaty Japan and the privileges and prerequisites to be granted them. The military was exerting great pressure to obtain for itself the widest possible privileges and fewest possible restrictions in the security arrangement. The State Department, however, tended to be more aware of Japanese sensibilities and was willing to settle for less by way of privileges.

Another interesting fact which stands out in the discussions over the peace treaty was that a very well-informed group in the State Department believed that the Japanese old clique was capable of reviving the military power of Japan. The 1947-48 and 1949 draft peace treaty sufficiently indicated this belief. This line of thinking, seen in the context of the attempts made by the Japanese conservative party to preserve the old and discredited institutions in that country, seemed plausible at that time.

In the next chapter we will see the reaction of the members of the Far Eastern Commission to the American proposals on the peace treaty. The two charts attached to this chapter were prepared by the author. They show in a brief summary the viewpoints on the peace settlement of the Three United States agencies concerned with the occupation.

REFERENCES

1. SCAP, n. 10 in Chapter 1, p. 765.
2. *The Washington Post*, 29 April 1949, p. 25.
3. SCAP, n. 10 in Chapter 1, p. 765.
4. Hugh Borton was chief of the Division of Japanese Affairs in the State Department. At that time he was engaged in drafting a peace treaty for Japan. In fact, in March 1947, he had gone to Tokyo to show the draft peace treaty to General MacArthur. See F.C. Jones *et al*, n. 4 in Chapter 1, p. 422.
5. Thc then Under-secretary of State Dean Acheson described MacArthur's suggestion as impractical. See Burton Sapin, n. 47 in Chapter 4, p. 753.
6. Ambassador Sebald, n, 103 in Chapter 4, p. 245.
7. Douglas W. Overton, *Reminiscens* (Oral History Research Office

Columbia University, New York, 1960) p. 30.

8. Frederick S. Dunn, *Peace-Making and the Settlement with Japan* (Princeton, 1963) p. 57.
9. *Ibid.*, pp. 58-9.
10. *Ibid.*, p. 60.
11. *Ibid*., p. 61.
12. Fearey, n. 68 in Chapter 2, p. 218.
13. Bernard C. Cohen, *The Political Process and Foreign Policy : The Making of the Japanese Peace Treaty* (Princeton, 1957) 107-9, Council on World Affairs Northern California, *Peace Making with Japan* 2 (San Francisco, 15 March 1948), p. 4.
14. R.N. Rosecrance, *Australian Diplomacy and Japan, 1945-1951* (London, 1962) pp. 72-4.
15. United States, Department of State, *Bulletin* 17 (27 July 1947) p. 182.
16. Dunn, op. cit., p. 66.
17. Sapin, n. 47 in Chapter 4, p. 753.
18. *The New York Times* 16 August, 1947, p. 12.
19. *Ibid.*, 26 September 1947, p. 16.
20. United Nations Department of Public Information, *Yearbook of the United Nations 1948-49* (New York, 1950) pp. 333-6.
21. Sapin, n. 47 in Chapter 4, p. 754.
22. *The New York Times*, 26 February 1949, p. 1.
23. *Ibid.*, 2 March 1949, p. 22.
24. *Ibid.*, 5 November 1949, p. 5.
25. Rosecrance, op. cit., p. 149.
26. *The New York Times*, 15 September 1949, p. 3.
27. Ambassador Sebald, n. 103 in Chapter 4, p. 247.
28. *The New York Times*, 12 May 1950, 4, *The New York Times*, 10 July 1950, p. 1 and 5.
29. Stanley I. Stuber, "Self-Defense for Japan" *The Christian Century*, 68 (5 September 1951) pp. 1010-1.
30. *The New York Times*, op. cit., p. 4.
31. The Far Eastern Commission laid down that "changes in the Japanese Constitutional structure or in the regime of control, or dealing with a change in the Japanese government as a whole will be issued only following consultation and following the attainment of agreement in the Far Eastern Commission" See SCAP, n. 10 in Chapter 1, p. 421.
32. *The New York Times*, op. cit., 4, Sapin, n. 47 in Chapter 4, p. 754.
33. *Nippon Times*, (Tokyo), 26 March 1950, p. 1.
34. Dunn, op. cit., pp. 83-6.
35. GARIOA and EROA stand respectively for Government and Relief in Occupied Areas, and Economic Rehabilitation of occupied areas.
36. John Robinson Beal, *John Foster Dulles : 1888-1959* (New York, 1957) p. 118.
37. Speech at Whittier College, Los Angeles, 31 March 1951. See *State Department Bulletin* 26 (9 April 1951) p. 576.

38. "Japan and the Philippines" address before the Philippine Institute of Pacific Relations. *Far Eastern Survey*, 20 (13 June 1951) p. 115.
39. Dunn, op. cit., p. 100.
40. Ambassador Sebald, n. 103 in Chapter 4, p. 253.
41. *Ibid.*, p. 255.
42. *Nippon Times*, 20 June 1950, 1, Beal, op. cit., p. 117.
43. John Foster Dulles, "Japanese Peace Treaty in Retrospect." Address delivered before the Governors' Conference, Gatlinburg, Tenn., 1 October 1951 (Washington, 1951) p. 43.
44. Sapin, 47 in Chapter 4, pp. 761-2.
45. Masao Maruyama, *Nationalism in Post-War Japan*, Document No. 1, 11th Conference of the Institute of Pacific Relations (Lucknow, India, 1950) p. 17.
46. United States Department of State, *Bulletin* 24 (26 March 1951), p. 578.
47. United States, Department of State, *Pacific Security : Its New Foundations*, Publication 4556, Far Eastern Series 48, (April 1952) p. 4.
48. United States State Department, *Bulletin*, 23 (4 December 1950), p. 881.
49. Department of State, *Japanese Peace Conference : San Francisco*, Publication 4355, International Organization and Conference Series 11, (September 1951) p. 5.
50. Department of State, op. cit., p. 3.
51. John Foster Dulles, "Security in the Pacific," *Foreign Affairs* 30 (January 1952) p. 183.
    The Vandenberg Resolution adopted by the Senate in June, 1948 stated that self help and mutual aid would be prerequisite fo r U.S. co-operation and association in regional and other collective arrangements for security. See Arthur H. Vandenberg, Jr. (ed.), *The Private Papers of Senator Vandenberg* (Boston, 1950) pp. 407-8.
52. Department of State, op. cit., pp. 6-7.

6

DIFFERENCES BETWEEN THE US AND THE ALLIES OVER THE PROPOSED PEACE TREATY

WHEN the United States circulated among the nations of the Far Eastern Commission a seven-point memorandum embodying the main principles it sought to write into the Japanese peace treaty, it created a strong reaction in the circle of its friends and foes alike. The Soviet Union was one of the countries which vigorously opposed the proposals. Russian participation or non-participation in the proposed peace conference would have profound effect both on the United States and Japan. Major differences of opinion existed between the Soviet Union and the United States with regard to procedure and substance of the Japanese peace settlement. Behind the legal positions taken by the two governments, there was a deep power struggle between the two war-time partners. As has been observed in the previous chapter, United States policy in Japan was to keep that country out of the Russian orbit, because, as John Foster Dulles put it "with Japan the Soviet Union would become invincible."[1] Therefore, "Peace making with Japan became a phase of the power struggle between the United States and U.S.S.R."[2]

Before World War II the Russians were tied with the Japanese in the contest for the domination of Northeast Asia. The Russo-Japanese tug of war was long and bitter and goes back to the time of the Tsars. The Soviets, who succeeded the Tsar, did not lose interest in Japan. Communists held Japan as a key to the victory of Marxism in Asia. More than forty years ago, Gregory Zinoviev, the leader of the Cominform had declared, at the first Congress of Toilers of the Far East in Moscow that "the only thing that really can solve the Far Eastern question is the defeat of the Japanese bourgeoisie and the final victory of the revolution in Japan."[3] Since the October 1917 revolution, Soviet policy toward Japan had undergone many phases, but the Russians never lost the hope of communising that country.

In 1941 the Soviet Union, in the face of a dire threat to her security both in Europe and in the Far East, tried to minimize the Japanese threat to its eastern flank by entering into a neutrality pact with that country. When Germany was on the verge of defeat and Japan showed unmistakable signs of surrender, the Russians reversed their policy toward Japan. Realizing that continued neutrality in the Pacific war would restrict her role in the Far East, the Soviet Union agreed at the Yalta Conference of February 1945 to declare war against Japan. After the defeat of Japan, the Soviet Union immediately occupied Sakhalin, and Kuriles, and other islands to the north and east of Hokkaido. At the same time, Moscow demanded an effective voice in the occupation of Japan. The Russian policy was to minimize American influence in Japan by controlling the occupation policy on the one hand. On the other hand, Moscow tried to weaken Japan economically and politically by insisting that the terms of surrender should be strictly applied and the Emperor should be tried as a war criminal. The Soviet Union calculated that a weak Japan would turn to Communism. However. MacArthur frustrated the Russian ambition by treating the Soviet representative as a 'piece of furniture' and by ignoring the FEC and the ACJ.[4]

During the first phase of the occupation, the Soviet Union silently co-operated with Supreme Commander for Allied Powers by supporting its democratic measures, because the reforms cut at the very root of Japanese feudal structure. Communists welcomed SCAP's effort to democratize Japan with the hope that it would promote revolutionary movement in the country. In the wake of Cold War and with the shift in American policy toward Japan, the Soviet Union changed its tactics. In 1948, when the

United States embarked upon a policy of economic reconstruction of its former enemy, the Russians intensified their attack on SCAP. Soviet representatives in the FEC and ACJ denounced the revision of the National Public Service Law and SCAP's nine point economic programme. During the same period the construction and expansion of the naval and air bases in the Japanese islands by the United States, convinced the Soviet Union that American influence in Japan would continue even after a peace settlement. Therefore, the Soviet Union decided to oppose any peace settlement with Japan which would promote American interest in the Far East. With a view to prevent such a development, the Russians insisted that a peace treaty for Japan be considered by the Council of Foreign Ministers, in which they enjoyed a vote.

In February 1949, Moscow studied with great interest the reported statement of Secretary of War Royal to the effect that some circles in Washington were seriously considering the withdrawal of United States forces in Japan. The Russians proposed an immediate meeting of the Council of Foreign Ministers to consider a peace treaty. The Soviet Union calculated that the United States would have to lay its cards on the table in the conference. If the United States prepared to leave Japan under the protections of the UN, as was suggested by MacArthur, the Russians would have a free hand in Japan. On the other hand, if the United States rejected the Soviet proposals, Moscow would lose nothing. In fact, it would gain the gratefulness of the Japanese. The Japanese would think that the Soviet Union rather than the United States was interested in ending the occupation. Also, it would put the United States in an awkward position.[5]

In short, both parties regarded the Japanese islands as a prize to be won. Since the Americans were in actual control of the islands, they ultimately succeeded in winning the Japanese to their side. Nevertheless, the Soviet Union did not consider the conclusion of a peace treaty at San Francisco in 1951 as a final victory for American interest in the Far East. In the face of formidable odds, Moscow simply postponed the Pacific battle for some other day. The following summation of the official position of the Soviet Union on the proposed peace treaty should be understood in the context of the foregoing account.

On the question of procedure and substance of the treaty, a number of notes were exchanged between the two governments. Clarification was sought on many points, and questions were raised. In spite of all these written explanations, and the personal talks between John Foster Dulles and J.A. Malik held in October 1950 at the UN, no satisfactory agreement was reached. The differences could be divided into two parts : (i) Procedure and (ii) Substance.

With regard to the procedure to be adopted for the preparation of the Peace Treaty for Japan, the Soviet Union, in an aide-memoir of 20 November 1950, said that the signatories of the Declaration by United Nations in Washington on 1 January 1942 undertook not to conclude a separate peace.[6] It enquired whether the United States possibly contemplated a treaty in which only some of the signatories would participate. The Soviet Union argued that the Peace Treaty with Japan could not be the affair of any one government but should be a joint affair of all those governments, as was provided for by appropriate international agreements. The right to draft a peace treaty with Japan had been assumed by the United States, USSR, China, and United Kingdom, that is, by those states which signed the Japanese Surrender document in accord with the Potsdam Agreement.

The Soviet note of 10 June 1951 to the United States cited the Potsdam Agreement—"the Council will consist of members representing those states which have signed surrender terms dictated to that enemy State which the given task concerns" and drew what it called indisputable conclusions.[7] In the setting up of the Council of Foreign Ministers composed of five powers, in August 1945 at Potsdam, preparatory work on a peace settlement was directly mentioned as its main task. Moreover, the peace settlement was not limited to Europe.

Consequently, the fulfillment of the Potsdam Agreement with respect to the preparation of a peace treaty with Japan required the calling of a meeting of the Council of Foreign Ministers, consisting of the representatives of the United States, USSR, Great Britain, and China. France was excluded because she was not a signatory to the Japanese terms of surrender. The Soviet Union said that the objection to this proposal on the part of the United States was not understandable.[8] The Russians further maintained that the United States intended to ignore the rights of the peoples of China and the Soviet Union, planning to dictate terms of treaty to Japan in accordance with its own judgement. The United States, it charged, did not want Japan to have a peace treaty with all the States that were in a state of war with her, but rather a separate peace treaty with the United States and its allies only.

The Soviet Union demanded that the peace treaty should be worked out on the basis of the Cairo Declaration, Potsdam Declaration, and Yalta Agreement.[9]

A.A. Gromyko, Deputy Minister of Foreign Affairs for the Soviet Union, speaking at the San Francisco Conference in September 1951, reiterated these views as follows :

> The procedure for the preparation of a peace treaty with Japan was provided for by the Potsdam Agreement which established the Council of Foreign Ministers of five Powers —the USSR, the US, China, Great Britain, and France —and by the well-known U.N. declaration of January 1, 1942, ensuring that no separate peace treaties be concluded with States that were at war with the Allied and Associated powers. In the Potsdam Declaration it was expressly stated that the Council of Foreign Ministers was being created first and foremost for "preparatory work on a peaceful settlement" and that while drawing up appropriate peace treaties "the Council shall be composed of members representing those states that have signed the terms of capitulation dictated to the enemy state concerned."[10]

The Soviet Union further observed that the United States government had arrogated to itself the right to prepare a peace treaty for Japan, which was a violation of the international obligation undertaken by the United States.

The Russians asserted that China, which was subjected during the course of many years to cruel aggression on the part of militaristic Japan, and bore the greatest sacrifices from the aggression of Japan, was excluded from participation in the drafting of the peace treaty. Without the participation of the Chinese People's Republic in the work of preparing a peace treaty for Japan, a real peace settlement in the Far East was not possible.[11]

The government of the United States, in its note of 19 May 1951, answered the points raised by the Soviet Union with regard to procedure. The United States argued that the Potsdam Agreement of 2 August 1945, contemplated that the Council of Foreign Ministers thereby established would "as its immediate important task, draw up treaties of peace with Italy, Rumania, Bulgaria, Hungary, and Finland, and propose settlements of territorial questions outstanding on the termination of war in Europe."[12] It was then provided that the Council should be utilised for the preparation of a peace settlement for Germany. It was finally agreed that other matters might from time to time be referred to the Council by agreement between the members. Thus the Potsdam Agreement between the governments of the Soviet Union, United Kingdom and United States did not mention the Japanese treaty. This was natural, the note said, for the war with Japan was then in full vigour and the Soviet Union was then neutral in that war. Consequently, the Potsdam Agreement contained nothing about the Japanese peace treaty. The Russians based their claim on a verbal understanding which they said had been reached between the leaders at Potsdam. The absence of a written agreement, they said, was due to the fact that the Soviet Union was neutral in the Far Eastern War and had to observe certain diplomatic norms. The Soviet contention was challenged in 1951, but seems to be supported by the record. Secretary of State James Byrnes was pleading at Potsdam for China's membership in the Council of Foreign Ministers, on the ground that China's presence on the Council would be of considerable help at the time of drafting a peace treaty for Japan. Churchill and Stalin at first did not share the American proposition but subsequently yielded to President Roosevelt's views.[13] It appears that Secretary of State Byrnes later changed his mind on the subject of verbal understanding when he saw the growing divergence of interest between the United States and the Soviet

Union on the role of Japan in the Pacific.

The United States' note of 19 May 1951, went on to say that "the United States has not agreed and does not agree to the reference to the Council of Foreign Ministers on the matter of making a Japanese peace treaty." The reason, among other things, the note said, was that the systematic misuse of veto power in the Council militated against the speedy achievement of an early peace treaty through the Council.[14] Furthermore, the procedure would give a secondary role to the Allied Powers which bore a great burden of the Pacific War than did the Soviet Union.

With regard to Chinese participation in the preparation of a peace treaty for Japan, the United States replied : "It is true that the United States does not seek guidance from a convicted aggressor."[15] This quotation referred to the intervention of Communist China in the Korean War. The real interests of China, the Americans argued, were fully reflected in the draft treaty. They pointed, for example, to the proposed Article Eleven, in which Japan was called in to renounce all special rights and interests in China and to the proposed Article Nineteen, which would make this renunciation automatically effective.[16]

As far as the substance of the draft treaty was concerned, the differences between the two governments centered around three main points : (a) Formosa and the Pescadores; (b) The Ryukyu and Bonin Islands; and (c) Safeguards against the rise of Japanese militarism :

(a) The Anglo-American draft of the Japanese peace treaty suggested that Japan should renounce all rights, title, and claim to Formosa and the Pescadores. The Soviet Union observed that according to the Cairo Declaration, the Islands of Taiwan and Pescadores should be restored to the Chinese Republic. In as much as the Chinese Republic had been transformed into the Chinese People's Republic and only the Chinese People's Republic expressed the will of the Chinese people, it was obvious that Taiwan and Pescadores should be transferred to the Chinese People's Republic. If it were not, the Cairo

Declaration would not be fulfilled, and the entire responsibility for this would fall on the government of the United States.

(b) The Soviet Union, referring to Article Three of the draft treaty, said that the Ryukyu and Bonin Islands were taken out from the sovereignty of Japan and placed under the trusteeship of the UN with the United States as the sole administering authority. Since the wresting away of the named islands from Japan was envisaged neither by agreement between the powers nor by decision of the UN in the person of the Security Council, "such wresting away does not have any justification."[17] These were deviations, it held, from international agreements.

(c) The government of the United States replied to this note and said that the territorial clauses of the surrender terms stipulated that the terms of the Cairo Declaration shall be carried out and "Japanese sovereignty shall be limited to the islands of Honshu, Hokkaido, Kyushu, Shikoku and such minor islands as we determine."[18] The draft treaty in fact, it held, limited Japanese sovereignty accordingly.

With respect to Formosa and the Pescadores, the United States argued that the Cairo Declaration provided that Manchuria, Formosa, and the Pescadores should be restored to the Republic of China. Furthermore, in view of the fact that the Soviet government had itself pointed out on numerous occasions that the "Republic of China should not be identified with the People's Republic of China," the United States enquired of the government of the Soviet Union whether it in fact desired that Manchuria, Formosa, and the Pescadores should be restored to the Republic of China. It further observed that the Japanese people ought not to be denied a state of peace because of differences of opinion among the Allied Powers as to the subsequent disposition of these territories.

With regard to the status of the Kurile and Sakhalin islands, the United States note maintained that it was in consonance with the surrender terms of the Allied Powers. It may be recalled that after the surrender of Japan the Soviet Union asserted her rights in the Sakhalin Islands, and occupied the Kurile Islands, which were promised to her by President Roosevelt at the Yalta Conference, held in February 1945.[19] The latter islands were offered to Russia by the United States as a price for her participation in the war against Japan.

The Soviet Union expressed its deep concern over the future rebirth of Japanese militarism. The Soviet note pointed out that no limitations were put on the armed forces of Japan. It quoted the example of the Italian Peace Treaty in which limitations were prescribed for the Italian army. Further, the Potsdam Declaration also laid down that the basic purposes of the Allied Powers was the task of obtaining "convincing proof that the capacity of Japan to wage war has been destroyed."[20] It was obvious, said the Soviet Union, that the period referred to in the Potsdam Declaration was not only the period of the occupa-rion, but the subsequent period also.

Moscow complained that the United States draft treaty did not contain any limitation on armed forces of Japan. The Soviet note of 10 June 1951 quoted the 19 June 1947 policy decision of the Far Eastern Commission, which stated that the task of the Allied Powers in Japan was to accomplish :

> The physical and spiritual demilitarization of Japan by means of the execution of a series of measures requiring the establishment of a period of strict control, including complete disarmament, the carrying out of economic reform the purpose of which would be to deprive Japan of the possibility of waging war, the eradication of militaristic influences and carrying out of strict justice with respect to war criminals.[21]

The Soviet Union insisted that the Far Eastern Commission decision was also meant to be continued after the peace settlement. Later the Russians changed their mind regarding the rearmament of Japan. During the peace conference at San Francisco, the Soviet delegate suggested that Japan should be allowed to rearm for self defense. However, the Soviet note stated that instead of preventing Japanese militarism, the United States was concluding a Security Pact between itself and Japan, "which would push Japan ever more toward the restoration of militarism."[22] And in the opinion of the Soviet Union the proposed Security Pact between the United States and Japan was directed against herself and China. All references to the Charter of the UN, to the right of individual and collective self-defense, in this case obviously had no substance and were false throughout.[23] The Soviet Union maintained that in refusing to set a time limit for the withdrawal of the occupation troops from Japanese territory, the government of the United States had broken one of its important obligations under international agreements. It also had contradicted the Potsdam Declaration of 26 July 1945, which provided for the withdrawal of foreign troops from Japan, and, by intending to continue the occupation after the conclusion of the Peace Treaty, the United States was aspiring to remain master in Japan for a long time. Therefore, the Soviet Union said that it was necessary that the time limit should be fixed for the withdrawal of foreign troops and that no foreign state should be allowed to have its troops of military bases in Japan.

The United States, in reply to this charge, said that it was a matter of profound concern to the United States, which bore the burden of Japan's war of aggression for nearly four years. In the opinion of the United States the most effective means to the desired end, would be to make the future security of the Japanese area a matter of collective international concern. In this way the measures which the Japanese might take for their own security would develop as a co-operative rather than as a purely national project. To the Soviet proposal that there should be established in the treaty a limitation in the armed forces of Japan, the United States replied that the Charter of the UN recognized the inherent right of collective as well as individual self-defense of nations. It was further pointed out that the suggestion of the Soviet Union that Japan should not have armed forces as required for its self-defense, coupled with the additional Soviet proposal that there be no other troops in Japan, seemed to be a reversion to the principle of letting Japan defend itself, and, consequently, as Stalin said, a 'conniving at aggression'. This phrase occurs in the statement of Stalin made on 10 March 1939 in which he said that :

Let each country defend itself from aggressors as it likes or as best it can. This principle, Stalin continued, meant, 'conniving at aggression'.[24]

The attitude of commonwealth countries toward the peace treaty
Most of the Commonwealth members had been victims of Japanese aggression during World War II. Therefore, at the end of the war it was but natural for them to demand an effective voice in the administration of their former enemy. Although most Commonwealth countries were members of the Far Eastern Commission and had collective representation on the Allied Council for Japan, their views regarding the occupation were mostly ignored by General MacArthur. Knowing General MacArthur's attitude toward the Allied Powers, and concerned with their own interest vis-a-vis Japan, the Commonwealth countries suggested an early peace settlement. In spite of considerable differences within the Commonwealth, the members agreed on certain fundamentals concerning the peace treaty. The various Commonwealth conferences held in Canberra in August 1947, in Colombo in January 1950, and in London in May 1950, urged that a draft treaty of peace be prepared by the members of the Far Eastern Commission. It should be noted here that in 1947 the consensus of opinion in the Commonwealth was that the draft treaty should be prepared by all members of the UN who had made a direct contribution toward winning the Pacific War. Later they came round to the 1947 American proposal on the procedure. Security against possible future aggression by Japan was a major concern of the Commonwealth.[25] Members expressed their doubt regarding Japan's unswerving acceptance of the Western democratic way of life. In order to prevent Japanese resurgence, in 1947 the Commonwealth proposed (1) limitations on Japanese armament, (2) restriction on her future industry and trade, and (3) enforcement of fundamental rights and the development and protection of trade unions.[26]

It appears that the Asian members of the Commonwealth—India, Pakistan, and Ceylon—were wary of physical control on Japanese freedom of action.[27]

It is interesting to observe that the recommendations of the

Commonwealth for the peace settlement coincided with those of the Borton group in the State Department. However, despite their strong protest against certain SCAP's policies and quiet canvassing for a strict treaty, the members of the Commonwealth had very little effect on the final outcome of the Japanese peace settlement. The contribution of the Commonwealth to the peace settlement with Japan was succinctly summarized by an editorial in a newspaper:

> The views of Britain, India, Australia and other such countries are in practice of less consequence to the future of Japan than the view of the various policy making groups in Washington . . . Military considerations are the prime factor and the debate on the future of Japan centres on the role that she may play in a possible war between the United States and Russia.[28]

The views of the British Government

In the first decade following the end of the war, Britain had to make difficult choices in her foreign policy. As far as the Far Eastern peace settlement was concerned, the United Kingdom was confronted with two dilemmas : (1) to reconcile her own political and economic interests with the needs of those members of the Commonwealth vitally concerned with Japan, (2) to arrive at a compromise in the conflict between her ambition to play a big role in peace-making and the compelling demands of the United States. It is doubtful whether Britain would have been a co-sponsor of the peace conference had she been uncompromising on the American condition for the peace settlement, that is, the American insistence on the retention of United States forces in Japan after the signing of the peace treaty. Recognizing these difficulties, the British government tried to strike a balance between its obligation to the Commonwealth and its own interest. As early as 1949, the British Foreign Secretary agreed to support the American proposal for a liberal peace treaty and a United States designed security arrangement for Japan. The draft peace treaty prepared by the British Foreign office in April 1951 indicated two trends. The British attempted to please the United States by acquiescing in the rearmament of Japan and by not pressing too hard on restrictions. On the other hand, the draft tried to satisfy the desires of Australia and New Zealand by calling for the suppression of undesirable political societies in Japan, by mentioning Japan's share of responsibility for the war, and by calling upon Japan to negotiate a fisheries convention with the Pacific nations.[29] However, neither of the latter provisions reached the final text. Britain gave up her fight against a possible revival of Japanese militarism in the face of strong American objections.

The deepest clash between the United States and Britain concerned the representation of China. The United Kingdom, supported by India and other states which had accorded recognition to the Chinese People's Republic, sought the representation of Communist China and the return of Formosa to that country. The United States Government, supported by the other states which still recognized the Chiang Kai-shek regimes as the *de jure* government of all China, wanted that government to sign the treaty with Japan. In order to resolve this major difference and other divergences between American and British positions, Dulles visited London on 2 June 1950, and after a series of meetings with Herbert Morrisson, the British Secretary of State for Foreign Affairs, arrived at a compromise. The two governments agreed that neither Chinese regime should participate in the peace conference, and Japan should through the treaty merely renounce her sovereignty over Formosa. Further, after the signing of the peace treaty Japan should decide for herself with which China to conclude formal peace. The British Government made it clear that any attempt by the United States to make its ratification of the treaty dependent upon a prior decision by the Japanese Government would be a violation of this understanding.[30] Hardly was the ink dry on the compromise document than the United Kingdom's Government was confronted with a *fait accompli*. In September 1951, the United States was facing difficulties in the matter of ratification of the treaty in the Senate. On 12 September 1951 fifty-six members of the Senate addressed a letter to the president stating that :

> We would consider the recognition of Communist China by Japan or the negotiation of a bilateral treaty with the Communist regime to be adverse to the best interests of the people of both Japan and the United States.[31]

The opposition on the issue in the United States Congress was so strong that Dulles had to go to Tokyo in December 1951 to extract a letter from Prime Minister Yoshida to the effect that Japan would recognize the Nationalist Government of China. According to an American diplomat who took part in the discussions, Dulles said during the talks with the Japanese officials that :

> American officials wished to know *now* whether Japan's foreign policy would parallel that of the United States or would be inimical to it. Parallel policies would simplify the solution of many problems. Divergences, however, would force the United States to review its position.[32]

The Japanese government was reluctant to take any action on the Chinese problem because of a division of opinion in the country on the problem. However, under pressure Yoshida handed over a letter on 24 December 1951 to the American visitors as desired by the latter.[33] That was the price Japan had to pay for the ratification of the peace treaty by the United States Senate. The State Department denied the charge that it pressured Japanese government to act according to its will. The foregoing account makes the State Department's denial meaningless. *The Washington Post* put the matter more clearly as follows :

> It is denied that the State Department exerted any pressure in getting this letter out of Premier Yoshida. The denial squares neither with the circumstances nor with Japanese characteristics, as is shown by the article that Mr. Yoshida worte in *Foreign Affairs* 12 months ago. "Red or white," he said, "China remains our next door neighbour . . . Economic law will, I believe, prevail in the long run over any ideological differences.[34]

The second major area of divergence between the British and American views was economics. The United Kingdom beset by its own post-war economic difficulties, feared Japanese industrial revival. In 1950 the British balance of trade was extremely unfavourable. The out-break of the Korean War in 1950 worsened the situation. It marked a sharp rise in the prices of imports on the one hand; on the other hand, the exports of coal and metal products decreased. The United Kingdom government planned to balance its trade by increasing the volume of exports, particularly the all-important textiles.[35] British traders saw Japan as a tough competitor in this field and also in pottery. By 1950 the Japanese, despite all their difficulties, had become top exporters of textile goods and were trying to increase volume by twenty-five per cent over the next four years.[36]

The British argued that Japanese competition in the years to come would be intensified by two factors. One was the combination of low wages of Japanese labour and American technical knowledge. United States businessmen, through their investment, were helping Japan to modernize its industrial plants. Further, a section of the British press was of the opinion that the Japanese conservatives were trying to revive its pre-war strength in the wake of removal of occupation controls. It reported that the Japanese conservative forces had progressively checked the liberation movement instituted by the occupation through its various reforms. Japanese labour unions had especially become the conservative target of attack.[37] The inference was that the Japanese would keep wages down by suppressing labour unions. This in turn would help the Zaibatsu to regain its pre-war position. As a result, Japan would again try to create a commercial empire for itself by using its old and familiar unfair trade practices. According to the British, another contributing factor to the situation was the continued exclusion of Japan from Chinese markets, because of American pressure on the Japanese to conclude a peace treaty with the Nationalist Government of China. The British calculated that this would force Japan to concentrate its export drive upon the markets of Southeast Asia, India, and Africa, which were at that time already witnessing a keen competition between British and Japanese products.[38] The United Kingdom also feared that Japan might get preferential treatment from the United States in allocations of raw materials, for which they would pay only the cost price of these materials.

In order to reduce Japanese competition in Africa, the British Government proposed that Japan should renounce her rights in the Congo Basin Treaties of 1919.[39] This treaty stipulated that equal treatment should be accorded to the commerce of all nations. Prior to World War II, the Japanese had cornered ninety per cent of the area's textile trade by exercising their rights under the treaty.[40] On the other hand, the United States, aiming to strengthen the Japanese economy, opposed any limitation on trade in the treaty. Ultimately the British view prevailed on this point. Again with a view to prevent Japan from practising unfair methods in the future, Britain, along with the other members of the Commonwealth proposed that Japan should express in the treaty her desire to adhere to internationally accepted practices in commercial relations. This suggestion finally found its way in the preamble of the treaty. The United Kingdom did not insist on any formal most-favoured nation treatment with Japan because she wanted a free hand to deal with the problem should it arise again.

The British Government also sought a treaty limitation on Japanese shipbuilding capacity.[41] The Japanese shipping industry was rapidly coming into its own and was likely to be a rival for the British vessels. The United States' position in this matter was that Japanese shipping industry would be a source of strength to the free world and therefore, should not be stifled by putting artificial fetters on it. Britain ultimately conceded to the United States on this point.

Britain also wanted Japan to negotiate a Far Eastern fisheries convention and, pending its conclusion, to prohibit Japanese nationals from fishing in certain conservation areas. This was a subject in which the United States, Canada, and other Pacific nations had primary interest. Since the United States was opposed to any prohibition written into the treaty, all the parties agreed to accept a voluntary statement by Japan to that effect outside the treaty.

Finally the British, in their draft treaty earmarked Japanese gold stock to be used to satisfy reparation claims, but this, too, was ultimately dropped in the face of American opposition.

The views of Australia and New Zealand

Australia had strong reservation regarding United States policy toward Japan in general and the American peace proposals in particular. The reasons behind the posture adopted by the Australians toward a prostrate Japan could be found in the history of the Pacific War. The swift Japanese advance southward after Pearl Harbor, the psychological effect of Japanese brutalities at Changi Prison Camp and along the Burma Railway, had left an indelible impression on the Australian mind. The memory of such incidents also produced an intense hatred of Japanese and a profound conviction that no such threat to Australian security must be allowed to materialize. At the end of the war Australians decided to seek protection against Japan by (i) insisting on the full and strict implementation of the terms of surrender (ii) by building an alliance with the like-minded Pacific powers against a resurgent Japan.[42] The first line of policy could not be put into practice unless Australia had a decisive hand in the occupation. With this conviction and also with a realization that her part in the Pacific War was second only to that of the United States, Australia sought a principal status in the policy making and in the control of the occupation.[43] Because of her major part in the war, the Commonwealth accorded Australia the honour to represent them in ACJ. Australia took active interests in the proceedings of the Far Eastern Commission and the ACJ.

In order to curb the political and economic strength of its former enemy, in 1946 Australia proposed that (i) Japan should be made to pay full reparations. (ii) War criminals should be severely punished. (iii) The Emperor should not be exempted from prosecution as a war criminal. (iv) Food should be supplied to China and the Philippines before being sent to the Japanese.[44] In the matter of reforms, Australia recommended in the Far Eastern Commission that the formation of trade unions in Japan should be encouraged and the unions should be permitted to take part in political activities. In short, Australian policy toward Japan was that "it [Japan] must never again be permitted to develop the means of waging war."[45] At the same time, she demanded that the Japanese whaling expedition in the Antarctic be prohibited. As had been pointed out, the Australian ambition was thwarted by the predominant position of the United States in all matters concerning the occupation and also by the irritating conduct of General MacArthur and his colleagues toward the allied representatives. In 1947 Australia indicated her growing concern at the shift in United States policy in Japan, which now envisaged that Japan should play an important role in American Far Eastern Policy as a powerful bastion against the Soviet threat in Asia, and as a 'work shop' for East Asia. Australia regarded the American thinking of Japan as a future ally against the Soviet Union as a leap from "the frying pan into the fire."[46] Since according to the Australians, both powers were dangerous.

Wishing to prevent Japanese economic build up by enforcement through a treaty, Australia called for an immediate conclusion of a peace settlement in March 1947, and in order to strengthen the influence of the Commonwealth in general and of herself in particular in a future peace conference regarding Japan, Australia suggested that the scheduled Commonwealth conference be held in Canberra in August 1947. Since the rest of the Commonwealth generally shared the views of Australia and New Zealand, the conference in its final communique recommended that a peace for Japan be written in conformity with the Potsdam Declaration. In its commentary on the peace settlement as suggested by the Commonwealth in September 1947, the New Zealand government asserted that the treaty must provide for maintenance of complete disarmament and demilitarization of Japan. Japan must not be permitted to retain or develop any armed force. It stated that Japan should be allowed to retain some non-military police force to keep internal peace and order, but that the peace treaty should place restriction on its strength and organization, and on the number and maximum calibres of weapons of foreign manufacture which might be held by the force. To ensure that this force did not become the nucleus of a secret army, the New Zealanders felt that it would be advisable to require that service in the force should by and large be forbidden to persons who had held certain positions under the old regime.[47]

It should be noted that the recommendations of the Commonwealth went unheeded. During 1948-49 the United States went ahead with the reconstruction of Japanese industry and certain sections in the United States began thinking in terms of eventual rearmament of Japan. In consonance with her original policy, Australia objected to the reversal of the earlier reforms by SCAP. For example she registered her opposition to the amendment of the Japanese National Public Service Law, the organization of a coastal patrol guard and the resumption of international contact by Japan.[48] Australian opposition to SCAP's policies was a cry in the wilderness. The policy makers in Washington and Tokyo turned a deaf ear toward the Australians.

American indifference to her views in Japanese matters put Australia in a dilemma. The United States, the only power which could help Australia decisively in a future Pacific war against Japan, was committed to the revival of Japanese industrial might. The Australian government tried to solve this dilemma by following a dual policy. While it made it clear that it was not pleased with many of SCAP's policies, it made concessions on many points concerning the economic development of Japan. But Australia remained firmly opposed to the rearmament of Japan until the final settlement at San Francisco in September 1951. On 21 June 1949, the Australian Foreign Minister, Dr. Evatt, expressed his country's concern with the problem as follows :

> It is quite a simple philosophy. You rearm Japan and remove all the restrictions to which it agreed in the Armistice and so develop its war potential, and you are quite satisfied that in any future struggle in the Far East Japan will do the bidding of the Western democracies. That is a fallacy.[49]

Australians of all hues seemed to have shared the feelings of their government. When Dulles visited Australia in February 1951, the newspapers in that country caricatured him "as a combination of Yankee missionary, deluded by Japanese pretenses of reform and eager to help 'the little brother,' and American imperialist, determined to use Japan for the political and economic expansion of the United States."[50]

Dulles argued that prescription of controls on Japanese armament in the treaty would drive Japan into the camp of the Soviet Union. The Australians answered that, if no controls were instituted, Japan could pretend to be on the Western side and then, after rearming, could swing over to the Communist camp.

The Australian Prime Minister, Robert Menzies, in a magazine article warned the United States against the possibility of Japan building long-range naval vessels. Admitting the force of arguments for Japanese rearmament, Menzies said :

> Are both defensive armament and offensive armament to be included in Japanese rearmament? Japan, to be defended against invasion, does not, for example, need long-range submarines. Nor does she need long-range surface ships of war. She may need them against us, or against you (Americans). But does she need them against the common prospective enemy? This is not an expression of fear. It is a note of warning."[51]

John Foster Dulles assured them that the United States would oppose any Japanese aggression and was willing to listen to any workable plan that they might advance. Addressing the Australian Institute of International Affairs on 19 February 1951, he attacked the demilitarisation school and said :

> If the democracies write into the Peace Treaty that Japan should not rearm, who is going to enforce it? I do not think there is enough power anywhere to do it.[52]

On returning to the United States he condemned the attitude of Australia, New Zealand, and the Philippines as out of date and resembling the mentality of the Versailles *diktat*.

Australia gave up the struggle for restriction on Japanese rearmament only when she found herself in a hopeless minority opposed to the principal allies. It did not end the story. Still the crucial problem before Australia and New Zealand was how to guarantee against future aggression by an economically strong and politically sovereign Japan.

The Korean War and the Communist Chinese intervention in that war changed the situation considerably. The United States decided to strengthen her military arrangement in the Far East by bringing Australia and New Zealand and other pacific nations into its fold. The tripartite security treaty, which has been described in the previous chapter, was tentatively agreed upon on 17 February 1951 during Dulles' visit to Canberra. "Anzus was the indispensable quid pro quo for Australian ratification of the Japanese peace treaty."[53]

The question that emerges from the foregoing material is, to what extent the fears of Australia and New Zealand from a possible future resurgent Japanese militarism were real? First of all it should be emphasized that the Australians and New Zealanders were not the only people who dreaded the possible rebirth of Japanese militarism. This contingency haunted the Americans, British, Indonesians, the Philippines, and the Chinese. A large number of Japanese themselves were alarmed by the activities of their conservative leaders. This actions and utterances of the Japanese rightists at the helm of affairs did not indicate that they repented the past. In fact, some of them openly stated, as has been observed in the previous chapter, that SCAPs' attempt to reform Japan was based on a mistaken notion of Japanese society. They thereby implied that there was nothing wrong with the old structure. At the same time, with a view to strengthening its bargaining position in the forthcoming peace settlement, the Japanese old guard attempted to play on anti-Communist feelings in the United States. In addition, in 1949 Prime Minister Yoshida was reported to have urged the creation of a 100,000 man internal security force and a four million ton merchant marine. Further, he is reported to have said that a peace treaty should allow Japan full control on internal airways and non-war production, and there should be minimum post-treaty supervision.[54] There is no authentic proof for these charges. However, these reports can not be completely discounted as baseless, especially if they are viewed in the light of the various attempts made by the Japanese conservatives to retain old institutions. On the other hand, Australia and New Zealand ignored the intense pacifist feelings prevailing in post-war Japan.

The real fear of Australia was that a revived and rearmed Japan would again be looking for room in the South Pacific, for its growing population. Again according to some Australian reports, the Japanese Population Council in its private appendix to its 1949 report suggested a planned migration of five million Japanese into the empty Pacific Islands.[55] It also stated that Dutch New Guinea was capable of absorbing twenty million Japanese. These reports may appear to be wild stories based on fancy. But to most Australians having had firsthand experience of Japanese militarism during the war, they seemed to be cold facts. Australians did not think it impossible that a strong Japan would force their country to absorb some of the Japanese surplus population.

On the purely economic side, Australian apprehension was that the economic recovery of Japan would bring intensified competition with Australian industry, both light and heavy. A too rapid revival of the textile industry, accompanied by a tidal wave of exports, could seriously dislocate industry in Southeast Asia as well as Australia.[56] There was also perhaps a concern with the possibility that a modernized and re-equipped Japan would entrench herself in the markets of Southeast Asia in the future. This was a long-term problem. Much more important immediately was the question of unfair trade practices by Japan, especially dumping and uncompetitive selling abroad as a result of concealed subsidies to industry and low labour costs. The danger of such practices had led to strong Australian support for the development of trade unionism in Japan. Therefore, Australia and New Zealand insisted in binding the Japanese in the treaty to the observance of fair practices in their trade and commerce.

Australia and New Zealand, in addition, wanted a clause to be written in the Peace Treaty providing guarantees for human rights and fundamental freedoms.

The views of India

Ever since 1947 India was in favour of an early peace settlement with Japan. In the Commonwealth conferences to which reference has been made, India advocated a liberal peace treaty and restoration of full sovereignty to Japan.[57] In keeping with its policy of non-alignment, the Indian Government suggested that Japan be left completely free to decide her future course in international relations. India, of course, hoped that a free Japan would remain un-aligned in the cold war and by doing so would help further the cause of the Asian-African nations, that is, to eliminate western imperialism and promote world peace. India also felt that Communist China, besides being a close neighbour of Japan, was one of the nations which suffered heavily in the hands of the Japanese militarists for half a century, and therefore, should be invited to participate in the peace conference. In the Indian view the consent of Communist China to the peace treaty was vital for the maintenance of a stable peace in the Far East. On territorial problems India took a strictly legal position. In doing so she seemed to overlook the Japanese claim to the Kurile Islands. Probably she did not want to displease her great neighbour, the Soviet Union.

Dulles accused India of playing "Asia for Asiatic."[58] This was an unfair charge. Indian leaders, particularly Prime Minister Nehru, had long been champions of close co-operation between the East and West. The American negotiator viewed every nation in his dogmatic belief that "those who are not with us are against us" and recipients of American aid should faithfully follow the line of the State Department. An American newspaper made the following comment on United States attitude toward India :

> India's refusal to take part in Japanese treaty negotiations has exposed a lack of statesmanship on our part. The upshot of published official comment is that, having given India some grain to ease on of her perennial famines, and having promised further 'economic aid,' India should have swallowed American Far Eastern policy, hook, line and sinker. Not only does this reaction reveal a crude political philosophy,

> it demonstrated the basic fallacy of those who have shaped much of our postwar foreign policy—the native belief that dollars can buy international friendship and persuade sovereign nations to dance to whatever, tune we choose to fiddle.[59]

In its reply to the invitation from the United States to attend the San Francisco Peace Conference, the Government of India expressed the view that any peace settlement with Japan should have two basic objectives in view. First, the terms of the treaty should concede to Japan a position of honour, equality, and contentment among the community of free nations. Secondly, they should be so framed as to enable all countries, especially those interested in the maintenance of a stable peace in the Far East, to subscribe to the treaty sooner or later.[60] After stating these two general principles, the note made certain comments on the draft treaty proper.

With regard to the Ryukyu and Bonin Islands, the Government of India was of the opinion that these islands had historic affinities with the people of Japan and Japan had not acquired them by aggression from any other country. Therefore, the keeping of these islands under the trusteeship of the UN with the USA as the sole administering authority would be a source of dissatisfaction to a large number of Japanese people and would carry the seeds of future dispute in the Far East. The matter was more clearly put by the *Times of India* as follows :

> Both territorially and historically these islands are Japanese and their severance from Japan lays Washington open to the charge of 'expansionism' which, whether motivated by economic or strategic reasons is in eastern eyes equally imperialistic.[61]

The Government of India recognized the sovereign right of Japan to defend herself and, in exercise of this right, to enter into a defensive agreement with a friendly power. But this right, it felt, should be exercised by the Japanese Government only after it had become truly sovereign. Referring to the provisions on security in the draft treaty, the Government of India said that they were "bound to give rise to the impression that the agreement does not represent a decision taken by Japan in the full enjoyment of her freedom as a sovereign nation."[62] India felt that the proposed security arrangement would have unfortunate effect on the people of Japan as well as Asia.

Furthermore, India held that international agreement among the great powers required that Formosa and the Pescadores Islands should be returned to China. The Indian note stated that the same argument *mutatis mutandis* applied to the Kurile and South Sakhalin Islands.

For the foregoing reasons the Government of India decided not to attend the peace conference and be a party to the peace treaty. However, it was the intention of the Government of India to put an end to the state of war between herself and Japan and to establish full diplomatic relations with that country as soon as possible.

The United States in its reply expressed surprise over the suggestions made by the Government of India and said that all along the announced goal of the United States had been to restore Japan to just such a position of "honour, equality, and contentment among the community of free nations."[63] The United States specifically answered the points raised by the Government of India.

With respect to the Ryukyu and Bonin Islands, the United States quoted the Potsdam Declaration and said that the acceptance of the Government of India's suggestion would involve a major departure from Potsdam surrender terms. The note further said that the Government of India never questioned those terms during the five and one-half years during which India served as a member of the Far Eastern Commission. The United States expressed its inability to understand why different tests were applied between the Kuriles and the Ryukyus.

On the question of security, the United States observed that it would be quite impracticable and totally unwelcome for the United States to help defend Japan, if that were not wanted by the Japanese people.

On Formosa, the United States pointed out that there could not be any final agreement among the Allied powers with respect to the future of Formosa. Therefore, it argued "to insist that a Japanese Peace Treaty be deferred until there is such agreement is, in fact, to postpone indefinitely the restoration of Japan to 'honour, equality, and contentment among the community of free nations,' which the Government of India agrees is an urgent requirement."[64]

In the end, the United States welcomed the decision of the Government of India to conclude a separate peace treaty with Japan on terms consistent with the principles of India's foreign policy.

The attitude of the Republic of China

Before World War II, Japan was the bitterest enemy of China. The Chinese did not forget the humiliation suffered in the hands of their former pupil. Despite Chiang Kai-Shek's official pronouncement of forgiveness after VJ Day, the prevailing opinion in China was one of vindictiveness.[65] The Chinese wished to reduce Japan to a status in which she would not again become a threat to Chinese security and would not challenge its international position. During the early years of the occupation the Nationalist Government of China sought to prevent the resurgence of Japanese expansionist militarism by advocating the destruction of Japan's war potential, the abolition of the Emperor system, and the purge of all school books. At the same time the Chinese expected a huge reparation from Japan.

In reply to the United State's peace proposals in 1947, Nanking suggested that the decisions in the Conference should be taken on the basis of a two-thirds majority including the concurring vote of the Big Four. When it appeared that the Soviet Union might not attend the proposed peace conference, the Nationalist government announced that it would not send its representative to the conference table in the absence of the Soviet Union. The Nanking regime did not wish to jeopardize the Sino-Russian treaty of 14 August 1945, which obligated the parties not to negotiate a separate peace treaty with Japan. In return the Soviet Union undertook to give aid, military supplies, and moral support exclusively to the nationalistic government as the central government of China.[66] Moreover, Big Four unity was considered essential by Nanking in order to boost its prestige. Its critics at home had charged that it was subservient to the United States. China's refusal to attend the peace conference indicated her independence of action. China also differed from the United States on the future status of Japan. The chief matters of contention were Chinese claims to the Ryukyu Islands, which were under United States occupation. The realization in the summer of 1947 that the United States had selected Japan instead of China as an anti-Soviet base, increased Chinese feelings of insecurity. All Chinese groups agreed at least on one issue—that is, opposition to American policies in Japan.[67] In the Chinese view, Japan, the old enemy, was once again trying to overshadow China with American backing. The Chinese charged that Japan was still imperialistic and the morale of the people was basically unaltered. They feared competition from Japanese trade. It was felt that foreign businessmen would prefer to invest their capital in a comparatively stable Japan than in the confused state of China. In the same year, the Chinese accused the Japanese of building armaments.[68] As an evidence they picked up the statement made in the spring of 1947 by Hitoshi Ashida, the then Foreign Minister of Japan, in which he had said that Japanese immigration rights and other prerogatives in the Kuriles, Pescadores, Ryukyus and Formosa Islands should be recognized by the allied powers. Ashida did not say anything in his statement regarding the rearmament of Japan. The Chinese inferred it from his statement.

The Nationalist government's policy toward Japan was in direct proportion to its position in China. Seriously challenged by the Communists in 1948, the Chiang Kai-Shek's government tried to soften its attitude toward Japan. It revived the idea of an early peace treaty for Japan and welcomed the SCAPs' policy of economic reconstruction of that country. An early peace treaty would provide solutions to some of the problems faced by the Nationalist government. It would lessen the tension between the United States and the Soviet Union. Relieved of Japan, the Americans would give more attention to China. If the conference did not materialize, it would at least give the impression that something was being done about the threat of Japan. Japan became a political football for both Nationalist and Communist China.

By 1950 the Chiang Kai-Shek's government in Formosa came around to the position of the United States concerning the peace settlement. It was prepared to waive reparations and concurred in the proposed security arrangement in the Far East. It was even prepared in accept the future of Formosa as undecided, provided Japan renounced all her title and rights in Taiwan.[69] Its dependence on United States support made the Nationalist government in Formosa swallow the bitterest pill. It hoped that it would be invited to represent the Chinese people in the peace conference. When the British and the Americans agreed to exclude both Chinas from the peace conference, Chiang Kai-Shek described the agreement as breach of international faith.[70]

Since its establishment in October 1949 the People's Republic of China on the mainland maintained that the peace treaty should be discussed by the Big Four including itself.

In December 1950 the Communist Government on mainland China demanded restoration of Taiwan and Pescadores to the Chinese People's Republic, destruction of Japanese capacity to wage war, and, the payment of full reparation by Japan. It also in turn condemned its exclusion from the peace conference. In a broadcast on 15 August 1951 Prime Minister Chou En-Lai made the following statement :

> For the sake of really helping to restore peace in Asia and to solve Far Eastern problems, the central people's government of the People's Republic of China firmly maintains that on the basis of the proposals of the Government of the Soviet Union, the peace conference should be convened with the participation of the representative of all the States that have participated with their armed forces in the war against Japan in order to confer on the problem of a joint peace treaty with Japan. At the same time on the basis of the UN Declaration, the Cairo Declaration, the Potsdam Declaration and agreement, and the basic post-surrender policy for Japan, adopted by the Far Eastern Commission, the Central People's Government of the People's Republic of China is ready to exchange views on the problem of a joint peace treaty with Japan with all the States that

participated in the war against Japan ![71]

He described the proposed Anglo-American draft treaty as "unacceptable to the Chinese People" and charged that it violated international agreements. Chou further stated that the treaty was a menace to the peoples of Asia and detrimental to the interest of the Japanese people.[72]

Reactions of Indonesia and the Philippines

Indonesia sought reparations for the damage done by Japanese occupation forces. In addition to requisitioning Indonesian natural resources, primarily petroleum products and rolling stock, the Japanese allegedly took millions of dollar's worth of gold and diamonds back to their homeland.[73]

To the Philippine Government, the most important features of the prospective peace settlement were, first, reparations and second, security. The Japanese had been driven out of the Philippines in 1944, but devastations wrought by them were still visible everywhere. The Philippines had gravely suffered from the cruel invasion and occupation by Japan. Almost every family had one or more members killed by the Japanese. It was only natural that there should be bitterness and a demand for at least material reparation. But for Washington the political needs of the free world in the present and future were more important than the past history and suffering of ex-colonial peoples. The mood of the Philippines was expressed by their foreign secretary when he said, "The proposed treaty has filled the Philippinos with profound disillusionment and dismay."[74]

The speaker of the Philippine House of Representatives, Eugenio Perez, said :

> The Philippino should not sit back and swallow the suicidal document. We shall refuse to sign the treaty. We shall still be technically at war with Japan.
>
> Mr. Perez further added that America seemed oblivious of the fact that the Philippino people, because of the patent justice they are about to receive, might conceivably turn to Communism even if only for the sake of empty promises of

better treatment."[75]

The Government of the Philippines insisted that a provision be made in the Peace Treaty to the effect that reparations should be subject to later negotiations. Moreover, they were just as concerned as the Australians about Japan's possible future emergence as a military menace or as an economic competitor.

The Philippines believed that Japan was an aritificial democracy of American make. The phrase used by the Americans with regard to Japan—"workshop of Asia"—had an unpleasant ring in the ears of Japan's neighbours.

The United States opposed further reparations. Washington held the view that it would be difficult for Japan with its limited resources to produce enough to meet the needs of its own eighty-five million inhabitants. Further strain would mean either increased American help, which the United States was not willing to guarantee, or a lower standard of living. The latter would increase social unrest and give rise to dangerous expansionist and explosive tendencies, which Japan's Communist neighbours would joyously exploit.[76]

On the same grounds, the United States had opposed in 1948, economic disabilities as for example, requiring a dismantling of part of Japan's industrial plants, particularly its shipbuilding capacity. The United States similarly had objected to fixing an upper limit to Japan's industrial output after 1948.

The foregoing account demonstrates that the United States through cajolery and by pulling the economic and military strings it possessed, imposed its will upon the reluctant allies. Despite the fact that almost all members of the Far Eastern Commission opposed the rearmament of Japan, the United States not only insisted in arming its former enemy, but also in excluding any limitation on the armament of Japan in the treaty. Again most members desired to limit Japanese industrial expansion for various reasons; mainly they feared an industrially resurgent Japan. Here again the United States prevailed over its allies in reversing their attitude. On matters concerning reparations the United States overlooked the interests of nations which had not only fought and suffered during the war, but had consistently supported the American position in the world.

It was only on minor points that the Americans conceded to their allies. The views of the major powers of Asia—India and China—were dismissed as "petty" and therefore, not worthy of consideration by Washington.[77] There was no common ground of agreement between the United States and the Soviet Union. Behind the facade of legality both powers tried to dictate their own terms to each other and regarded Japan as a prize to be won.

In brief, the hundred talks and thousand papers exchanged between the United States and Far Eastern Commission members did not change the original blueprint on the peace treaty issued by the State Department in November 1950. It very much remained as the brain child of the United States. In the next chapter we will see how the United States managed to get the treaty signed at the San Francisco Peace Conference.

REFERENCES

1. U.S. Congress, n. 89 in Chapter 4 p. 6.
2. Claude A. Buss, "Making Peace with Japan, U.S. Policy on the Japan Treaty," *Ear Eastern Survey* 20 (15 June 1951) p. 113.
3. Swearingen *et al*, n. 248, p. 13.
4. See p. 14.
5. Baron E. J. Lewe Van Aduard, *Japan : From Surrender to Peace* (The Hague 1953) pp. 124-5.
6. United States State Department, *Bulletin* 23 (4 December 1950) pp. 881-2.
7. *Ibid.*, 25 (23 July 1951) p. 142.
8. *Ibid.*
9. *Ibid.*, p. 141.
10. United States Department of State, n. 32 in Chapter 4, pp. 116-7.
11. United States State Department, *Bulletin*, op. cit., p. 142.
12. *Ibid.*, 24 (28 May 1951) p. 852.
13. Byrnes. 23 in Chapter 1, pp. 71-2.
14. United States State Department, *Bulletin* op. cit., p. 852.
15. *Ibid.*
16. *Ibid.*
17. *Ibid.*, p. 857.
18. *Ibid.*, p. 853.
19. U.S. Department of State, *Foreign Relations of the U.S., Diplomatic Papers, the Conferences at Malta and Yalta 1945* (Washington, 1955) p. 984.

20. United States State Department, *Bulletin* op. cit., p. 138.
21. *Ibid.*
22. *Ibid.*, p. 139.
23. *Ibid.*
24. U.S. Department of State, n. 32 in Chapter 4, p. 81.
25. New Zealand Departmental External Affairs, *Japanese Peace Settlement* 38 (Wellington, 1947) p. 5.
26. *Ibid.*, pp. 5-6
27. U.S. Department of State, n. 32 in Chapter 4, p. 148.
28. *The Hindu* (Madras), 26 June 1950, p. 4.
29. Dunn, n. 8 in Chapter 5. pp. 137-9, Ambassador Sebald, n. 103 in Chapter 4, p. 265. The United Kingdom has not so far published this draft treaty referred by Professor Dunn.
30. Anthony Eden, *The Memoirs of Anthony Eden, Full Circle* (Boston, 1960) p. 21.
31. U.S. Government, *Congressional Record, Proceedings and Debates of the 82d Congress, First Session* 97 (Washington, 1951) p. 11371.
32. Ambassador Sebald, n. 103 in Chapter 4, p. 285.
33. *Ibid.*, p. 286.
34. *The Washington Post*, 22 January 1952, p. 8.
35. *The Times* (London) 27 November 1951, p. 4.
36. *The Economist* 160 (London, 7 April 1951), p. 789.
37. *The Times* (London) 23 April 1951, p. 5.
38. *Ibid.*, 13 April, 1951, p. 7.
39. The United Kingdom, *Draft Peace Treaty with Japan*, Cmd 8300 (London, July 1951) p. 4.
40. Beal, n. 36 in Chapter 5, p. 123.
41. *The Times* (London), 16 April 1951, p. 3.
42. Rosecrance, n. 8 in Chapter 5, pp. 60-1.
43. Byrnes, n. 23 in Chapter 1, p. 102.
44. Rosecrance, n. 8, in Chapter 5, pp. 25-6.
45. Australia, *House of Representatives Debates* 190 (1946-7) p. 170.
46. Rosecrance, n. 14 in Chapter 5, p. 105.
47. New Zealand Department of External Affairs, op. cit., p. 12.
48. Rosecrance, n. 14 in Chapter 5, p. 110.
49. Australia, *House of Representatives Debates* 202 (1949), p. 1225.
50. Dunn, n. 8 in Chapter 5, p. 125.
51. Robert Gordon Menzies, The Pacific Settlement Seen from Australia, *Foreign Affairs* 30 (January 1952), p. 190-1.
52. *The New York Times*, 20, February 1951, p. 4.
53. Rosecrance, n. 8 in Chapter 5, p. 241.
54 N.D. Harper, *Australia and the Peace Settlement* (11th Conference of the Insitutte of Pacific Relations (Lucknow, India, 1950) p. 33.
55. *Ibid.*, p. 31.
56. Peter Calvocaressi, *Survey of International Affairs*, 1951 (London, 1954), p. 405.

57. U.S. Department of State, n. 32 in Chapter 4, p. 92.
58. *The New York Times*, 3 December 1951, p. 5.
59. *The Christian Science Monitor*, 29 September 1951, p. 14.
60. United States State Department, *Bulletin*, 25 (3 September 1951), p. 386.
61. *The Times of India* (Bombay), 28 August 1951, p. 4.
62. United States State Department, *Bulletin op. cit.*, p. 386.
63. *Ibid.*, p. 387.
64. *Ibid.*, p. 388.
65. Thurston Griggs, "Chinese Views on Japan," *American Perspective* (Washington, D.C., 2 January 1949), p. 388-405.
66. United States State Department, *Bulletin*, 17 (23 November 1947), p. 1005.
67. Griggy, *Op. cit.*, p. 400.
68. *Ibid.*, p. 399.
69. Dunn, n. 8 in Chapter 5, p. 144.
70. *The Times* (London), 17 July 1951, p. 3.
71. *The New York Times*, 16 August 1951, p. 6.
72. *Ibid.*
73. Buss, *Op. cit.*, 115, U.S. Department of State, n. 32 in Chapter 4, p. 220-1.
74. *The New Times of Burma*, 21 July 1951, p. 4.
75. *The Hindu*, 26 July 1951, p. 5.
76. United States State Department, *Bulletin*, 24 April 1951, p. 578.
77. *The Times of India*, *op. cit.*, p. 4.

7

THE SAN FRANCISCO PEACE CONFERENCE

SECTION I

DURING his trip to London in June 1951, Dulles invited the British government to join the United States in sponsoring the treaty of Peace for Japan. British Foreign Secretary Herbert Morrison accepted the invitation. The Anglo-American draft treaty was made public on 13 July 1951. The idea behind the move was to show allied unity in the face of Soviet opposition to the peace proposals made by the United States.[1]

As we have already seen, there was a deadlock between the western powers and the Soviet Union on the procedure to be adopted for drawing up the terms of the proposed treaty. Dulles evaded the obstacle by giving up the idea of using a conference method for negotiating the terms of the treaty. Instead, he resorted to the procedure of negotiation on a bilateral basis through diplomatic channels. The negotiations which began in September 1950 had continued almost until the time of the San Francisco Conference a year later. The long and difficult business of negotiating the terms of the treaty was now nearing its end. In the course of these negotiations Dulles had flown three times to Japan and had visited nine capitals of countries especially interested in the peace settlement. This enterprise had been spoken of by Dulles as an "eleven months peace conference."[2] The final draft was ready in Jully 1951, and the problem then was to get the treaty concluded and signed by as many states as possible. On 22 August 1951, the United States sent invitations to fifty-five countries for the Peace Conference to be held in San Francisco on 4 September 1951. Fifty-two countries accepted the invitation, and three countries, India, Burma, and Yugoslavia, expressed their inability to attend the Conference. In order to prevent further discussion and delay in adopting the treaty, it was made clear in the invitation that the business of the Conference would be to sign the text. The Statement, made orally to each recipient country at the time of delivery of the invitation, said :

> These 10 months of preparatory work of consultation, discussion, and negotiation have developed a large measure of agreement and reconciliation of divergent viewpoints and should be considered as replacing what would normally be the controversial phase of substantive discussions at a peace conference. Accordingly, the conference to be held at San Francisco will be for the purpose of signing the August 13 text.[3]

This statement was meant to discourage the members of the Soviet block from reopening negotiations on the terms of the peace treaty, thereby causing an indefinite delay.

To the surprise of some people who doubted whether the Soviet Union would care to attend the conference, the Russians accepted the invitation and sent a large delegation headed by their Deputy Minister of Foreign Affairs, A.A. Gromyko.

It was in this setting, and under these conditions, that the Conference was opened on Tuesday night 4 September 1951, at the San Francisco Opera House. Immediately after the customary welcoming ceremonies the Conference resolved itself into a battle of words between the Soviet bloc and the Allied powers. The strategy of the sponsors of the treaty was to get a set of rules of procedure which was designed to leave little ground for discussing any possible modifications of the draft treaty. Dean Acheson, the temporary president of the Conference, told his audience in preliminary observations that he would conduct the proceedings in such a way as to realize the purpose for which the Conference was called, namely, the conclusion and signature of the Treaty of Peace with Japan on the terms of the text submitted to the Conference.[4]

After the motion to adopt the rules of procedure had been proposed and seconded by the delegates of New Zealand and Cuba respectively, Gromyko tried to raise a prior question of the representation of the People's Republic of China in the Conference. The proposal of the Soviet delegate was ruled out of order by the temporary president of the Conference on the ground that the subject under discussion at that time was the adoption of the rules of procedure which had already been moved and seconded, and the Soviet delegate was trying to introduce another matter into the discussion. Gromyko appealed from the ruling of the chair. At this stage, the Polish delegate, Stefan Wierblowski, intervened and made a strong speech in favour of Communist China's representation accusing the United States of oppressing the countries of Asia. He further said that the denial of representation to Communist China, which had fought Japanese aggression for many, many years, was a matter of shame.[5] After this sharp interchange, the ruling of the chair was put to vote, it was sustained by the Conference by a vote of thirty-five for, and three against.[6] Fourteen states did not vote. The Soviet delegate again rose on a point of order and said that he reserved his right to raise the question of Communist China's representation after the adoption of the rules of procedure.

The Polish delegate then proposed that the rules of procedure be discussed thoroughly before being acted upon, and that a committee of seven members be appointed to study the procedure submitted by the sponsors of the Conference, along with any other proposals that might be made by other delegates. Gromyko expressed his agreement with the Polish proposal and said that a committee on procedure might be composed of ten or fourteen or even twenty representatives. He also proposed a number of amendments to the rules of procedure that were under discussion. In the course of discussion on the rules of procedure, the Soviet Union assumed a position of defending the rights of small as well as big nations to have a voice in the Conference. The delegate from Ceylon, J.R. Jayawardene, reminded Gromyko that a few years previous the Soviet Union had suggested that the peace treaty should be drafted by the four powers belonging to the Council of Foreign Ministers and the position of the Soviet delegate in the Conference was contrary to his country's views in the past.[7] The Polish proposal and the Soviet amendments were put to vote and were rejected. Later on, Gromyko requested the chair to take the opinion of the Conference on his proposal to invite Communist China. Acheson ruled that, under the rules of procedure just adopted, the proposal of the Soviet delegate was out of order. Article Seven of the rules of procedure provided that :

> Representation at the conference shall be confined to the plenipotentiary delegations accredited respectively to the governments of allied powers invited by the Government of the United States of America to participate in the Conference. The Japanese Delegation shall be entitled to be present without vote at all public meetings of the conference and shall be afforded by the presiding officer appropriate opportunity to be heard prior to the ceremony of signing the Treaty.[8]

The Soviet Union immediately challenged the ruling of the chair and said that the Soviet Union wished to see the Conference, rather than the president, take a decision on the question of seating Communist China in the Conference. The ruling of the chair was put to a vote. The vote sustained the ruling by forty-six to two.[9] On demand of the delegate of the Soviet Union, the vote was counted again to record the number of those who had consciously abstained. This time thirty-six voted in favour of sustaining the ruling of the chair, three opposed and two abstained.[10] This whole drama vividly brought out the basic conflict between the two blocs. The Soviet group was trying to delay the peace treaty, whereas, the Westeren group was attempting to go ahead with the peace treaty according to its own procedure and proposals. The Russians wanted to turn the meeting into a traditional peace conference in which all the terms of the treaty were examined. This could be done on the plea that all participants had a right to be heard and that United States strategy was designed to bloc any debate. The quarrel between the Western powers and the Soviet bloc, seemingly over procedure, probably convinced the assembled delegates in the Conference that under the circumstances, the treaty submitted to the Conference was probably the best that could be achieved. Certain allied powers who were dissatisfied with various terms of the treaty seemed to have realized that it would be very difficult to achieve unanimity, and the British-American treaty was far better than no treaty at all. By the end of the first plenary session, everything seemed to be going well for the Western powers.

From this point on, the Conference went through routine procedure. Formal statements were made by each delegation on the draft peace treaty. According to the plan adopted, the two sponsors of the treaty—the United States and the United Kingdom—first made statements presenting the treaty to the members of the Conference. This was followed by the comments of the other delegations.

The delegate of the United States, John Foster Dulles, explained the purpose of the peace treaty and gave a brief account of the various steps taken by Supreme Commander for Allied Powers from time to time to prepare the former enemy for an eventual peace settlement. In his view it was the duty of the United States to initiate the peace negotiation. At the time of victory, the allies had given the United States exclusive power to name the Supreme Commander for all the Allied Powers and to direct the occupation, whose main purpose was to prepare Japan for the peace to come. This allied act, Dulles asserted, gave the United States a unique position to judge when the Japanese were prepared for peace and to take timely steps to bring the occupation to its predestined end. Explaining why the United States abandoned the conference method of making peace, Dulles observed that the conference method afforded excessive possibilities of obstruction. Regarding the authorship of the treaty, the United States delegate pointed out that every nation which had constructively interested itself in the treaty could claim authorship of important parts of the final draft. Dulles claimed that the treaty was the most broadly-based peace in all history.[11] In substantiation of this Dulles produced a comparative study of the March 1951 draft of the treaty and the August 23, 1951 text, which was finally circulated. These indicated that no article of the earlier draft escaped some modification in the later one and in many instances the changes were important.[12]

The peace treaty, according to Dulles, was a step toward breaking "the vicious cycle of war—victory—peace—war."[13] Further, it was a peace of justice and reconciliation. The preamble of the treaty contained the Japanese desire to adhere to the principle of the Charter, to observe fundamental human rights, and to conform to internationally accepted fair practices. Explaining why these were not written into the treaty, Dulles said that there were good reasons for not doing so. Eighty million people of Japan could not be compelled from without to respect the human rights and fundamental freedoms of their fellow beings. Fair trade practices could not be made a formal obligation when they were not spelled out in international conventions. The ultimate sovereignty of the territories renounced by Japan was not specified in the treaty because of the lack of agreement between the allied powers. According to Dulles, the choice before the allies was either to give Japan peace on the Potsdam Surrender Terms, or deny peace to the former enemy while the Allies argued about the ultimate location of sovereignty of the territories Japan was prepared to, and required to, give up. In the view of the United States delegate, the wise course was to proceed with the peace treaty, leaving the future to resolve doubts by invoking international principles rather than invoking the treaty.[14]

Security provisions in the peace treaty were necessary if the treaty was to restore sovereignty to Japan, Dulles said. The delegate of the United States asserted that "to give a sovereignty which cannot be defended was to give an empty husk."[15] Dulles denied that the United States compelled Japan to accept the security arrangements.[16]

The delegate of the United Kingdom, K.C. Younger, presented the text of the treaty to the Conference. His country was the co-sponsor of the treaty. Regretting India's absence from the Peace Conference, Younger observed that India, which had played a conspicuous part in the defeat of Japan and had strongly advocated a liberal peace treaty, did not participate in the Conference because of her sincere concern with certain items of the peace treaty. Explaining why Communist China was not invited to the Conference, the British delegate said that China, because of her long and bitter experience of Japanese aggression, had a better claim than any country to take part in the making of a peace treaty. Since the two Chinas could not decide among themselves as to what government possessed the lawful and practical authority to commit the whole Chinese nation to permanent engagement, and since there was no agreement among the allied powers on the question of the representation of China, that country was not invited to the Peace Conference.[17] Putting off the treaty until the allied powers reached an agreement on the question of Chinese representation would have been inconsistent with the general agreement on the urgent need for a peace treaty. Speaking on the rearmament of Japan, the delegate from the United Kingdom observed that the treaty did not put any limitations on Japanese rearmament because experience in regard to such restrictions in previous treaties had shown that in the course of time they had become a dead letter. Such restrictions in the past had also provided a breeding ground for the germs of nationalism in its most dangerous forms.[18]

The Soviet delegate, A.A. Gromyko, made a long statement on the text of the peace treaty, probably the most critical of all statements made on it. Gromyko said that the authors of the American-British draft were anxious to clear the path for the rebirth of Japanese militarism and to push Japan again along the path of aggression and military adventure.[19] The Government of the United States had its own special plans in regard to Japan. These plans had nothing in common with the interests of a real peace settlement with Japan, with the interest of maintaining and strengthening peace in the Far East. The draft treaty did not contain any guarantees against the re-establishment of Japanese militarism and, also, the security of the countries which had suffered Japanese aggression was not ensured in the treaty.

The Soviet delegate pointed out that the Potsdam Declaration of 1945 and the resolution of the Far Eastern Commission on the Basic Post-Surrender Policy for Japan provided for the eradication of Japanese militarism and prevention of conditions which would permit the rebirth of militarism in Japan. The Basic Post-Surrender Policy of 19 June, 1947 imposed rigid restrictions on the armed forces of Japan, whereas, the draft treaty did not do so. The peace treaties concluded after World War II with the former enemy states—for example, the peace treaty with Italy—contained clear and specific provisions restricting the armed forces of that country. Japan was placed in a privileged position in this respect without any reason. Therefore, the American-British draft treaty was contradictory to the decision of the Far Eastern Commission.[20] Gromyko made reference to the argument of the authors of the treaty that the decision of the Far Eastern Commission was valid only for the period preceding the conclusion of a peace treaty with Japan. This argument, the Russian delegate pointed out, was inadequate in view of the fact that the decision of the Far Eastern Commission outlined measures which would deprive Japan of power to make war, and this decision covered the entire post-war period.

Gromyko maintained that the American-British draft treaty legalized steps that were being taken by the occupation authorities in Japan, such as the construction and expansion of military, naval and air bases in Japan, the re-establishment of the land, naval, and air forces, and the expansion and modernization of former Japanese military arsenals. All these actions on the part of the United States showed that the United States ignored the obligations undertaken by her together with other allied powers to prevent the rebirth of Japan as an aggressive state.[21]

The American-British draft, Gromyko observed, provided for the participation of Japan in a military bloc created under the aegis of the United States. The purpose of this arrangement had nothing to do with the maintenance of peace in the Far East. The Soviet representative argued that by inserting Article Six (a) the United States made provision for retaining armed forces in Japan. The article provided that :

> All occupation forces of the Allied Powers shall be withdrawn from Japan as soon as possible after the coming into

> force of the present treaty, and in any case not later than 90 days thereafter. Nothing in this provision shall, however, prevent the stationing or retention of foreign armed forces in Japanese territory under or in consequence of any bilateral or multilateral agreements which have been or may be made between one or more of the Allied Powers, on the one hand, and Japan on the other.[22]

Gromyko declared that the United States, instead of preventing the revival of Japanese militarism, was herself performing the task of the Japanese militarists by inserting Article Six in the treaty. In the view of the Russian delegate the purpose of the military pact was to encourage the activities of the militaristic circles in Japan, who were prepared to start new military adventures against their neighbouring states. The treaty imposed on Japan an obligation to join a military arrangement directed against Japan's neighbours and particularly against the Chinese People's Republic and the Soviet Union. This was clear from the fact that the military agreement provided by the peace treaty excluded the participation of the Chinese People's Republic and the Soviet Union.[23] The draft treaty not only failed to provide the obligations that Japan should not join any coalitions directed against any of the states which participated in the war against militarist Japan, but, on the contrary, was clearing the path for Japan's participation in aggresive blocs in the Far East created under the leadership of the United States. This motive of the United States, the Soviet delegate asserted, could not be concealed by any false phrases such as the right of Japan for "individual and collective security." In view of the fact that there existed no threat to Japan from her neighbours, any reference to the necessity for Japan to join a military bloc allegedly for the purpose of self-defense was groundless. It was a well-known fact that Japan had not been subjected to any attack for centuries from anybody. Therefore, it was ridiculous to talk of the protection of Japan from imaginary attacks.[24] Speaking on the provision in the draft treaty which provided for the retention of armed forces on the territory of Japan after the signing of the treaty, the Soviet delegate said that the peace treaties concluded after

World War II, including the peace treaty with Italy, specifically provided for the withdrawal of occupation forces within ninety-days from the date of the coming into force of the peace treaty. The British-American draft made provision for the withdrawal of the armed forces in Article Six, but the same article made it possible for the occupation forces to remain in Japan under a bilateral treaty. It was an empty phrase which conveyed nothing, and was meant to mislead naive people regarding the real meaning of the article. Military agreements were imposed on Japan under which it undertook in advance to yield its territory for the establishment of American military, naval, and air bases in accordance with the aggressive plans of the United States in the Far East. The negotiations between the Japanese Government and the United States were going on over a long period of time on the question of the retention of American forces and military bases in Japan after the peace settlement, and during the course of these negotiations the Japanese government was being subjected to flagrant pressure by the United States, who actually controlled the political and economic life of Japan.[25] This provision in the draft treaty contradicted the proclaimed purpose of the peace treaty, namely the restoration of full sovereignty to Japan. Dealing with the territorial questions in the peace treaty, Gromyko said that the omission on the part of the authors of the treaty to mention the ultimate fate of Taiwan, the Pescadores, the Paracel, and other islands over which Japan renounced all claims and rights grossly violated the indisputable rights of Communist China to these territories.[26]

Similarly, said the Soviet delegate, the draft treaty merely mentioned the renunciation by Japan of rights, claims, and title over the Kurile Islands and the Southern Sakhalin and the islands adjacent to it. The treaty made no mention of the indisputable obligation on the part of Japan to recognize the sovereignty of the Soviet Union over these territories. By introducing such proposals on territorial questions, Great Britain and the United States violated the obligations undertaken by them in the Cairo and Potsdam Declarations as well as the Yalta Agreement on territorial adjustments.[27] The draft treaty also provided for the exclusion of the islands of Ryukyu,

Bonin, Rosario, Volcano, Parece Vela, Marcus, and Daito from the sovereignty of Japan and their transfer, under the sole administration of the United States as trust territories of the UN. Such a severance of the said islands from Japan, asserted Gromyko, was provided for neither by any international, agreement, nor by the decision of the Security Council, which alone had the right to make decisions regarding trusteeship over territories of strategic importance. The Soviet Union considered this arrangement as arbitrary and illegal.[28]

The Soviet official argued that the draft treaty did not contain any provision pertaining to the democratisation of Japan. The Potsdam Declaration and the decision of the Far Eastern Commission required the Allied Powers to encourage the formation of democratic institutions in Japan, and to inculcate in the Japanese people respect for fundamental human rights. These decisions were not written into the peace treaty. On the contrary, at the time of the signing of the peace treaty, repressive measures were being adopted by the Japanese Government against the trade unions, the democratic parties, outstanding democratic leaders of Japan, and the progressive organs of the Japanese press, with the approval and direct encouragement of the occupation authorities.

Gromyko said that the provisions on economic matters in the peace treaty deserved serious attention. He was of the opinion that the peace treaty safeguarded the economic privileges obtained by certain states in general and by the United States in particular in Japan during the period of occupation. The draft treaty made provision for the foreign monopolies to maintain a commanding position in the Japanese economy, especially in the fields of industry, shipping, and foreign trade. The treaty did not mention Japan's right to have access to raw materials as provided for by the Potsdam Declaration.

The obligations undertaken by Japan under the peace treaty to pay reparations to the Allied Powers in terms of the labour of her people was described by the Soviet delegate as a "slavery like form of redeeming the damage."[29] This long statement was summed up by Gromyko by saying that :

> "the American-British draft is not a treaty of peace but a treaty for the preparation of a new war in the Far East."[30]

According to Gromyko, the Soviet Union took part in the San Francisco Conference to voice publicly the truth about the American-British draft treaty and oppose it with demands for a new peace treaty which would serve the cause of a universal peace.

The Soviet delegate than proposed a number of amendments to the draft treaty. In his reply to a question put by the chair whether the Soviet delegate was proposing amendments to the draft treaty, Gromyko said that he was making a declaration. Later in the debate Gromyko asserted that the declarations were amendments and should be treated as such. His most important amendments were as follows :

(1) All armed forces of the Allied and Associated Powers should be withdrawn from the territory of Japan within ninety days of the coming into force of the treaty and after that there should be no foreign troops or bases on the territory of Japan.

(2) Japan should recognize the sovereignty of China over Manchuria, Formosa, and various other islands off the China coast.

(3) Russia should have full sovereignty over the southern part of Skhalin and adjacent islands as well as over the Kurile Islands.

(4) The Sovereignty of Japan should extend to the four main islands mentioned in the treaty as well as to the Islands of Ryukyu, Bonin, Rosario, Volcano, and various other Islands then being administered by the United States.

(5) Japan should undertake to remove all obstacles to the revival and strengthening of democratic tendencies among the Japanese people and to secure for them the enjoyment of human rights and fundamental freedoms.

(6) The resurgence of fascist and militarist organizations should be prohibited.

(7) Japan should not enter any coalition or military alliance directed against any power which had participated

in the war against Japan.

(8) Japanese land, air, and naval forces should be closely restricted to the minimum size necessary for self defense, and so forth.

(9) A new article should be added to Chapter 3 in the treaty as follows :

> 1. The Straits of La Perouse (Soya) and Nemuro, along the entire Japanese coast, as well as the Straits of Tsugaru and Tsushima shall be demilitarized. These Straits shall always be open for the passage of merchant ships of all countries.
> 2. The Straits named in paragraph (1) of this article shall be open for the passage of only such warships as belong to the powers adjacent to the Sea of Japan.[31]

Later in the debate, replying to the Soviet criticism of the treaty, Dulles said that the sum total of the Soviet proposals was to create a situation where Japan would be defenseless both internally and externally and thereby would rapidly fall a victim to any strong, dynamic power in her vicinity. The United States representative asserted that there existed such a power in close proximity. Referring to the Soviet amendment Number Nine, quoted above, Dulles said that proposal, if accepted, would mean that only the Russian naval force based upon Vladivostok could use the Straits of La Perouse, Nemuro, Tsugaru, and Tsushima. This Soviet naval force would patrol the waters in and about Japan, which would cut Japan into two and divide Japan from Korea, so that not even the United Nation's Force could operate in the Straits between Korea and Japan. Dulles further observed that the Soviet proposals contained 'the Jokers' with which the United States had to put up with for eleven months, and were the kind of proposals which made it impossible for the United States to cooperate with the Soviet Union.[32]

Towards the end of the Conference, the Soviet delegate inquired of the President in what order the Soviet amendments to the treaty would be taken up for the consideration of the Conference and whether a vote was intended on these amendments and in what manner. Acheson reminded Gromyko that at the time of his original statement on the draft treaty the chair had asked the Soviet delegate whether he was proposing any amendments and Gromyko had said at that time that he was making a statement. Therefore, Acheson said that he did not have from Gromyko any proposal before the chair to make any amendments to the treaty. Gromyko said that the amendments were a part of the declaration of the Soviet delegation and maintained that they should be treated as amendments and voted upon by the Conference. There was at the time a motion before the Conference moved by Ceylon and seconded by Cuba that would permit only a few more statements and then the Conference would be deemed closed except for the signing of the treaty and other routine matters. The chair ruled that if the resolution was adopted the opportunity to propose amendments to the treaty was foreclosed. After further discussion, the motion moved by Ceylon was put to vote. It was adopted by a vote of forty-one to one.[33] Gromyko immediately contended that the adoption of the resolution did not alter the situation and insisted that his amendments be considered. The chair ruled the Soviet proposal out of order. The ruling of the chair was challenged, and, after a heated debate, a vote was taken. The conference upheld the ruling of the chair by forty-six to three votes.[34]

The Australian delegate, P.C. Spender, while describing the peace treaty as benevolent and magnanimous, doubted whether freedom was in full flower in Japan, whether militarism had been completely eradicated, whether the evil of Zaibatsu had been utterly destroyed, and whether the roots of the police state had been completely removed from the soil of Japan.[35] The Australian delegate further maintained that his country recognized Japan's right to defend herself but at the same time Australia wished to see included in the treaty some limitations upon Japan's right to rearm, the range and composition of her defense forces, her ship building capacity, the manufacture of atomic weapons, and other related matters.

The delegate from New Zealand, Sir Carl Berendsen, described the draft treaty as a peace of good hope and good will, which contained no elements of revenge. However, the wanton aggression against New Zealand by Japan during World War II and the consequent sufferings of the New Zealanders, observed Sir Carl Berdensen, made some people in his country doubt the future policy of Japan in the Pacific. New Zealand willingly took a risk in allowing the Japanese to rearm because New Zealand wanted to play her part as a good neighbour in the Pacific. Further, it was important from the point of view of the security of New Zealand to maintain and consolidate the democratic reforms introduced in Japan during the period of occupation.[36]

The delegate from Poland, Stefan Wierblowski, described the peace treaty as dangerous not only to the Asiatic neighbours of Japan but also for peace in the entire world. Speaking on the procedure adopted by the United States for the conclusion of the peace treaty, the Polish delegate said that the United States violated its international commitments "openly, callously and shamelessly."[37] He asserted that a peace treaty for Japan should be drafted by the Council of Foreign Ministers as provided by such international documents as the United Nation's Declaration of January, 1942. Wierblowski ridiculed John Foster Dulles' remark that it was "a peace conference for eleven months" and observed that it was a strange Conference consisting of the United States and a number of other governments corresponding with each other, while the United States retained the exclusive authority to decide which opinions should find recognition in the provisions of the treaty. In the opinion of the Polish delegate, it was a distortion of facts to say that conversations were held with the Soviet Union, whose demands were completely ignored. Further, the peace treaty was dictated by the United States and the confirmation of this fact could be found in the numerous statements made in the Conference by the representatives of the countries concerned.[38] Wierblowski insisted that the aim of United States policy in the Far East was clear from the very beginning. In Japan, the United States decided to apply a modernized and enlarged Monroe Doctrine which tried to extend American influence over new territories in the world. This could be found in the United States decision to include Japan in the American system of bases and territories in which the United States intended to station its armed forces.[39] The Polish delegate supported all the amendments proposed by the Soviet Union to the draft treaty.

The delegate from the Philippines, Carlos P. Romulo, while giving general support to the draft peace treaty, expressed profound dissatisfaction with certain aspects of it. He reminded the Conference of the acts of cruelty and destruction committed by the Japanese against his countrymen during World War II and said that the Philippines craved no pity from any one. All they wanted was justice. According to Romulo, the Philippine Government pursued three objectives in its policy towards post-war Japan; first, to make sure that Japan would never again become a menace to the Philippines and other countries; second, to secure equitable reparations for the damage caused by Japan to the Philippines and other countries; and third, to welcome a democratic and non-militarist Japan at a proper time.[40] In the light of these principles, the Government of the Philippines considered that the peace treaty fell short in certain respects of what it deemed to be just and necessary.[41] Romulo said that his government wished to see written into the treaty the reforms of the political and educational system instituted during the period of occupation. He doubted the opinion of those people who held that Japan during a brief period of six years had transformed itself from the aggresive, feudal, militarist police state, which it had been for centuries, into a practicing and thoroughgoing democracy. The Philippine delegate expressed dissatisfaction with the provision in the treaty on reparations and observed that depriving Japan of certain overseas territories under Articles Two and Three and the confiscation of the Japanese overseas assets under Article Fourteen (a) benefitted only the great powers.[42] On the other hand, the reparations to be paid to the smaller countries for the damage caused by Japan during the war were severely restricted under the treaty. He further observed that :

> The Philippine Government cannot accept the theory that the payment of a due amount of reparations from Japan is an act of vindictiveness. The principle of indemnification for damage willfully caused can no more be renounced in the relations between states than it can be relinquished in the ralations between individuals.[43]

Romulo quoted statistics to show the progress made by Japan in the field of economics during the period of occupation and indicated that country had the capacity to pay reparations. He was of the opinion that the restrictions put on the form of reparations would make the claimant countries subservient to the Japanese economy as mere suppliers of raw material for the Japanese industrial machine. Furthermore, in view of the pre-war predominance of Japanese industry over the economy of Asia, these fears should not be lightly dismissed. Romulo reserved his government's right to negotiate with the Japanese Government concerning the kind and forms of reparation.

The delegate from Egypt, Mohamed Kamil Bey Abdul Rahim, also referred to the omission on the part of the Allied Powers of the fates of the territories over which Japan renounced her sovereignty. With regard to the territories under Article Three, which were to be administered by the United States as trust-territories, the Egyptian delegate remarked that it would have been advisable to leave the whole matter to the General Assembly of the UN. He further observed that by making a provision for the retention of the occupation forces in Article Six (a), the condition of freedom of choice was not fulfilled.[44] The government of Egypt reserved its right to impose additional taxes on Japanese imports, should the circumstances so demand, and insisted that this should not deprive Egypt of the economic privileges granted by the treaty. The delegate from Indonesia also expressed his government's dissatisfaction with the provisions in the treaty on reparations and moved a number of modifications to Article Fourteen which dealt with the reparation problem.[45]

The Japanese Prime Minister, Shigern Yoshida, was the last speaker in the Conference. Yoshida, while welcoming the treaty, described it as 'an instrument of reconciliation' and not a 'treaty of vengeance'.[46] However, he stated that the territorial arrangements in the treaty were unfair to the Japanese people. He welcomed the American recognition of Japanese residual sovereignty over Ryukyu and Bonin islands. On the other hand the Prime Minister questioned the Russian contention that Japan occupied the Kuriles and South Sakhalin by force. He asserted that, at the time of the opening of diplomatic and commercial relations with Japan by the Russians, the then Tsarist government did not question Japanese ownership of the islands of Etorofu and Kunashiri. Further, the North Kuriles and the Southern half of Sakhalin were open to both Japanese and Russian settlers. Yoshida pointed out that under the Russo-Japanese agreement of 7 May, 1875 Japan ceded South Sakhalin to Russia in exchange for the North Kuriles. In accordance with the treaty of Portsmouth of 1905, South Sakhalin became a Japanese territory. He also claimed that Habomai and the Shikotan Islands were parts of Hokkaido, the northern part of Japan.[47]

On the question of reparations, Yoshida pleaded for understanding. He stated that reduced in territory Japan was hard pressed to pay reparations, but with the help of the Allied powers, the Japanese Government would fulfil her obligations. He hoped that the doors of the Allied nations would be opened for Japanese trade. Prime Minister Yoshida also sought the aid of the allies for a speedy repatriation of 340,000 Japanese prisoners of war in the Soviet Union.

He regretted the absence of India and Burma from the Conference and said that Japan was anxious to cultivate friendly relations with her Asian neighbours. With regard to China, Yoshida said that the role of the mainland of China in Japanese trade had been exaggerated and that the six years following the end of the war had proved that Japan could prosper without Chinese markets.[48]

Yoshida alluded to the menace of totalitarianism and implied that the Soviet Union presented a threat to Japanese security. Therefore, according to Yoshida, the Japanese Government decided to conclude a security treaty with the United States under which American forces would be retained in Japan as long as a Communist threat continued. He assured the Allied nations that his country, beaten and battered by the war, would not become a menace to her neighbours. Further, "Japan of today is no longer the Japan of yesterday. We will not fail your expectations of us as a new nation dedicated to peace, democracy and freedom."[49] Yoshida concluded his speech by saying that his countrymen passionately desired to live in peace with their neighbours and save "succeeding generations from the scourge of war."[50]

The events and the speeches described above point out two things :

(1) The rivalry between the United States and the Soviet Union over Japan continued to the last moment; and

(2) The widespread dissatisfaction among the members of the Western bloc provided further proof for the conclusion drawn in the last chapter, that the United States military and economic power prevailed over the interest of the allies.

The proceedings of the Conference further strengthened the conclusion arrived at in the preceeding chapter, that both the United States and the Soviet Union desired to bring Japan into their respective spheres of influence by signing a peace treaty on their own terms. The Soviet Union along with Poland and Czechoslavakia tried hard to reopen the entire problem of the peace settlement with Japan in the San Francisco Peace Conference. The Soviet delegate used all the means available to him to turn the Peace Conference into a conventional peace-making body. The purpose was to drag out the Conference by bringing in the question of Chinese representation and finally to create disorder and disunity among the Western powers, which would mean the end of the Conference. The Soviet ambitions in Japan were revealed when her Foreign Minister proposed that the peace treaty should give the Russian war ships the exclusive right to patrol the straits surrounding Japan. Had the proposal been accepted, it would have given the Russians the means to control Japan from the North. On the other hand, the United States, along with Britain and other countries represented in the Conference, wanted to block any discussion on the draft treaty and reduce it to a formal signing ceremony. The United States, through careful preparation and skillful management, defeated every Soviet move to reopen negotiations on the peace settlement. Whenever, Gromyko raised a procedural point, Dean Acheson used his thorough knowledge of parliamentary procedure to put the Soviet delegate on the wrong side. When Gromyko found himself hopelessly out-maneuvered and out-numbered in a conference of partisan men, he gave up the fight as futile.

The formal statements made by the delegates from Australia,

New Zealand, and the Philippines, to mention a few, showed a good deal of dissatisfaction among the members of the FEC over certain provisions of the peace treaty. In spite of the eleven months peace negotiations and in spite of certain prior agreements on security arrangements between the United States and other Pacific nations, some of the conflicting interests of these countries were not reconciled. This disunity among the members of the FEC apparently made questionable John Foster Dulles' claim that the treaty was "the most broadly based peace treaty in all history." The delegate from the Philippines implied in his speech that the peace treaty mainly served the interest of the United States.[51] The fact of the matter was that the allies, dependent on the military and economic support of the United States could not afford to displease the Americans.

SECTION II

On 8 September 1951, the peace treaty was signed by forty-nine nations, including Japan. The three Communist states—the Soviet Union, Poland and Czechoslavakia—refrained from signing. On the same day the security treaty between Japan and the United States was also signed. A year later, in April 1952, the administrative agreement concerning the disposition of American forces in Japan was concluded. These three agreements together formed the peace settlement for Japan, and they were regarded as inseparable. For the sake of convenience, first we shall deal with the peace treaty and then the other two agreements will be taken up. The peace treaty, as we have seen, was praised by some delegates and condemned by others in the Conference. The United States and the other members of the Western bloc described the treaty as conciliatory, generous, and magnanimous. The Soviet Union and her friends declared it as dangerous and as a treaty for the preparation of a new war in the Far East. Although it would be difficult to pass any definitive judgement on the treaty, in the following pages an attempt is made to point out certain contradictions between the war-time agreements and the treaty and the implications of these contradictions to Japan.

I. The peace treaty formally repudiated the ideas and the

agreements signed at Cairo, Yalta, and Potsdam, and by so doing finally opened the way for the incorporation of Japan into the American defense perimeter in the Pacific.[52] First of all, the treaty did not put any limitation on Japanese rearmament and research concerning atomic weapons. On the contrary, a reluctant Japanese Government, in the face of a strong public opinion against rearmament, was forced to organize a 100,000-man police force after the outbreak of the Korean War. Also, the security treaty between the United States and Japan, which was regarded as an integral part of the peace treaty, openly encouraged Japan to mount its armed strength by stating that :

> Japan will itself increasingly assume responsibility for its own defense against direct and indirect aggression . . . ."[53]

In addition, the treaty said that Japan would give every assistance to the UN, which could in theory mean to include assistance by armed forces. After the signing of the peace treaty, the United States cajoled and threatened the Japanese to accept military build up targets that they considered economically unrealistic and politically undesirable.[54] These provisions and threats were not only against the Potsdam Declaration, which required complete demilitarization of Japan, but also' as several Japanese intellectuals have claimed, against Article Nine of their country's Constitution, which renounced war as an instrument of national policy.[55] The treaty imposed the economic burden of rearmament on the country. The 1952 Japanese national budget appropriate nearly twenty-one per cent for defense.[56] It was done at the expense of public welfare projects such as housing, relief, and other items designed to raise the living standards of the Japanese people. For several post-war years the Japanese hoped that their days of paying for a military machine were over. Far from that, the rearmament of the country was going to cost them more and more each passing year. For the Japanese Government proposed to increase the strength of the National Police Force to 310,000 by 1954. It is interesting to note that before Japan invaded Manchuria the Japanese army was only 230,000 men.

Again, the year before Japan attacked Manchuria, the nation's military expenditure stood only slightly higher at thirty per cent of the national budget.[57] The government's blueprint on national defense prompted even a pro-rearmament Japanese newspaper *The Jiji Shimpo* to declare that military figures presented in 1952 "exceeded the bounds of mere strengthening police forces."[58] The paper advocated that a spade be called a spade and it described the government's defense programme as rearmament in a big way. Alarmed by the prospect of a rearmed Japan, critics denounced the peace treaty as a road to war rather than to peace.[59] Some sections in Japan feared that the army would again pose a threat to democracy in the country.

II. The territorial arrangements were unfair to the Japanese. Article Three gave the United States an indefinite control over the Ryukyu and Bonin Islands. However, the United States recognized Japanese residual sovereignty over those islands. Under Article Two (c) Japan relinquished all right, title, and claim to the Kurile Islands, and South Sakhalin. The Kurile, Ryukyu and Bonin Islands legally belonged to Japan and were not acquired by aggression. Therefore, the severance of these territories from Japan was not only contrary to the Atlantic and Cairo Declarations, which stated that the Allied powers "covet no gain for themselves and have no thought of territorial expansion,"[60] but also to the declared objective of the peace treaty, that is, to restore full sovereignty to Japan. This unjust disposition of Japanese territories exposed both Moscow and Washington to the charge of expansionism. Though the Soviet Union refused to be a party to the treaty, she insisted that the peace settlement explicitly recognize her legal claim over the Kurile and other islands occupied by her. In terms of resources, speecially in fishing and manpower, these territorial losses meant much to Japan. The Japanese claimed that the Habomai and Shikotan Islands were parts of Hokkaido and were not included in the Kurile Islands. They asserted that the Russian occupation of these islands was illegal. The Japanese argued that since their country was not a party to the Yalta Agreement, and since the agreement was not mentioned in the documents concerning Japanese surrender, they were not bound by it.[61]

III. The treaty did not make the reforms introduced by SCAP in the early years of the occupation binding on the Japanese Government. It may be recalled that in June 1948 the Chief of the Government Section in GHQ had stated with regard to the purge programme that "final action taken under the purge programme is regarded to be of a permanent nature for which the Allied Powers will unquestionably hold future Japanese Governments fully responsible."[62] This statement was in consonance with the terms of the Potsdam Declaration upon which rested the whole superstructure of the purge programme. A clause to the effect should have been included in the peace treaty in order to have made effective the permanency of the reforms. One might ask why these reforms were not made enforceable through the treaty. It may be again recalled that the Japanese conservative parties, especially that of Prime Minister Yoshida, considered most of the occupation reforms such as the deconcentration of Zaibatsu, the decentralization of police power, the trade union movement, and the purge measures as excessive and unsuitable to Japan and wanted to modify them. The writing of these measures in the treaty would have made it difficult for Yoshida to undo the post-war democratic reforms. The result was that "After the peace treaty went into effect Yoshida's Liberal Party Cabinet set about revising or abolishing those SCAP-imposed laws which it claimed were not appropriate to the needs of Japan. Rather than reexamining all of the occupation policies, the Liberal Party Cabinet concentrated upon maintaining and strengthening the conservative line which the Supreme Commander for Allied Powers had laid down during the latter part of the occupation period and suppressing those policies of the early occupation days which had been aimed at democratization".[63] The Japanese Government issued ordinances revoking the purge in its entirety, restricting the activities of labour unions and public school teachers, centralizing education, strengthening the police system, revising the system of pensions for war veterans and so forth.

The ink was hardly dry on the peace treaty in March 1952, when the Japanese Government introduced the Subversive

Organizations Control Bill, which was designed to check the activities of public and private associations. Ominous signs were increasing on the right, in the revival of ultranationalistic societies and the entrance of certain military leaders into politics as rearmament progressed. College graduates seeking jobs in big banks and commercial companies were required either to endorse the peace treaty or keep quite. Furthermore, the conservative forces began to assert themselves in their drive to keep the Emperor remote from the people.[64]

IV. The provision which constituted the heart of the controversy over the peace settlement both in Japan and abroad was Article Six, which provided for the retention of the American armed forces in Japan, under the pretext of Japan's right to individual or collective self-defense referred to in Article Fifty-one of the Charter of the United Nations. It was stated by American spokesmen that in accordance with this provision, the Japanese Government concluded the security pact between itself and the United States in its capacity as an independent sovereign government. It was hard to believe that Japan, still under the occupation at the time the treaty was being drafted, took an independent decision without being influenced by the United States Government. Moreover, the stationing of foreign troops in Japan ran counter to the provisions on sovereignty. The fact of the matter was that the Japanese conservative leaders had to give their consent, knowing as they did that there would not be an early peace settlement with the Western powers unless the American armed forces were allowed to be retained in Japan after the conclusion of the peace treaty. As one author put it :

> In place of requiring Japan as a condition of peace to allow American troops to remain indefinitely in Japanese territory, the proposed treaty provision was put in the form of a request by Japan for American military aid and an acceptance by the United States. This appeared to give Japan the initiative in the arrangement and hence did not formally impair the grant of full sovereignty to Japan.[65]

The illusory character of Japanese independence was further

illustrated by the extraction of a letter by Dulles from Yoshida to the effect that the Japanese Government would recognize the Chinese Nationalist Government of Formosa.[66]

The serious question that arises from the text of the treaty was the one which concerned the basic objective of the peace settelment. Did the peace treaty bring the state of war that existed between Japan and those powers who were at war with her to an end ?

The Soviet Union, and other Communist states bitterly opposed the terms of the treaty, and by refusing to sign it were still at war with Japan. Communist China, the most populous neighbour of Japan, was not invited to the Conference. India, the next most populous state, and Burma, which had suffered under Japanese aggression in World War II, though invited, preferred to abstain from the Conference. Moreover, the treaty left the ultimate disposition of certain territories undecided. In view of these facts, it was doubtful whether the treaty really established peace between Japan and her immediate neighbours. As *The London Times* put it, "A Far Eastern settlement that excludes Soviet Russia, the Chinese People's Republic, India, and Burma was conspicuously incomplete . . ."[67]

On the other hand, the economic provisions of the treaty had been variously described as liberal and 'soft'. Certain critics have charged that by leaving the economy unrestricted the treaty did not destroy the potential warmaking capacity of Japan as required by the Potsdam Declaration.

There was nothing in the treaty or in its accompanying declarations and undertakings to prevent Japanese industrialists, traders, and ocean carriers from becoming once again formidable rivals of their counterparts in the Allied countries.

Japan was required to pay only token reparations to the Allied Powers for the damage and suffering caused by her during the war. These reparations were to be paid in the form of manufacturing and technical services. Unlike Germany in World War I, Japan was very fortunate in this respect. Her merchant fleet had not been taken from her. Her shipbuilding capacity had been left unlimited. Due to disagreement among the Allied Powers, the early policy of earmarking for removal as reparation, plants then considered surplus to a peaceful economy, was stopped. The favour shown to Japan in these provisions of the treaty could be explained in terms of Japanese domestic demands.

The Japanese ruling party, which represented generally well-to-do businessmen, landlords, and other conservative elements in the country, pleaded that no restrictions be put on the Japanese economy. It argued that economic unrest resulting from restricted economic growth would give rise to explosive tendencies among the people, which the Japanese Communist Party and Japan's neighbours would skillfully exploit. This was exactly the thing the United States feared and wished to prevent. Moreover, business groups in the United States opposed treaty restrictions on Japanese industry. For they wanted free trade and investment in Japan. As has been pointed out, after the Korean War the United States decided to gear Japanese industry to American military needs in the Far East. In July, 1951, the United States Defense Mobilization Director Charles E. Wilson, actively canvassed for United States-Japan economic co-operation.[68] Furthermore Dulles believed in a treaty of 'magnanimity based on power.'[69] The result was that the United States first opposed reparations completely, but later, in deference to the strong feelings of the Philippines, Indonesia, and the other Allied powers on this problem, agreed to token reparations.

THE SECURITY PACT, ADMINISTRATIVE AGREEMENT AND THEIR IMPLICATIONS

The Security Pact and the Administrative Agreement were two very important documents. They had special significance for the Japanese and these agreements created a widespread opposition to the government in Japan. Some of the important provisions of the agreements could be summarized as follows :

Under the Security Treaty, the United States agreed to maintain its land, air and sea forces in and about Japan for the protection of that country. The United States forces were to assist the Japanese Government to put down internal disturbances instigated by outside powers. The Security Treaty would expire whenever, in the opinion of both governments, an alternative security arrangement (such as United Nations protection or any other individual or collective arrangement), had been made which would maintain international peace and security in the Japanese area.[70]

Under the Administrative Agreement, the United States armed forces enjoyed a number of privileges.

(1) The armed forces were granted priorities equivalent to the priorities enjoyed by the ministries and agencies of the Japanese Government.
(2) They were exempt from Japanese laws and regulations on the registration and control of aliens.
(3) All material supplies and equipment imported to Japan by the United States armed forces and their dependents were exempted from customs duties and other such charges.
(4) They were not liable to pay any Japanese taxes to the Japanese Government or to any other taxing agency in Japan.
(5) Pending an agreement between the two governments over criminal jurisdiction, the United States Service Courts and authorities were given exclusive jurisdiction over all offenses committed by the members of the United States armed forces and their dependents in Japan.
(6) Any member of the United States armed forces and their civilian components arrested for an offense by Japanese were to be immediately turned over to the United States authorities in Japan.
(7) If a member of the armed forces violated any Japanese laws, he was to be tried by the United States Service Courts and authorities.
(8) Japan was to pay $115 million per year for the purpose of procurement by the United States of transportation and other services and supplies in Japan.[71]

The crucial point in the security Treaty, the one that gave rise to serious controversy in Japan, appeared in Article One, which says that :

such forces may be utilized to contribute to the

> maintenance of international peace and security in the Far East and to the security of Japan against armed attack from without. . . .

It meant that the United States armed forces in Japan were not maintained exclusively for the protection of that country against external aggression, they were an integral part of the United States military posture in Asia. It suggested that the United States forces could not only move freely up and down the Japanese islands but also they could be flown to any trouble spot in the Far East such as for bombing of Manchuria and China, which would automatically involve Japan in an act of belligerency without its assent. Thus the treaty committed the Japanese to the cold war as well as to direct combat. The treaty also gave the United States the right to bring atomic weapons into Japan without consultation or the assent of the Japanese Government. The provision for the United States to intervene in certain cases of internal disturbance in Japan was obviously designed to deter a Communist-led revolt supported either by the Soviet Union or Communist China. It had two implications : (i) It gave the impression that any support on the part of the population to the Communists could be considered as subversive activity likely to disturb public peace and security, and such an occasion would give the Japanese Government an execuse to bring the United States forces into action (ii) The conservative leaders could also use the United States forces to suppress any popular uprising by branding it as Communist inspired. This provision harmed Japan's prestige as a soverign and independent nation. It implied that the Japanese Government was incapable of performing its primary function, that is, the maintenance of peace and order in the country, and depended instead on foreign forces for its very existence. In normal times such a government could not be considered worth its name. It resembled colonial administrations in Asia and Africa. It may be recalled that in some of the colonies the reactionary native rulers called upon foreign forces to quell popular uprisings against the government.

The treaty prescribed no time limit for its expiration. By so doing it gave the Americans a blank cheque; they could withdraw their armed forces at their convenience.

In the notes exchanged between the Secretary of State Dean Acheson and Prime Minister Yoshida, on the same day the Pact was signed, the latter gave an assurance that :

> if and when forces of a Member or Members of the United Nations are engaged in any United Nations action in the Far East after the Treaty of Peace comes into force, Japan will permit and facilitate the support in and about Japan, by the Member or Members of the forces engaged in such United Nations actions. . . .[72]

Thus, the note assured the UN forces of the continued use of Japan as a base, if such a need arose. In addition, the note was so worded that any future UN action in the Far East would be granted the same facilities in and about Japan as the Korean operation.

The Administrative Agreement was a particular target of resentment in Japan. It denied the Japanese Government criminal jurisdiction over the United States armed forces, civilian components, and their dependents. This exemption included all kinds of offenses, whether committed while on duty or off duty. The privileges bestowed upon the American forces in Japan were more extensive than those granted in similar agreements. For example, the British forces stationed abroad did not enjoy such extraordinary prerogatives, not to mention privileges accorded to American and other armed forces under the North Atlantic Treaty Organization.[73] The position of foreign forces in their country recalled in the minds of many Japanese the deep memories of the 'unequal treaties' of the Meiji times. As one American scholar has put it :

> In particular the semi-extraterritorial status of the American military, with all the unfortunate nineteenth century associations of extraterritoriality, is a specific irritant stimulating this fear of American colonialism.[74]

In other words the United States considered Japan as her 'back yard' as one Japanese scholar has put it.[75] According to another

Japanese scholar the security pact amounted to 'military control of Japan' by American imperialism.[76] The United States bound the succeeding governments in Japan to guarantee the special status given to the American armed forces by inserting a provision to the effect that Japan would cooperate with the United States :

> in taking such steps as may from time to time be necessary to ensure the security of the U.S. armed forces, the members thereof, the civilian components, and their property. The Japanese Government agrees to seek such legislation and to take such other actions as may be necessary to ensure the adequate security and protection within its territory of installations, equipment, property, records, and official information of the U.S. and for the punishment of offenders under the applicable laws of Japan.[77]

In law and theory the United States forces in Japan were supposed to be 'considerate' guests on the people of that country. In fact they were a constant reminder to the Japanese that the occupation had not really ended. The mere change of terminology from "members of the occupation forces" to "members of the security forces" did not substantially alter the attitude of the GI's and the civilians toward the Japanese and their government. American military personnel tried to hang on to the physical facilities such as the Dai Ichi building and the Imperial hotel, the two symbols of the occupation, choice housing in certain areas, golf courses, resort hotels and to their former status in the country. Moreover, hundreds of military bases retained by the Americans created social and political problems for the Japanese. The Japanese charged that the American bases in their country constituted an infringement on human and individual rights. The appropriation of farm land for the expansion of American bases in Sunakawa, a suburb of Tokyo, in September 1955, led to a clash between students and police.[78] The sense of pride and consciousness of independence made the Japanese resent the presence of foreign forces in their country.

The peace settlement did not improve Japan's international

position either. It left her "virtually isolated in Asia."[79] The Soviet Union and Communist China looked upon her as a colony of the United States and declared that there could be no friendship between them and the Japanese Government until the latter became really independent by revoking the Security Pact with the United States and by getting rid of the American military forces. The Philippines were disappointed with the peace treaty and feared a revival of Japanese expansion. The non-committed Asian nations regarded Japan as a "tail to the American kite." They thought that Japan could gain more by being non-aligned in the cold war. The Australians and the British were concerned with Japanese competition in trade. The passionate desire of the Japanese people to be a member of the UN and a part of the Asian community were not fulfilled immediately, because their government put all its eggs in one basket. The Soviet Union opposed Japan's membership in the UN and the newly independent nations of Asia showed reluctance to accept her as full fledged member of a resurgent Asia.

To sum up, United States troops remained in the main islands as garrison forces. Japan was heavily dependent on the United States for raw materials and markets. There was a ban on Japan's trade with Communist China.[80] Enjoying extraterritorial rights the foreign armed forces continuted to hold the Japanese as second class citizens in their own country. Japan was deprived of certain islands which legally belonged to her. Finally, she stood isolated in Asia. In view of all these facts, it is highly doubtful whether Dulles' claim that the peace treaty conceded to Japan a position of honour and equality in the family of nations was accurate. In the words of a former U.S. Ambassador to Japan Douglas MacArthur II "Japan's restoration of sovereignty and independence was not complete."[81] The fact of the matter was that it was an unequal treaty which accorded semi-independence to the country, and was so regarded by the Japanese both of the left and of the right. Even those Japanese who supported the peace treaty doubted its usefulness. For example, "It is natural that all Japanese should feel uneasiness over whether such a peace treaty can really guarantee the independence and security of Japan.[82] Yet another respected

Japanese scholar characterized the peace treaty as "unilateral and illogical" and said that "under this unilaterality or inequality Japan has neither the appearance nor the standing of an independent country, but is in a position of subservience to the United States."[83]

Commenting on the Administrative Agreement, a conservative newspaper, *The Nihon Keizai*, wrote as follows :

> Frankly speaking we get the impression that the will of the US has been forcibly imposed upon Japan. This is a fact we cannot overlook in criticising the results of the US-Japanese negotiation of the agreement.[84]

The Asahi, a leading newspaper made the following remarks on the peace treaty :

> friendship between Japan and the United States will become everlasting only when the two peoples stand in equal autonomy.[85]

The President of Tokyo University, Mr. Yanaihara in an interview with Joseph Alsop of *The New York Herald Tribune*, described Japan under the Security Pact as "America's barking dog." "We now bark or bark not as the signal may be given."[86] The late Asanuma Ineihiro, the then General Secretary of the Japan Socialist party, echoed the sentiments of all leftist groups in Japan when he said that :

> we must struggle for peace and independence, and carry on the strugle—for the return of Okinawa to Japan, the struggle for restoration of normal relations with Communist China and the struggle against nuclear bombs. We must combine all these struggles into one struggle for revision of the unequal Security Pact and connect the struggle with the struggle for the people's welfare.[87]

In the next chapter we will see why the Japanese Government accepted such a treaty.

REFERENCES

1. John Foster Dulles, *A Peace Treaty in the Making, Japanese Peace Conference, San Francisco, September 4-8, 1951* (Washington, 1951) p. 49.
2. *Ibid.*, p.3.
3. Department of State, n. 32 in Chapter 4, p, 20.
4. *Ibid.*, p. 38.
5. *Ibid.*, p. 43.
6. *Ibid.*,p .45.
7. *Ibid.*, p. 56.
8. *Ibid.*, p. 69.
9. *Ibid.*, p. 70.
10. *Ibid.*, p. 71.
11. *Ibid.*, p. 76.
12. *Ibid.*, p. 74.
13. *Ibid.*, p. 77.
14. *Ibid.*, p. 78.
15. *Ibid.*, p. 80.
16. *Ibid.*, p. 81.
17. *Ibid.*, p. 92.
18. *Ibid.*, p. 20.
19. *Ibid.*, p. 104.
20. *Ibid.*, p. 109.
21. *Ibid.*, p. 110.
22. *Ibid.*, p. 112.
23. *Ibid.*, p. 111.
24. *Ibid.*
25. *Ibid.*, p. 112.
26. *Ibid.*
27. *Ibid.*, p. 113.
28. *Ibid.*
29. *Ibid.*, p. 108.
30. *Ibid.*, p. 116.
31. *Ibid.*, p. 112.
32. *Ibid.*, p. 304.
33. *Ibid.*, p. 286.
34. *Ibid.*, p. 292·
35. *Ibid.*, p. 244.
36. *Ibid.*, p. 201.
37. *Ibid.*, p. 264.
38. *Ibid.*, pp. 266-7.
39. *Ibid.*
40. *Ibid.*
41. *Ibid.*
42. *Ibid.*, p. 228.
43. *Ibid.*

44. *Ibid.*, p. 145.
45. *Ibid.*, p. 221.
46. *Ibid.*, p. 277.
47. *Ibid.*, p. 278.
48. *Ibid.*, p. 279.
49. *Ibid.*, p. 280.
50. *Ibid.*, p.p. 280-1.
51. John Foster Dulles, op. cit.
52. Richard P. Stebbins, *The United States in World Affairs, 1951.* (New York, 1952) p. 186.
53. *Department of State, United States Treaties and other International Agreements* Vol. 3 Part 3 (Washington, 1955) p. 3331.
54. *The New York Herald Tribune*, 29 April 1955, p. 14.
55. The Japanese government has maintained since 1951 that renunciation of War did not mean renunciation of the right of self-defense. It is interesting to note that former Prime Minister Yoshida speaking in a debate on the interpretation of Article Nine of the Constitution in the House of Representatives on 29th June 1946 stated that "Japan had renounced war even in self-defense." See Saheki Kiichi, "The Building of Japan's Self-Defense," *Japan Quarterly*, 4 (January March 1957), p. 107. See also, Makoto Hori, "Yoshida Shuso No Ito," in The National Diet Library (ed.), *Kowa Mondai Ni Kansuru Kokunai Roncho*, 2 (Tokyo, 1951), p. 154-7. There are others who hold the contrary view. See Keishiro Irie, "Senso No Hoki to Nihon," in The National Diet Library (ed.), *Kowa Mondai Ni Kansuru Kokunai Roncho*, 1 (Tokyo 1951) p. p. 45-6.
56. *The Christian Science Monitor* (Boston), 15 February 1952, p. 9. The national budget for 1952 was F8, 739M. Out of this, F1, 802M. was spent on defense which amounted to 20.6% of the national budget and 3.5% of the estimated national income. The national income in 1952 being F51, 945M. These figures are found in Kiichis's article. *ibid.*, p. 104.
57. *Ibid.* Taken from *The Christian Science Monitor*.
58. Quoted by *The Christian Science Monitor* 15 February 1952, p. 9.
59. Yoshishige Abe, "For the Sake of Peace of the World, Asia and Japan," *Sekai* 70 (Tokyo, October 1951) p. 64.
60. United States Department of State, *Foreign Relations of the US Diplomatic Papers, 1941* I (Washington, 1958) p. 368, and *Foreign Relation of the US, Diplomatic Papers: The Conferences at Cairo and Tehran 1943* (Washington, 1961) p. 448.
61. Japan, House of Representatives, *The Official Gazette Extra*, 12th Session, 9 (27 October 1951) p. 28.
62. SCAP, n. 10 in chapter 1, p. 4183.
63. Oka, n. 4 in chapter 3, p. 20. Also see Yoshihiko Seki, n. 253 in chapter 3 p. 5.
64. *The Washington Post* 11 February 1953, p. 13. See also, Kanichi

Fukuda. "The Fate of Monarchy in the *Twentieth Century*," *JSPIJ*, n. 83 in chapter 2, p. 28.

65. Dunn, n. 8 in chapter 5, p. 106.
66. Ambassador Sebald, n. 33 in chapter 6.
67. *The Times* (London), 27 November 1951, p. 1.
68. *Nippon Times*, 25 July 1951. p. 1.
69. Beal, n. 421, p. 118.
70. Department of State, op. cit., p. 3331.
71. *Ibid.*, p. 3342-62.
72. *Ibid.*, p. 3328.
73. Yuichi Takano, " Foreign Armed Forces and Criminal Jurisdiction of Japan" *The Japanese Annual of International Law* 2 (Tokyo, 1952) p. 29.
74. Edwin O. Reischauer, *Japan and America Today* (Stanford, California, 1963) 8. See also Junzo Inamura, "The Peace Movement and The Platform of the Socialist Party," *JSPIJ* 3 (April 1964), p. 45.
75. Makoto, Saito, "A New Beginning for American Diplomacy" *JSPIJ* 2 (April 1963) p. 83.
76. Koshiro Okakura, "Afro-Asian Concept of Independence and Peace" *JSPIJ* n. 9 in chepter 3, p. 109.
77. Art. XXIX of the Administrative Agreement. See State Department, op. cit., p. 3361-2.
78. Oka, n. 4 in chapters, p. 19, *The New York Herald Tribune*, 25 April, 1955, p. 18.
79. James W. Morley, "Japan's Position in Asia," *Journal of International Affairs*, XVII, (Columbia University, New York, 1963) p. 143. The Journal does not mention the month.
80. Under the US Mutual Defense Assistance Control Act of 1951 Japan put total embarge upon the shipment of strategic goods to the Soviet bloc including China. See US Congress, n. 89 in chapter 4, pp. 10-11.
81. Douglas MacArthur, "The Evolution of the Japanese-American Partnership," address made before the American-Japan Society of Tokyo, 7 March 1961, *News Release* 61-65 (Embassy of the United States of America, Tokyo) pp. 2-3.
82. Kane Hatano, "In Rebuttal of Those Who Oppose Both the San-Francisco Peace Treaty and Mutual Security Agreement" *JSPIJ* op. cit., p. 43-4.
83. Royama Masamichi, "The US-Japanese Security Treaty—A Japanese View." Japan Quarterly, op. cit., p. 288 and 294.
84. *The New York Times*, 3 March 1952, p. 3.
85. *Ibid.*
86. *The New York Herald Tribune*, 25 April 1955, p. 18.
87. Kikuo Nakamura, "Party Politics" *New Leader* 2 Supplement (New York, 28 November 1960) p. 22.

8

JAPANESE VIEWS ON THE PEACE SETTLEMENT

AT THE time of the peace negotiations in 1950, there was a sharp division among the politically conscious Japanese on the problem of the peace settlement. This division could be found in the attitudes and reactions of the Japanese political parties and groups to the peace treaty and the security pact. This chapter is devoted to the study of such reactions in historical perspective.

Three themes seemed to have strongly influenced the political attitudes of the people in post-war Japan—peace, independence, and democracy.[1] These themes may be defined as follows.

Peace

Peace had a special meaning for the Japanese. The tragic effects of the atom bombs on Hiroshima and Nagasaki in World War II left an indelible mark on the nation. The Japanese desire for peace found its concrete expression in Article Nine of their constitution which renounced war as a means of national policy. Knowing that their country took a wrong turn, that is, a turning towards military control at home and aggression abroad, the Japanese resolved that there would be no more adventures in militarism in the future. Men and women saw Japan's best hope in peaceful progress and co-operation with the countries of the East and the West. Moreover, the

Japanese argued that nuclear war transcended both victory and defeat, since such a war would mean the annihilation of human society. Therefore, the maintenance of peace in the world should take priority over the ideological rivalry between Communism and democracy. Anything which threatened the peaceful image of the nation represented by Article Nine of the constitution was opposed by the Japanese and was regarded as unconstitutional. This attitude gave a clue to the understanding of the psychological resistence of a large section of the population in Japan to the type of defense system contemplated in the United States-Japanese Security Treaty. This also explained the people's resentment against the organization of a 100,000-man police force after the outbreak of the Korean War. The very word rearmament had a hateful ring in the Japanese mind, for it suggested going back to something evil that was dead and gone. Representing the Japanese Women's Disarmament Committee, the women members of the House of Councillors sent a letter to the United States Senate saying "We wish the Senate to keep on record that we, the women of Japan, had eagerly desired that our nation be left out of the armament race."[2]

Independence

The last few years of the occupation witnessed the Japanese longing for independence. The extreme nationalist sentiments, having for a time disappeared from the surface, began to emerge at about the time of the Korean War. With the economic recovery of the country, national sentiments were again kindled; dormant anti-foreign feelings came to the fore. Both the rightist and leftist political groups utilized these natural feelings of the nation for partisan purposes. For example, in January, 1951 in a New Year message to the nation Prime Minister Yoshida called upon his countrymen to keep "a flaming spirit of patriotism and independence, it would," he said :

> be cowardly to look to the right and to the left in doubt and indecision and seek to preserve ourselves by expedients and makeshifts, nor would it be becoming of a great nation

to be frightened by baseless rumours and false alarms.[3]

The simple fact that the country lay under foreign occupation for seven years could not but arouse a certain measure of nationalist resentment and, as years passed, exasperation. The business group in the country was anxious to revive its pre-war trade relations with China and other countries. The conservative ruling party being unhappy with the democratic reforms of the occupation, sought freedom to put the clock back. The Socialists and the intellectuals felt isolated from the Asian movement against colonialism and desired freedom to follow a neutral policy in world affairs and consolidate the democratic gains at home. The Communists were hoping for a proletarian revolution to follow the termination of the occupation. Regardless of the motives, the attainment of independence was a powerful national aspiration.

A large number of people in Japan opposed the security arrangement with the United States on the ground that Americans, by making the peace treaty and the security pact inseparable, intended to continue the occupation.[4] Therefore, the security treaty was against the Japanese national aspiration for the restoration of full sovereignty to their country.

Democracy

Democracy was the third theme which caught the imagination of the people in post-war Japan. All the major political parties in the country professed their belief in democracy. But the word democracy did not have the same meaning to all its adherents. To the conservative party democracy meant the restoration of the old order with minor modifications in the Meiji constitution. The Socialists believed in democratic Socialism. To the Communists democracy was only a stepping stone to a proletarian revolution.

American emphasis on the strategic importance of Japan in the fight against Communism gave the impression that the United States was no longer interested in the development of democratic institutions in Japan. The United States seemed to be going back on many of the ideals it tried to teach the Japanese. Americans had spent a vast amount of money and time teaching the Japanese the folly of nationalism and militarism. Then after 1950 the same Americans reversed themselves and forced the Japanese Government to rearm. This led to a sort of disillusionment over the ways of the West, especially among the people who had enthusiastically welcomed the initial liberal policy of the occupation. In the words of one Japanese author.

> the more the Japanese wanted to be loyal to democracy the more strongly they rejected American policy.[5]

The attitude and reaction of the political parties in Japan to the peace settlement should be understood in the light of the appeal these themes had for the people. However, there was no agreement among the parties concerning the precise meaning of the themes or regarding the means to achieve them.

THE ATTITUDE OF THE RULING CONSERVATIVE PARTY

The ruling party in Japan played a major role in the dramatic events that led to the signing of the peace treaty at San Francisco. The peace treaty was designed partly to further the interest of the conservative groups in the country because they professed to be friends of the Western powers. The fact of the matter was that the old guard was longing to reverse what they described as accessive reforms of the occupation.[6] Meanwhile they reluctantly co-operated with the occupation and seemingly proclaimed their faith in democracy and individual liberty.[7] They maneuvered in thousands of ways to achieve their aim. The peace treaty could be considered as a crowning achievement of their manipulations. The ruling groups worked in co-operation, but the man who officially led them through the occupation and more than anybody else was responsible in restoring the country to a semi-independent status was Shigeru Yoshida. A word about this spokesman of the old guard may not be out of place here. Both the Japanese and the foreigners who had watched Yoshida in close quarters described him as an autocrat, a bureaucrat and an aristocrat.[8] Yoshida was a carrer diplomat. In the years preceeding World War II his profession had taken him to China, London, Rome, and Washington. In between he had served as a vice minister in Giichi Tanka's cabinet. In the 1930's he was offered a cabinet post, disliking Yoshida's father-in-law, Count Makino, the army turned him down. This refusal proved to be a blessing in disguise. After two years, when he reached sixty, Yoshida retired and did not take active part in the ultranationalistic adventures of the militarists. In 1945, when the war was going very badly for his country, Yoshida desired to bring the conflict to an end. The militarists accused him of secret dealings with the enemy and put him behind bars for a short time in 1945.[9] Again this incident proved to be fortunate, for it saved him from being purged after the war.

Yoshida was a dyed-in-the-wool conservative and an ardent anti-Communist. At the end of the war he suggested to the founder of the Liberal Party, Hatoyama, who later became Yoshida's bitter critic, that "it might be a good idea if the new party (Liberal Party) were openly to advocate anti-Communist policy and make it one of its chief features."[10] When Supreme Commander for Allied Powers (SCAP) released the Japanese Communist leaders in October 1945, Yoshida described MacArthur's action as a blunder. He earnestly desired to suppress the Communist Party of Japan root and branch. This Communist baiting in Yoshida led him to denounce Socialist and all leftist groups as little better than reds. He branded the reform enthusiasts in SCAP as idealists and new-dealers and openly described SCAP reforms as foolish.[11] His anti-radical phobia brought him close to the anti-Communist group in GHQ, headed by men like General Willoughby, General Eichelberger, and other like-minded officials about whom reference had been made in previous chapters. General Willoughby and Eichelberger, sharing Yoshida's anti-Marxist passion, provided him with escorts and secret police during the latter's tour in the country for protection against the local Communists.[12] He also befriended SCAPs' diplomatic advisers George Atcheson and his successor William Sebald. In due course of time Yoshida developed close relationships with MacArthur and hailed the Supreme Commander as a great statesman. He considered MacArthur's views on Communism as superior and wholeheartedly supported the latter's stern policy toward the Japanese

Communist Party.[13] In the words of an American observer Yoshida used MacArthur just as MacArthur used him.[14]

Yoshida had nothing but an unconcealed contempt for the parliament he headed and for the party politicians over whom he presided. At the same time it should be noted that Yoshida was a shrewd politician who understood the postwar situation in Japan and desired to mold his country on the model of British constitutional monarchy which he admired.[15] In fact, some observers have described him as an outstanding statesman of postwar Japan.[16] Being a bureaucrat by training he was cautious and slow in his approach to the postwar political and socio-economic problems of his country. As a result at times he found himself unable to cope with the revolutionary situation in Japan during the unsettled years of the occupation. Yoshida took keen interest in the working of the Japanese Ministry of Foreign Affairs. Being well-versed in the Japanese pre-war diplomatic tactics, he preferred personal understanding with American diplomats.[17]

It may be recalled that as early as 1946 the conservative leaders had realized that their primary objective of preservation of the traditional order of things in the country could be achieved only by bringing the occupation to an end, and a favourable peace treaty could be obtained by exploiting division in the ranks of the allied powers. The old guard calculated that the Russians would propose severe terms in the peace treaty and the only power which could counter the Soviet Union in the peace conference would be the United States. Americans could also soften the attitude of Australia, New Zealand, and other powers which were hostile toward Japan. Therefore, toward the end of 1946, Yoshida and his colleagues seemed to have taken a decision to the effect that the United States should be made the spokesman for Japan in the Far Eastern Commission and in other allied meetings concerned with the occupation. The question that confronted the oligarchs at that time was how to make the United States a spokesman for traditional Japan.

Yoshida and the top bureaucrats in the party and in the foreign office watched the international situation closely and mobilized all their diplomatic skill to open a window in the

Pentagon and the State Department.

The cold war that was developing in Europe, and the vacuum theory, which was fashionable in the United States came in handy for the rulers of Japan.[18] The Japanese oligarchs were delighted to read Sir Winston Churchill's speech at Fulton, Missouri, in March 1946. It was one of those occasions when the old clique could turn back and say 'we told you so'.

The statement of the American representative in the Allied Council in November 1946 that "Japanese aims have become virtually identical with American aims" heartened the conservative elements in Japan.[19] The enunciation of the philosophy of containment of Communism by President Truman in February 1947 further strengthened their convictions. Being aware of anti-Communist feelings in the United States, Yoshida and his associates constantly played on the theme of anti-Marxism to prove their trustworthiness in the American eyes. They played their cards well. Yoshida Stated :

> The world had now reached a stage where we have to choose one of two paths—a pro-American-British or a pro-Soviet policy. We take the former.[20]

This was an effort to make domestic capital out of differences between the war-time Allies. The conservative leaders attempted to build a circle of sympathizers in G2 Section of GHQ and were pleased by General Willoughby's response. Yoshida and his friends also tried to win over MacArthur to their side by exploiting his weakness for flattery. It is difficult to say how far the Supreme Commander was influenced by the Japanese Gevernment leaders. However, MacArthur out of his own convictions consistently advocated an early peace treaty for Japan.

In the early years of the occupation, Yoshida and his colleagues seemed to have realized from their talks with General MacArthur and with other high officials in SCAP that the key to an early peace treaty was largely in the hands of the military authorities in Washington.[21] With a view to influencing the powers in Washington the Japanese foreign office began the work of compiling very useful material on the economic, political, and social conditions in the various islands belonging to Japan.[22] This material, which ran into nearly sixty volumes, was sent to the State and Defense Departments. There is ground to suspect that several of these volumes contained intelligence information regarding Soviet activities in the Far East. Presumably this information was gathered by the pre-surrender Government of Japan and was laying in the foreign office. According to Yoshida, the high officials in the two departments in Washington were pleased to receive those volumes. It is also possible to speculate that this information was sent at the suggestion of Yoshida's friend General Willoughby who employed the Japanese militarists in his office to co-ordinate Japanese-American intelligence work. It may be recalled that Willoughby was interested in convincing high officials in Washington that SCAP's policies in Japan at that time were harming the anti-Communist cause in the Far East and that the Soviet Union could not be trusted. Another purpose behind this supplying of the material was to create an impression in Washington that the Japanese conservative leaders could be counted upon as strong supporters of the Western Powers against the Soviet Union.

When, in March 1947, MacArthur announced that the occupation should be ended by concluding a peace treaty, the Japanese foreign office, anticipating an early peace conference, prepared a secret peace treaty of its own, entitled "preparatory Measures of the Japanese for the Presumed Conditions which the Allied Powers will present at the Japanese Peace Treaty Conference."[23] This document further revealed the intentions of the Japanese conservatives. Its thoroughness also suggested that the top bureaucrats in the foreign office had spent considerable time and had given careful thought in preparing the document. It proposed that there should be no restrictions on Japanese economy, Japan should have the right to repeal occupation measures and laws, the country should be permitted to increase the strength of the police force, there should be no supervision on the implementation of the peace terms by the Japanese, and so on. At the same time the Japanese foreign office also dreamed of building an army of 100,000 men and a sizable air force.[24] The document anticipated that some of the allied powers would propose to acquire certain Japanese islands for security purposes and stated that the Japanese Government would acquiesce to them if their primary needs as described above were met.

The patriarchs continued to influence Washington on the matter of the peace treaty by sending letters and dispatches. On 28 July 1947, Foreign Minister Ashida sent an identical letter to George Atcheson and General Whitney explaining the Japanese position on peace treaty and security problems. Knowing that the ruling clique was trying to capitalize on cold war tension, General Whitney refused to acknowledge the letter on the ground that "time was delicate and the problem was not urgent."[25] It may be recalled that General Whitney was one of those officers in GHQ in SCAP who advocated thorough reform of Japanese society, and for this reason the old guard did not like him. Rebuked by General Whitney, the conservatives turned to one of their influential friends, General Eichelberger, commander of the Eighth Army. On 13 September 1947, they entrusted the General with a message and a semi-official letter to be delivered to authorities in Washington. In that letter the ruling group again requested the United States to permit the Japanese Government to strengthen the island and coastal police force. They also expressed a desire to have a security arrangement with the United States for the protection of the country against external aggression. The nature of the security proposed in the letter "was the same as that on which the United States-Japan security was later to be based."[26]

However, to the great disappointment of the conservative leaders, the proposed peace conference in 1947 did not materialize. But the attempts made by the ruling group to influence the content of the treaty did not go in vain. The United States slowly came to rely upon the conservative forces in the country and stopped the tide of reforms. The old guard was of course happy to see the change in the United States attitude toward them. With the American backing, the Zaibatsu gradually came into its own and the other ruling groups put themselves strongly in the saddle. As has been observed, the cold war and the direct conflict in Korea brought forth an alliance between the conservatives and the policymakers in Washington. With the economic boom in the country created by the Korean War, the old guard began to foresee a new role for the country. For example, Yoshida while speaking in the Diet in 1950 said:

> It is my cherished aspiration that, if she can, Japan will lead the group of free nations in the Far East or in Asia.[27]

They began to look to Asia again as a vast reservoir of essential raw materials. Japan with her highly developed industries and technical skill could build a new commercial empire in Asia, and regain a political status in the world. This ambition could be achieved only by an independent Japan and therefore was to be a long-range programme. The ruling group secretly continued to dream of building an army by amending Article Nine of the Constitution. The constitutional provision was a great hindrance for their ambition to play a big role in international politics.[28] However, there was a division in the ruling group on the question of implementation of the rearmament programme. One group led by Yoshida and Ikeda argued that, in view of the emotional opposition to rearmament in the country, the suspicion of Japan's neighbours concerning the revival of militarism, and the limited economic resources of the country, the rearmament programme should be achieved gradually.[29]

The opposite group was led by former Prime Ministers Ashida and Kishi. It favoured the rearmament of the country on the ground that it was imcompatible with the dignity of an independent country to depend on a foreign power for its protection.[30] Moreover, the United States, with her heavy military commitments in Europe and Asia, would not be able to devote sufficient attention to the defense of Japan. This group also considered the security pact as one-sided and declared that the treaty made Japan a protectorate of the United States.[31] If Japan wished to gain her freedom, her independence, and her place in the family of nations she should pay the price of freedom by rearming herself. Obviously in 1950 the first group prevailed over the second.

However, the ruling party's immediate problem was internal danger to the establishment and a possible external threat. Political conditions in the country greatly disturbed the Japanese conservative leadership. With the passage of time and with the inauguration of the reverse course in American policy in Japan, the progressive movement for democratization, led by the Socialists and other leftist organizations gained momentum. The repressive measures adopted by the Japanese Government with SCAPs' backing, against the Japanese Communist party, labour unions, and other progressive groups, gave rise to stronger opposition to the ruling party. It seemed to threaten the very existence of the traditional pattern of authority in the country. Moreover, the younger generation showed sings of revolt against the rigid social system, reverence for the emperor, and so forth. What upset the ruling party more than anything else was the distrust and contempt in which the conservative leadership was held by intellectuals, students, socialists, communists and other leftist elements in the country. The Liberal-Democratic Party seemed to have come to the conclusion in the early years of the occupation, that this anti-conservative movement, if allowed to grow, would one day explode and would destroy the traditional Japan. Therefore, it was essential, in the interest of the ruling party, to prevent this movement from growing. But this could not be done while the country was under occupation. Therefore, there was an imperative need to gain freedom of action through the conclusion of the peace treaty.

The conclusion of the Sino-Soviet treaty of alliance and friendship in 1950, which was directed against Japan, also seemed to have influenced the thinking of the conservative leaders on the problem of peace and security. The ruling party held the view that the Soviet Union and the Chinese Communists would seek to control Japan with the help of the Japanese Communist Party and the Japanese prisoners of war detained in the Soviet Union.[32] In view of these internal and external threats, the Japanese ruling party sought protection from enemies within and without.

Yoshida and his colleagues in the government knew that military leaders in Washington held a veto on the peace settlement and that the Defense Department was strongly in favour of the continuation of the occupation. In the light of this knowledge, the Japanese Government leaders concluded that there could not be an early peace treaty with the allied powers, unless the American armed forces were allowed to be stationed in the country. The presence of American soldiers in the country might put certain restrictions on Japanese sovereignty. But the delay in the conclusion of a peace treaty would greatly strengthen the leftist movement in Japan. The leftist parties would arouse the people by appealing to their nationalist sentiments against foreign domination and by describing the conservative party as a puppet in the hands of the American authorities. These possibilities put the conservative leaders in a dilemma.

It may be recalled that in the middle of June 1950, United States Defense Secretary Louis Johnson, General Omar Bradley the chairman of the United States Joint Chiefs of Staff, and John Foster Dulles visited Japan. It has also been noted, in Chapter 5, that during their stay in Tokyo these civilian and military leaders of the United States made a decision on the security arrangements in the Pacific.[33] At that time, when MacArthur and Dulles tried to persuade the Defense Department officials to agree on an early peace treaty, the latter insisted that they would give their consent to the peace settlement if their condition were accepted. The military high ups demanded that Dulles should get a complete assurance from the Japanese Government to the effect that after the signing of the peace treaty American forces in Japan "could hold on to the military bases without fear of being renounced by a subsequent Japanese Government or cut off by domestic Communists as the Hukbalahap Clark field in the Philippines".[34] The essence of this condition was that Japan should remain as a protectorate of the United States indefinitely.[35] MacArthur, being the spokesman of the Japanese conservatives, agreed to convey the message to the Japanese leaders.

Understanding the logic of the situation, Yoshida tried to reach a consensus of opinion in the ranks of the ruling party. The Japanese Prime Minister hurried to meet the speaker of the House of Representatives, Kijuro Shidehara, and the President of the House of Councillors, Naotake Sato, and he also conferred secretly with Democratic Party leader Hitoshi Ashida.[36] In their parleys, the patriarchs agreed to accept the American conditions. On 22 June 1950, the Mainichi commented in its editorial that

> the mystery surrounding their meeting gives one the impression that some shady deal is under way in the political circle . . . . National unity in foreign policy is desirable but the methods to create that unity should not be kept secret from the people.[37]

After their meeting, the Japanese leaders held conferences with Dulles and arrived at an informal agreement with the American diplomat. Under this agreement Japan was to enjoy internal autonomy, defense and foreign affairs were to be looked after by the United States, and there was to be no restriction on the Japanese ruling party as far as domestic policy was concerned.[38] In other words, no restrictions were to be prescribed in the peace treaty. Yoshida, while speaking in the Diet in February 1951, stated that "an understanding satisfactory to both sides has been reached".[39] Probably the Japanese Prime Minister was talking of the secret understanding reached with American officials. It should be observed that both right wing and left wing parties in the parliaments protested at the vagueness of the statement and charged Yoshida with conducting secret diplomacy. In the words of a Tokyo businessman, "Yoshida sold Japan from under his Kimono like a Parisian selling dirty pictures".[40]

The explanations and defense of the peace treaty and the security pact by the Japanese Government should be seen in the context of this probable historical meeting of minds between the Japanese conservative leaders and the United States authorities.

The terms of the understanding implied that the peace treaty was to be signed without the participation of the Soviet Union and Communist China. The Soviet Union could not possibly be expected to be a party to a treaty which allowed the United States to retain her armed forces in Japan. The ruling party, having made a deal with the Pentagon and the State Department was willing to accept any decision the United States might take with regard to the formal signing of an agreement. A large section of the Japanese population was opposed to a separate peace treaty and was in favour of a peace treaty with all the nations which had fought against Japan. Therefore, Yoshida and his colleagues had to defend their secret diplomacy.

The ruling party's views on a separate peace treaty, security, rearmament, and other allied subjects could be summarized as follows.

In the first place, a peace treaty including all states concerned, though desirable, was not possible to conclude in view of the Soviet Union's refusal to accept the procedure proposed by the United States. Therefore, under the circumstances, the conclusion of a peace treaty with those who were willing was the best that could be achieved. Second, Japan, not being a party to international agreements among the big powers, had no right to choose the parties to a treaty.[41] Third, the continuation of the occupation until an agreement was reached between the Soviet Union and the Western powers, was obviously not in the interest of Japan.

The Japanese Government considered the problems of peace and security inseparable. Independence had no meaning to a country which did not have the means to defend its independence. Since Japan had no army, it was proper that the country should join a collective security system for its protection. For collective security was recognized by the UN. With regard to the proposition made by the opposition parties that Japan should remain neutral in world conflict, Yoshida stated that the idea of permanent neutrality for Japan was 'only a fond dream'.[42]

There was a danger of Communist aggression in Japan. The invasion of South Korea by the North Korean Communists was a case in point. Further, the Sino-Soviet alliance of 1950 was directed against Japan. The Communist Party of Japan also posed a threat to the internal security of the country. Moreover, according to Prime Minister Yoshida, diplomatic relations with the Communist states were impossible as long as they remained Communist. For peaceful relations with totalitarian countries would amount to an invitation to them to create Communist propaganda centres in Japan.[43] If the Communist states ceased to be totalitarian, then it would be a different matter. It was an extraordinary statement on the part of a seasoned diplomat like Yoshida. Probably it was meant for the consumption of his supporters in the countryside.

Since Japan was mainly under the American occupation and the United States was responsible for introducing democracy into the country, it was therefore a historical necessity for Japan to join the United States and other free countries in their fight against Communist expansion. How deep the faith of Prime Minister Yoshida and his party in democracy was can be judged by the record of the Japanese Government since the conclusion of the peace treaty! As we have observed in Chapter 3, soon after the conclusion of the peace treaty the conservative government attempted to pare down or abolish those early occupation reforms which were aimed at democratization.[44] Furthermore, the pro-American policy of Prime Minister Yoshida was not a product of this professed attachment to democracy. "It was strictly a matter of expediency."[45] The prosperity of the Zaibatsu depended on American support for raw materials and market. As Sulzberger of *The New York Times* put it recently "And our economic hold is so strong that when Wall Street sneezes Tokyo has pneumonia".[46] If circumstances permitted, the old guard would "like nothing better than tell Americans to go to hell and launch into an aggressive foreign policy."[47] It may not be aggressive in the military sense but it would certainly be aimed at making Japan a great power.

When the peace treaty and the security pact came before the Diet for ratification, quite a few members of the ruling party expressed their dissatisfaction with the security pact. Some members were of the opinion that the security arrangement should have been made after the signing of the peace treaty.[48] Another member of the ruling party described it as unequal and suggested that the security treaty should be abrogated and should be replaced by a new United States-Japan treaty of mutual security based on equality and fairness[49]. Others declared the administrative agreement as inconsistent with the independence of Japan.

Despite these objections, the peace treaty was generally supported by the members of the ruling party in the Diet. They described it as just and generous. However, a general criticism was voiced against the territorial adjustment in the treaty. It was asserted by several members that the Kurile Islands and the Habomai and Shikotan Islands, historically, racially, and geographically belonged to Japan, and the Soviet Union was in illegal occupation of them. Article Five of the treaty, under which Japan was to assist the UN in any action in took, was declared by a member as contrary to Article Nine of the Japanese constitution.[50] Confiscation of Japanese property under Article Fourteen of the treaty was characterized by a member of the ruling party as against the recognized principles of private international law.

VIEWS OF THE LEFTIST GROUP ON THE PEACE SETTLEMENT

In the post-war years, the main stream of Japanese society was divided into two diametrically opposite groups. In the first Chapter these groups have been described as the conservatives and the progressives. With the passage of time the gap widened between the establishment, the top bureaucracy and business-man on the one side, and the intellectuals, writers, scientists, students, socialists, workers, and communists on the other. They seemed to speak different languages. In fact, there was little trust and respect between them. This whole attitude was symptomatic of the ideological gulf that existed within Japanese society. The two groups had different values and different pictures of the future of Japan. There was no central core of ideals on which all groups could agree. Under such circumstances, no real dialogue was possible between the conservatives and the progressives.[51]

The intellectuals, working with the socialists and the communists, set the intellectual tone of the progressive group. They advocated three principles of peace on which there was common agreement. They were as follows : (i) a peace treaty with all the powers which had fought against Japan; (ii) neutrality in the cold war between the East and the West; and (iii) opposition to Japanese rearmament and to the lease of military bases to the United States.[52] It should be noted, as will be explained later, that the right wing of the Socialist Party and the Communists had slightly different views on the problem of security.

A summary of the beliefs and fears entertained by the progressives will help us to understand better their point of view on the peace settlement.

The progressive group believed that the concepts of democracy and Socialism were closely intertwined.[53] During the 1930's when militarism was at its height in Japan, the only group which seemed to have stood resolutely against the militarists and the ultranationalists was the Communist Party. The so-called liberal democrats were lukewarm in their opposition to the militarists and stood as silent spectators. Therefore, the progressive group came to believe that Marxism rather than liberal democracy was the chief enemy of militarism and authoritarianism.[54] Moreover, Marxist theory allegedly explained scientifically the contradiction between imperialism and peace and imperalism and socialism. This theory was widely accepted by the progressives.

It might be recalled that the progressive group had enthusiastically welcomed the occupation troops and had supported the initial liberal policy of Supreme Commander for Allied Powers. But the generally continued conservative leadership of the government in post-war Japan, and, in the latter half of the occupation, the changed attitude of Supreme Commander for Allied Powers toward labour unions, convinced the progressives that there was no real change in the establishment. They also came to believe that the post-war conservative parties were nothing but a regrouping of the old pre-war leadership. In other words, it was the old wine in a new bottle. Further, it held the opinion that the leadership of the Liberal and the Democratic Parties was dedicated to recreating the authoritarian, militaristic system of pre-war Japan.[55] The progressives refused to accept the conservative majority in the Diet. For the conservative majority, they believed, did not represent the wishes of the Japanese people.

The progressives argued that the general mass of the people in Japan was totally opposed to authoritarianism and militarism. They maintained that the conservatives manoeuvered to win a majority in the Diet by using dubious methods such as traditional authority, open bribery, and the skilful manipulation of the less-awakened strata of society. Moreover, Japan was far from being a democracy. However perfect the external forms might be, the inner realities were not there.[56]

The progressive group placed little confidence in American profession of faith in freedom and the United States leadership in foreign affairs. The United States, they held, seemed to be more interested in the strategic importance of Japan against communism than in democratic reforms. Supreme Commander for Allied Powers violated the constitution it wrote by rearming the country. The United States encouraged the conservatives, who were anti-democratic. In short, the progressives came to believe that the Machiavellian tactics of their former military rulers were being continued by the Americans. In other words, only the master, not the system, had changed. Furthermore, before World War II, when the Americans disliked the Japanese, the United States bestowed on the Chinese every conceivable favour. Within a few years after the end of the war, the United States lost trust in the Nationalist government and was calling it "corrupt in the extreme."[57] Then in 1950, when the Korean War broke out and the Chinese Communists began to grow stronger and threatened the American military bases in Formosa, the United States suddenly brought Chiang Kai-Shek into favour and treated him as if he was the representative of the six hundred million people of China. The Japanese progressives wondered when this attitude would change.

There was also an economic explanation to the conflict between the conservatives and the progressives. The progressives believed that the manifestation of clashing economic interests could be found in the post-war trade union movement. The ruling conservative party seemed to be opposed to organized labour's right to strike and the right to collective bargaining. In the opinion of the progressives, who encouraged and led the trade union movement, this opposition of the conservatives was a pure and simple example of classical capitalism versus socialism. In other words, it was a manifestation of a class war between the capitalists who dominated the government and the labourers.

The outbreak of the Korean War in June 1950 brought an economic boom to Japan. Japanese businessman profited by

United States contracts for the procurement of military goods in Japan. The Korean War also saw a growing economic cooperation between Japanese and United States businessmen. To the progressives, businessmen as capitalists were suspect by definition. This Japanese-United States business co-operation was, therefore, a design of the capitalists to exploit cheap Japanese labour by keeping the trade union movement under control.

To sum up, the progressives believed that the security treaty between the United States and Japan was designed to continue the occupation of Japan. United States-Japanese economic co-operation was against the Japanese trade union movement. The rearmament of the country increased the danger of a revival of the Japanese pre-war militarism. The conservative party was becoming more anti-democratic with the encouragement of United States. The combination of these forces went against the three pillars of the progressive movement in Japan—peace, independence and democracy.

The three principles of peace advocated by the progressive group, therefore, should be studied in the light of this background.

The arguments in favour of an overall peace treaty went in this way. Japan surrendered to the five allied powers on the basis of the Potsdam Declaration. The terms of the Potsdam Declaration implied that Japan should sign a peace treaty with all the powers which fought against her. Therefore, the signing of a peace treaty with the Western Powers with the exclusion of the Soviet Union, China, India and Burma was against the surrender terms.[58] It meant the continuation of a state of war between the Soviet Union and China on the one side and Japan on the other.[59] It was a strange peace treaty which did not end the war.

Communist China also had a romantic and emotional appeal to the Japanese progressives. Feeling deeply their geographic propinquity, racial affinity, and above all, their cultural relationship, the Japanese had a tremendous yearning for the re-establishment of friendly contact with China. An unspoken but keen feeling of guilt over Japanese war-time conduct in China heightened this attitude of friendship.[60] The conservative leaders, instead of correcting past mistakes, were joining hands with the reactionary forces which opposed the people's Republic of China. Prime Minister Yoshida was against the Communist Government on the mainland and accepted American informal restrictions on trade with Communist China. These acts of the conservative leadership provided another proof of the militaristic policy of the ruling party.

The progressive group felt that it was the moral duty of Japan to reject a peace treaty to which China was not a party. Similarly, the non-participation of India and Burma in the peace conference was a serious matter for the country. A peace which did not have the support of the major Asian countries was against the interests of Japan[61] Moreover, the Anglo-American treaty, by denying the Japanese their right to establish trade relations with Communist China, made the country dependent on the United States.

The idea of a separate peace treaty was based on the suspicion and the distrust of the communist countries. This kind of Communist baiting did not solve the problem of peace. Instead, it intensified the cold war. The Japanese people, with their sad experience in the war, wished to see a lessening of cold war tension in the world. Therefore, in the interest of world peace and in her own interest, Japan should sign a treaty with all the powers which fought against her in World War II.[62]

The conclusion of an overall peace treaty would also facilitate the pursuit of a neutral policy in world affairs. The arguments in favour of neutralism could be summarized as follows.

The progressive group questioned the containment philosophy and its assumption that the world was divided into two mutually hostile camps. They also questioned the thesis that the struggle between the two blocs was one of ideology. The progressives contended that the picture of the world painted by both the Communist and the Western Powers was an extremely simplified version of a complicated international situation. They believed that the ideological struggle was only a mask behind the conflicting national interests of the great powers. Moreover, from the theoretical point of view, it would be hard to identify purely liberal democratic, or out and out Communist states in the world. For example, one could find in the western camp extremes ranging from fascist states and military juntas to liberal democracies. Similarly in the Soviet bloc one could detect deviations.[63]

The progressives also repudiated the concept held by the Japanese conservatives and by some of the Western Powers that the danger to world peace came from Communist-inspired revolutions and Communist-led nationalist movements. They believed that imperialism posed a main danger to world peace and the major struggle in the world was between nationalism and imperialism. They pointed out that the Communists in the colonial and dependent countries were as much nationalists as they were anti-imperialists. Moreover, recognizing that revolutions could not be imported or created from without, the world communist movement repudiated Trotsky's concepts of a permanent revolution. In view of these developments, Communists could not be considered as a danger to world peace. On the other hand, the progressives argued that the fascist movements which were raising their ugly heads in Japan and in other parts of world really threatened world peace. They also saw the possibility of a direct conflict between the two super powers, which might come as a result of miscalculation of each other's intentions on the part of authorities in those countries. According to the progressive, there also existed side by side some encouraging forces which tended to draw the super powers closer to each other. For example, there was a realization on the part of the nuclear powers that there would be no winners, and no losers in a war between them.

The progressive argued that the existence of both the hopeful and the depressing trends in the world situation created an imperative need for the organization of a third force, which could play the role of a reconciliator. They were of the opinion that India was playing such a role by remaining outside the power bloc. The progressive group held Prime Minister Nehru in high regard and believed that Nehru championed the cause of Afro-Asian nations and served the cause of world peace by widening the area of co-operation between the two camps.[64] The progressive group held it to be a moral duty of all progressive elements in Asia and Africa to work for the elimination of imperial influence from the world, especially from Asia and Africa, and establish permanent peace in the world.

The progressive group advocated that Japan become a force for peace and liberation by remaining independent of the power blocs. It was a moral obligation of the Japanese to help bring the forces of peace together. For she alone in the whole world knew the terrible effects of nuclear weapons.

The progressives argued that the security treaty with the United States would not really provide protection for the country. The American forces and military bases would merely serve to invite relationship upon Japan from the opposite camp. In view of this possibility, they believed that neutrality would provide the best possible defense for the country.[65] Being against the rearmament of the country, the progressives advocated an unarmed neutrality. They hoped that the UN would guarantee Japan's security. The United Nations had a great appeal to the Japanese. They regarded the world organization as the crystallization of the universal desire for peace.[66] However, the progressives did not seem to have a clear idea of the kind of protection they sought from the United Nations.

In summary, the policy of neutrality was partly based upon the thesis that the national interest was best guaranteed by a policy of internationalism which made no military commitments to either of the two blocs. To the Japanese progressives, neutralism was pacifistic nationalism in international affairs, as Sakamoto has put it.[67]

Differences in the Social Democratic Party: The Social Democratic Party was divided into two groups on the problem of the security of Japan. The right wing in the party believed that the Communist bloc posed a threat to the security of Japan. They suggested that Japan should seek her security through the UN. It should be done, moreover, *after* the country recovered its full independence by concluding a peace treaty with those who were willing to sign it. The right wing regarded the Anglo-American Peace Treaty as a step toward independence.[68] The left wing of the party, however, emphasized the danger from the colonial powers to the independence of the Asian countries and implied that Communist China and the Soviet Union posed no threat to Japan.[69] A split took place in the Social Democratic Party at the time of the ratification of the treaties as a result of long standing differences of opinion between its right and left wing factions on many matters including the issue of Communist threat to Japan. The right wing voted for the peace treaty and rejected the security pact, while the left-wing rejected both.

The following comments were made by the members of the Social Democratic Party at the time of the ratification of the treaties by the Diet. Socialist members in the Diet described, the peace treaty and the security pact as one-sided, unequal and slavish, and maintained that the treaties reduced Japan to a colonial status.[70] They were unanimous in declaring the territorial arrangements in the treaty illegal. The Socialist members demanded that the Kurile Islands, the Bonin Islands, and the Ryukyu Islands should be returned to Japan.[71] The administrative agreement which was to be concluded after the ratification of the treaties without the consent of the Diet was considered as a challenge to the constitutional law of Japan.[72] The socialists accused the ruling party of having indulged in secret diplomacy. A socialist member agreed with the opinion of a member of the ruling party that Article Fourteen in the treaty concerning the confiscation of Japanese property, was a breach of international law.[73]

Views of the Communist Party. The Communist Party of Japan generally supported the Soviet line, including the Soviet advocacy of rearmament of the country. The communist members in the Diet characterized the peace treaty as humiliating and shameful.[74] A communist member said that the security treaty was similar to the Japan-Manchuko agreement of 1931.[75] The Communist Party rejected both the treaties.

REACTION OF THE GENERAL PUBLIC TO THE PEACE TREATY AND THE SECURITY PACT

At this stage, a question may be asked as to how the general public in Japan reacted to the peace settlement. In the following pages an attempt is made to answer this question.

On 10 October 1951, the peace treaty was approved by the House of Representatives by a vote of three hundred and seven to forty-seven. In the house of Councillors the treaty was adopted by a vote of one-hundred and seventy four to forty-five.[76] The security treaty did not fare so well. In the lower house the voting on the security treaty was two-hundred and eighty-nine to seventy-one and in the upper house it was passed by a vote of one-hundred and forty-seven to seventy-six.[77]

A public opinion survey based on a random sample was conducted by the National Public Opinion Research Institute in Tokyo in May, 1952. One thousand persons were chosen for the purpose and answers were received from 786 of them.[78]

Fifty-one per cent of those questioned believed that the peace treaty was satisfactory in view of the fact that Japan was a vanquished nation (in Table 8.1). Twenty per cent found fault with the treaty but felt that they had to accept it because their country was defeated in the war.[79]

TABLE 8.1 : **Japanese reaction to the peace treaty**

Response	per cent
Complete satisfaction	51
Satisfied because there is no alternative	20
Not satisfied	12
Don't know	17
	100%
	n.=786

The principal points of complaint were the Security Pact, the extraterritorial rights given to the American forces under the administrative agreement, and the unsatisfactory territorial provisions. Most of those dissatisfied people felt that their government did not make enough effort to obtain a treaty signed by all nations (Table 8.2).

Further, sixty-four per cent of those questioned said that there was little enthusiasm among the people on effectuation of the peace treaty.[81] Thirty-two per cent of those seeing little enthusiasm attributed the lack of enthusiasm to the hard living conditions in the country and twenty-three per cent criticized it for such reasons as the stationing of the American forces in Japan even after the conclusion of the peace treaty and

TABLE 8.2 : **Reasons for dissatisfaction among those who were dissatisfied with the treaty or thought there was no alternative**

Main reasons	Per cent
Because of the security pact, administrative agreement, extra-territorial rights, etc.	24
Because of a separate peace treaty	18
Because of territorial problems	14
Because of greater powers given to the US	11
Dissatisfied for no reasons	6
Feared that Japan would be involved in a war	2
Other reasons	7
Don't know	18
	100%
	n.=252

the conditions under which the peace treaty was signed (Table 8.3).[82] The security pact between the United States and Japan and its consequences on the latter seemed to have been upper most in the minds of the majority of respondents in the sample survey. For example seventy-four per cent of those

TABLE 8.3 : **Public enthusiasm on the implementation of the peace treaty**

	Per cent
There is little enthusiasm	64
There is enthusiasm	23
Don't know	13
	100%
	n.=786

questioned feared that Japan would be involved in a future war as a result of her alliance with the United States (Table 8.4).[83] When asked to suggest remedies for the predicted danger of Japanese involvement in a war a surprisingly high twenty-eight per cent of those who saw a danger suggested rearmament of the country, and sixteen per cent favoured neutrality

TABLE 8.4 : **Danger of Japanese involvement in a future war**

	Per cent
There is danger	74
There is no danger	14
Don't know	12
	100%
	n.=786

and adoption of diplomatic, educational, political and other measures to avoid such an involvement (Table 8.5).[84]

TABLE 8.5 : **Suggestions for avoidance of a possible Japanese involvement in future war (asked only of those seeing a danger)**

	per cent of those seeing a danger	per cent of total sample
Rearmament of Japan	28	20.7
Adoption of a policy of neutrality between the two blocs and a policy of maintenance of peace	16	12.0
Others	56	41.3
	100%	74.0%
	n.=581	n.=786

If this survey can be taken as an indication of the general feelings of the Japanese people as a whole on the peace settlement, one is compelled to conclude that only one half of the nation accepted the peace settlement. It is also clear that three fourths of the population doubted whether the security arrangement with the United States would provide real protection for Japan in a future war. It is interesting to note that twenty-one per cent suggested rearmament of the country as an alternative for the security pact, and only twelve per cent favoured a policy of neutrality. A great number of people were, however, concerned with the economic conditions in the country.

There seemed to have prevailed a sense of resignation in

the nation regarding the peace settlement. Mindful of their country's defeat in the war, the Japanese did not expect equal treatment from the Allied Powers. Most of them, however, seemed to have been disappointed with their government's handling of the problem.

REFERENCES

1. Sakamoto, n. 111 in Chapter 4, p. 153.
2. US Congress, n. 360, p. 81.
3. *The Times* (London), 19 February 1951, p. 7.
4. Sakamoto, n. 382, p. 154.
5. *Ibid.*
6. Noboru Sato, "Socialism and Neutralism" *JSPIJ*, n. in Chapter 3, p. 62. The Japanese ruling party "from the beginning disliked the democratization policies of the occupation." See Takashi Ota, "A Study of Educational Policies in Post-war Period," *JSPIJ*, in Chapter 2, p. 118.
7. Sakamoto, in Chapter 3, p. 44.
8. Ambassador Sebald, n. 103 in Chapter 4, p. 97. When Yoshida became the Prime Minister of Japan in May 1946, a Japanese newspaper commented that Yoshida was "a feudalistic, bureaucratic politician who had particularly close relations with a great financial clique, and who received the portfolio of Prime Minister upon the recommendation of high quarters." See *The Yomiuri Hochi Shimbun*, 7 May 1946, quoted in GHQ SCAP, *Press Translations* 16, (editorial series 905) p. 3.
9. Yoshida, n. 9 in Chapter 1, pp. 24-6.
10. *Ibid.*, 164-5. It is interesting to note that when SCAP requisitioned Yoshida's house for the use of the Soviet mission in Japan, he approached the American diplomat William Sebald and was reported to have said, "You see, I am an anti-Communist and I don't like to have Bolsheviks in my home." See Ambassador Sebald, n. 103 in Chapter 4, p. 98.
11. Yoshida, n. 9 in Chapter 1, pp. 54-55.
12. *Ibid.*, pp. 228-9.
13. *The Asahi Evening News* (Tokyo), 11 September 1961, p. 1.
14. Gunther, n. 34 in Chapter 1, p. 158.
15. Yoshida, n. 9, p. 118.
16. Ambassador Sebald, n. 374, p. 99.
17. According to some Japanese scholars the top bureaucrats in the Japanese ministry of Foreign Affairs believed that "they are the only ones who know anything about foreign policy." In other words the Japanese diplomats did not think that public discussion of foreign affairs was useful. This view is supported by the manner in which

Prime Minister Yoshida and his colleagues tackled the problem of the peace settlement with the United States and other Allied Powers, which is explained in the subsequent pages of this dissertation. Masataka Kasaka, "An Appeal to the Liberal Democratic and Socialist Parties: Japan, A Nation without a foreign policy," *JSPIJ* 2 (December 1964) 59. Also see Junnosuke Masumi, "A Profile of the Japanese Conservative Party," *Asian Survey* 3 (August 1963) p. 390.

18. Yoshida, n. 9 in Chapter 1, pp. 263-4. See also Sakamoto, n. 49 in Chapter 3, p. 44.
19. *The New Statesman and Nation* (London), 23 November 1961, p. 13.
20. *Newsweek*, 9 June 1947, p. 42.
21. Yoshida, n. 9 in Chapter 1, p. 246.
22. *Ibid.*, p. 247.
23. *World Reports* (New York, 9 December 1947), pp. 33-6.
24. John C. Campbell, *The United States in World Affairs 1947-1948* (New York, 1948) p. 166.
25. Shigeru Yoshida, *Kaiko-Junen* 3 (Tokyo, 1957) p. 112. This version of the story does not appear in the English translation.
26. Yoshida, n. 9 in Chapter 1, p. 113.
27. Japan, House of Representatives, *The Official Gazette Extra* 12th Session, 4 (16 October 1951) p. 4.
28. Douglas H. Mendel, Jr. *Japanese People and Foreign Policy* (Berkeley, 1961) 73. It is interesting to note that recently in a magazine article former Prime Minister Kishi stated that the Liberal Democratic Party desired to eradicate completely the consequences of Japan's defeat and of the American occupation by amending Article Nine of the constitution. See Nobusuke Kishi, "Political movements in Japan, "*Foreign Affairs* 44 (October 1965) 93. See also Jun Eto, "The Bankruptcy of Our Idealistic Intellectuals," *JSPIJ*, n. 30 in Chapter 3, p. 103.
29. Japan, House of Councillors, *The Official Gazette Extra* 12th Session, 4 (13 October 1951) pp. 6-7. The author was also given this information in Tokyo 1961-62 by Kumao Nishimura, the then Director of the treaty section in the Japanese Foreign Ministry.
30. Hithoshi Ashida, "Japan: Communist Temptation," *Contemporary Japan* XX (Tokyo, January-March 1951) p. 24.
31. Japan, House of Representatives, *The Official Gazette Extra*, 11th Session, 2 (18 August 1951) p. 3.
32. *Ibid.*, 12th Session, 8 (27 October 1951) p. 24.
33. John Foster Dulles, n. 43 in Chapter 5.
34. *Nippon Times*, 23 June 1950, p. 1.
35. *Ibid.*, 24 June 1950, p. 1.
36. *Ibid.*, 22 June 1950, p. 1.
37. *Ibid.*, p. 4.
38. *Ibid.*, 24 June 1950, 4, Yoshida, n. 9 in Chapter 1, p. 251, Japan, House of Representatives, *The Official Gazette Extra*, the 12th

Session, 4 (17 October 1951) p. 9.

39. *The Times* (London) 14 February 1951, p. 3.
40. Elizabeth and Victor A. Velen, (ed.) *The New Japan* (New York, 1958) p. 86.
41. Japan, House of Representatives op. cit., 12th Session, 8 (27 October 1951) pp. 5-6.
42. Japan, House of Councillors, op. cit., p. 9.
43. *Ibid.*
44. Oka, n. 63 in Chapter 7,
45. *The New York Herald Tribune*, 2 May 1955, p. 14.
46. *The New York Times*, 18 May 1966, 40M. This description of Japanese financial situation is supported by a Japanese scholar who has pictured the Zaibatsu as "one wing of American imperialism." See Inamura, n. 74 in Chapter 7, pp. 46-7.
47. *The New York Herald Tribune*, 2 May 1955, p. 14.
48. Japan, House of Representatives, op. cit., p. 30.
49. Japan, House of Councillors, op. cit., 5 (17 October 1951) p. 3.
50. *Ibid.*
51. Edwin O. Reischauer, "The Broken Dialogue with Japan," *Foreign Affairs*, 39 (October 1960) 19. See also Kishi, op. cit., p. 90.
52. See the statement issued by the Heiwa Mondai Kondankai, entitled "Tainichi Kowa Mondai ni Tsuiteno Seimei" in *Kowa Mondai ni Kansuru, Kokunai Roncho*, 1 n. 55 in Chapter 7, p. 32.
53. The author heard this line of argument in his talks with Japanese intellectuals in Tokyo during his visits in 1961-62. Also see Seiichi Katsumata, "The Japanese Socialist Party Should Oppose Both the San-Francisco Peace Treaty and the Mutual Security Agreement," *JSPIJ*, 3 (April 1965) p. 41.
54. See the Introduction entitled "Japanese Intellectuals Their View of International Politics," in *JSPIJ* 1 (April 1963) pp. 4-5.
55. Sakamoto, n. 111 in Chapter 9. This line of argument is found in Professor Sakamoto's original article which the author of this dissertation had the privilege to read in Tokyo. This particular version is omitted in the printed article.
56. The author in his talks with many university professors, especially with Professors Sakamoto and Kyogoku of Tokyo University in 1961-62 came across this kind of agrument frequently. See also Reischauer, op. cit., 19, Kosaka, op. cit., p. 58.
57. Sakamoto, n. 260 in Chapter 3, p. 45, Lawrence Olson, *A Japanese Intellectual's view of American Policy* (Japan LAO, American Field Staff Report, Kyoto, 30 October 1955) pp. 2-3.
58. Yoshitaro Hirano, Symposium, "Kowa no Hori" in *Kowa Mondai Ni Kansuru Kokunai Roncho* 2, n. 55 in Chapter 7, pp. 16-21.
59. India and Burma were prepared to sign a bilateral peace treaty with Japan separately, which would end the state of war between India and Burma on one side, and Japan on the other.

60. Yoshitaro Hirano, "Kowa Ni Kansuru Kihon Mondai" in *Kowa Mondai Ni Kansuru Kokunai Roncho*, 2, n. 55 in Chapter 7, pp. 13-5. See also Soichiro Ohara, "Exportation of a Vinylon Plant to China" *JSPIJ*, n. 9 in Chapter 3, pp. 108-9.
61. See Katsumata Seiichi's speech in the Diet, Japan, House of Representatives, op. cit., p. 32.
62. Yoshishige Abe, "Nihon no Saigumbi ni Tsuite," in *Kowa Mondai Ni Kansuru Kokunai Roncho* 2, n. 55 in Chapter 7, pp. 48-52.
63. Peace Problems Discussion Circle, on Peace: "Our Third Statement," op. cit., p. 15.
64. *Ibid.*, p. 17.
65. Hori, n. op. cit., pp. 154-7, Philip W. Quigg, "Japan in Neutral," *Foreign Affairs* 44 (January 1966) pp. 253-7.
66. *Ibid.*
67. Yoshikazu Sakamoto, "Neutralism and the Idea of Peaceful Coexistence" *JSPIJ*, 1 (April 1963) p. 66.
68. Japan, House of Representatives, op. cit., pp. 22-3, Oka, n. 215, p. 18.
69. *Ibid.*, p. 31.
70. Japan, House of Councillors, op. cit., 6 (18 October 1951) p. 3.
71. Japan, House of Representatives, op. cit., p. 1.
72. Japan, House of Representatives, op. cit., p. 23.
73. *Ibid.*, p. 22.
74. Japan, House of Representatives, op. cit., p. 12.
75. Japan, House of Representatives, op. cit., p. 5. (17 October 1951) p. 9.
76. The Institute of World Economy, *The Japan Annual 1954* (Tokyo, Japan Annual Publications) p. 115.
77. *Ibid.*, p. 138.
78. Kokuritsu Yoron Chosa, *Kowa ni Kansuru Yoron Chosa* (Tokyo, June 1952) p. 1.
79. *Ibid.*, p. 17.
80. *Ibid.*, p. 20.
81. *Ibid.*, p. 23.
82. *Ibid.*, p. 24.
83. *Ibid.*, p. 30.
84. *Ibid.*

9

CONCLUSIONS

THE occupation of Japan which lasted for six and a half years was a very important event in the history of international relations. Japan was the first major country in the east to be occupied by the United States after the end of World War II. Soon it became a testing ground for American foreign policy in Asia. Its outcome was closely watched by the Asian people. The occupation of Japan became the yardstick for the Asians with which to measure the alleged gap between the practice and the preaching of the great powers. The occupation was also an absorbingly interesting international drama played on the stage of Japan. The setting was eastern but the main characters in the drama were western. What made it so interesting was the blending of so many incompatible elements into it. To begin with, the great powers—the United States and the Soviet Union—stood in direct conflict with each other, in national interest. The advocates of democracy and Communism regarded Japan as a testing ground for their ideologies. The towering personality of General MacArthur and the exaggerated importance he attached to his role in the occupation also contributed to the drama. In the preceding chapters we have seen the play un-folding in its various acts.

It is very hard to make any definitive judgments over the success or the failure of the occupation. However, the occupation of Japan provides us with a case study in the field of international relations and certain tentative conclusions can be drawn from it. In the following pages such an attempt is made. It should be remembered that the conclusions are based on a single case study. Therefore, they need to be verified by other similar studies.

1. This case study confirms the general practice in international relations that states use disguises to conceal their true national interests. There are numerous examples in the occupation of Japan where American officials resorted to such a general practice. For instance, when in late 1947, the United States began to change its policy towards Japan from reform to rehabilitation, she justified her action in the name of protecting democracy in that country. In fact from this point on the United States policy was to make Japan a bulwark against Communist expansion by reviving that country's industrial power and by reversing the liberal democratic trend. Restrictions were put on labour unions. The policy of deconcentration was brought to a sudden end. The purge policy was reversed. A red purge was put underway. The basis of this red purge was, interestingly enough, stated as belonging to category C of the original directive, which had referred to "ultranationalistic terroristic or secret patriotic societies." It would be farfetched to imagine that the authors of the original purge directive also meant it to be applied to Communist party members. The fact of the matter was that the original policy was used as a disguise to justify the constitutionally dubious policy of a red purge. The rearmament of Japan was against Article Nine of the constitution and was also contradictory to the Potsdam Declaration. Yet it was justified under the disguise of protecting democracy.

The controversy between the United States and the Soviet Union with regard to procedure to be adopted for the peace settlement is again an example of how states use certain set terms to further their national interest. In this particular case the Soviet Union insisted on the procedure laid down by the United Nations' Declaration of 1 January 1942 for the conclusion of peace treaties with enemy states. The U.N. Declaration said :

> Each government pledges itself to co-operate with the governments signatory hereto and not to make a separate armistice or peace with the enemies.[1]

The Soviet Union argued that the Japanese peace treaty should be discussed in the Council of Foreign Ministers in accordance with international agreements. The probable intention behind the Soviet move was to squeeze concessions from the Western powers by using the veto power. The United States sought to circumvent the Soviet tactics by by-passing the Council of Foreign Minister, although the United States had agreed at the Potsdam Conference that the Japanese peace treaty should be drafted by the Council of Foreign Ministers. Both sides argued endlessly on procedural matters, using it as a disguise.

Again, the Soviet insistence that fundamental human rights should be written into the Japanese peace treaty, that Japan should be allowed to rearm for self-defense, and her concern about the Japanese labour movement, and so on, seemed to have been used as disguises for something else. The real motive of the Soviet Union appeared to be the furtherance of the Communist cause.

Similarly the United States utilized the Japanese right to individual and collective security under the UN charter in order to keep her armed forces in Japan after the peace settlement. Examples of this kind can be multiplied.

2. Another tentative conclusion is that decisions concerning post-war arrangements made by the great powers, during wartime, assume questionable validity in peace-time. The decisions made by the Allied Powers during the war regarding post-war arrangements in Japan were found inadequate to solve the peace-time problems of that country. In the preceding conclusion we have seen how in late 1947 the United States changed her policies in Japan one by one, and by so doing she contradicted the Potsdam Declaration. The part of the Yalta agreement concerning the territorial arrangements between China and the Soviet Union was denounced by the United States within a few years after the end of the war.[2] It should be noted that we are not concerned with the merit of the cases cited here. We are concerned only with the validity of

the war-time decisions.

In view of cold war developments the United States had to adjust her commitments made during the war with regard to Germany, Italy and the Soviet Union. Similarly, the Soviet Union denounced her commitment to hold free elections in the East European countries immediately after the end of the war.

3. Another conclusion is that a foreign power can achieve only limited socio-economic objectives in the country it occupies.

By the end of 1947, Supreme Commander for Allied Powers had achieved impressive results. A new constitution had been promulgated. Japan had been disarmed. The ultranationalists had been purged. The hated police organization had been abolished. At that time it appeared that the United States wanted to remake Japan in her own image and the United States seemed to be in a hurry. Credit should be given to the United States for having brought about a fundamental change in the formal political structure of Japan. For the first time in their long history the Japanese were given a thoroughly democratic constitution. It is hard to believe that the Japanese ruling class, left to itself, would have adopted a new constitution at all.

However, the working of the constitution in Japan during the last eighteen years has shown that a foreign power can create external forms of democracy, but it cannot compel the people to work them out. The sudden stoppage of the programme of deconcentration of economic power in 1948 limited the scope of the reform designed to dissolve the Zaibatsu system. The policy of depurge adopted by SCAP in the latter half of the occupation similarly restricted the political reforms in the country. The rearmament of Japan in 1950 further nullified the corrective and reformative measures of the occupation. It seems to be in the nature of occupations that only a limited objective can be achieved by an alien power in an occupied country.[3]

4. After a war, when military establishment is still powerful, military considerations are likely to have disproportionate influence over political considerations on foreign policy-making.

In the post-war period, the United States was pre-occupied with the problem of Communist expansion. The Truman Doctrine, the North Atlantic Pact, and so on, were designed to contain Communism and to protect the members of the western camp. As the United States came to be more and more involved in the security of her allies in the world, the Pentagon assumed more and more importance in the United States Government. Military authorities began to play a more vital role in the formation and implementation of United States foreign policy. At times it appeared that the Pentagon rather than the State Department had the final say in matters concerning foreign policy. The Japanese peace treaty was a good case in point. We have seen how the Defense Department consistently blocked an early peace settlement for Japan under the disguise of security. In fact from 1947 to 1950, when John Foster Dulles was entrusted the task of treaty-making, almost all the State Department proposals on the peace settlement were vetoed by the Defense Department. The fact of the matter was that the Pentagon wanted to continue the occupation. The central point of the case is that the civilian branch of the United States Government allowed itself to be dominated by the Defense Department on vital policy matters. The American public seemed to have given their tacit consent to this rather undemocratic procedure by keeping silent on the subject. In view of the fact that the United States is generally considered as an advanced democratic country, the decisive role of the military personnel in foreign policy matters produces a disturbing note.

In recent times the military seems to have had a major hand in the formation of governmental policies in most European as well as Asian countries. France is the most outstanding example both because of her liberal tradition and because of the influence she used to wield in the world.

5. This case study also confirms the great power concept in international relations. Responsibility and power go hand in hand. Since the solution of the problems of war and peace in the world depend on the decisions of the great powers, those powers carry great responsibility on their shoulders. During the 19th and the early 20th centuries, Great Britain,

along with the other European powers, made decisions affecting the life of the people in most parts of the world. In the mid-20th century the United States and the Soviet Union have replaced the European powers. The difference between the past and the present is that the United States and the Soviet Union appear to be more sensitive to world public opinion than their predecessors.

Although theoretically Japan was under the Allied occupation, in practice it was an American undertaking. The Allies simply concurred with the United States' decision regarding the occupation. For instance the United States Basic Post-Surrender Policy for Japan was approved by the Far Eastern Commission without any change. It is hard to find a single example in the entire administration of the occupation where the United States allowed any opposite view of the allies to prevail on matters concerning Japan. In the face of strong opposition from Australia, New Zealand and the Philippines, the United States went ahead and rehabilitated Japanese industrial power, rearmed the country and encouraged the pre-war leadership. Again on the problems of the peace settlement the United States encountered opposition from the same quarter. But nothing happened. The Allies could not change the mind of the American policy-makers. This is well illustrated by the fact that Australia, New Zealand and the Philippines took their grievances to the conference hall at San Francisco, despite Dulles' claim that the Allied Powers had talked with the United States for eleven months on the peace settlement. But even at San Francisco, the United States' position prevailed.

6. A further conclusion is that one-power and one-man control of an ex-enemy country seem to work better than a collective occupation. It is doubtful whether Japan could have fared as well if it had been divided into zones of occupation as was the case in Germany. Japan was saved from the misfortunes of Germany and Korea, because she was occupied practically by only one power. General MacArthur's forceful personality and his tight control over the affairs of Japan also seemed to have contributed to the relative success of the occupation. It should be remembered that this is a tentative

conclusion and needs to be confirmed by other similar studies.

7. The Japanese peace treaty confirms the general idea in international relations that careful preparatory work is a prerequisite to the success of a conference. The so-called eleven months peace conference claimed by Dulles seemed to have been useful to a certain extent in thrashing out the differences among the Allies in private. Although some of the Allied nations voiced their dissatisfaction in the peace conference, they did not vote against the peace treaty. No changes were made in the Anglo-American draft treaty in the conference at San Francisco.

8. It also appears that a peace conference is regarded by the great powers as a forum for propaganda. In view of the fact that no changes were allowed to be made in the draft treaty, one wonders why the United States thought it necessary to hold the peace conference at San Francisco at all. The treaty could have been signed by the ambassadors of the countries presented at the conference in some convenient place like Washington where all of them were available. It would have saved considerable money and time. However, the conference served the purpose of propaganda. The difference between the United States and the Soviet Union was dramatized in the conference on television for public review.

9. Another tentative conclusion is that an alien power which occupies a country generally hands over the reins of government to the groups or a group in that country which is likely to follow for a considerable time the general line of the policy laid down by the alien power.

It is doubtful whether the United States would have agreed to sign a peace treaty with a socialist government in Japan. As we know, the Japanese Socialists were opposed to the policy of alignment with the western powers. The transfer of power to the conservative leadership in Japan in 1951 ensured the United States interest in that country.

In the immediate past, Great Britain was most successful in transferring power to generally conservative groups in most of her colonies. At present, most of the former colonies of Britain are members of the Commonwealth. The other European colonial powers were also successful in transferring power to the groups in their colonies who were friendly to the colonial powers.

It is interesting to speculate whether the labour government in Britain in 1947 would have agreed to leave India or any other former colony in the hands of the local Communists.

Since the end of World War II the United States had generally transferred political power to conservative leaders in the areas which were under her control. Japan, Germany, and Italy are the outstanding examples, and they seem to confirm the hypothesis mentioned above.

10. Another conclusion is that after a short period of setback, the conservative leadership in an occupied country generally aligns itself with the foreign power. This strange alliance then tries to suppress any progressive movement which threatens the combined interest of the aliens and the conservative class in that country. This does not suggest by any means that the conservative elements in an occupied area do not desire the independence of their country. They would certainly like to be independent of the foreign power provided the governmental authority is retained in their hands. For example, the strongest supporters of the British rule in India were the Maharajas, the Nawabs, the big landlords and the estate holders. They wanted the British Government to transfer the power to them and expressed their dissatisfaction when power was transferred to the congress party.

In Japan also the same alignment of forces took place during the occupation. The Japanese conservative leaders, with the active support of the United States, tried to curb the march of the progressive movement in Japan. In almost all occupied countries in Asia and Africa the conservative forces have tried to maintain themselves in power with the help of the foreigners. And foreign powers have found it profitable to align with the conservative forces in the countries under their control. Economic and political interests seem to be the common factors between them.

The foregoing are some of the tentative conclusions. Some of them only confirm what is known; others are far from definitive. A comparative study of the German, the Italian, and the Japanese occupations can provide us with certain guidelines for the future.

REFERENCES

1. United Nations, Office of Public Information, *Everyman's United Nations* (New York, 1964) p. 4.
2. The concessions made to the Soviet Union at Yalta were as follows:

   (i) The commercial port of Dairen shall be internationalized, the pre-eminent interest of the Soviet Union in this port being safeguarded, and the lease of Port Arthur as a naval base of the USSR restored. (ii) The Chinese-Eastern railroad, and South-Manchurian Railroad, which provide an outlet to Dairen, shall be jointly operated by the establishment of a joint Soviet-Chinese Company, it being understood that the pre-eminent interests of the Soviet Union shall be safeguarded and that China shall retain full sovereignty in Manchuria. United States, Department of State, *Foreign Relations of the US Diplomatic Papers, the Conferences at Malta and Yalta 1945* (Washington, 1955) p. 984.
3. The conclusion numbered three explains what happened in Japan during the occupation. Some of the reasons why the allied powers could not transform the Japanese society in their image are explained in Chapter 3.

BIBLIOGRAPHY

DOCUMENTS AND MEMOIRS

Primary sources

Ackerman, Lauren V. *The Reminiscence* (Oral History Research Office, Columbia University, New York, 1961).

American Federation of Labor, Report of the Proceedings of the Sixty-Seventh Convention, November 15 to 22, 1948 (Cinncinati, 1948).

Baldwin, R.N. *The Reminiscence* (Oral History Research Office, Columbia University, New York, 1961).

Ballantine, Joseph. *The Reminiscence* (Oral History Research Office, Columbia University, New York, 1961).

Blakeslee, George H. *The Far Eastern Commission, A Study in International Cooperation: 1945 to 1952.* (Washington, 1953).

Byrnes, James F. *Speaking Frankly.* (New York, 1947).

Crane, Burton. *The Reminiscence* (Oral History Research Office, Columbia University, New York, 1961).

Eichelberger, Robert L. *Our Jungle Road to Tokyo.* (New York, 1950).

General Headquarters, Supreme Commander for Allied Powers. *Education in New Japan.* (Tokyo, 1948).

General Headquarters, SCAP and Far Eastern Command. *Two*

Years of Occupation. (Washington, 1947).

Gordon, Joseph. *The Reminiscence.* (Oral History Research Office, Columbia University, New York, 1961).

Grew, Joseph Clark. *Ten Years in Japan.* (New York, 1944).

Harold, John. *The Reminiscence* (Oral History Research Office, Columbia University, New York, 1962).

Henderson, Herald, *The Reminiscence* (Oral History Research Office, Columbia University, New York, 1962).

Institute of Pacific Relations. *Some Japanese Views on American-Japanese Relations* (New York, 1952).

Japan, Kokkai Sangiin. *Minutes of the Proceedings in the House of Councillors of the National Diet 1st-13th session, 1947-1952* (Tokyo).

——. *Minutes of the Proceedings in the House of Representatives of the National Diet 1st-13th sessions, 1947-1952* (Tokyo).

Japan, Ministry of Education, *Progress of Education Reform* (Tokyo, 1950).

——. *Japan in the World Today* (Tokyo, 1952).

Japan, Ministry of Foreign Affairs. *Japan, her Security and Mission* (Tokyo, 1950).

——. *Present Condition of Japan* (Tokyo, 1950).

——. *The Northern Islands, background of territorial problems in the Japanese-Soviet Negotiations* (Tokyo, 1955).

——. *Documents concerning the Allied occupation of Japan* 2 (Tokyo, 1949).

Kokuritsu Yoron Chosa. *Kawa ni Kansuru Yoron Chosa* (Tokyo, 1952).

Kume, Ai. *The Reminiscences* (Oral History Research Office, Columbia University, New York, 1962).

MacArthur, Douglas. *Reminiscences* (New York, 1964).

Maruyama, Masao, "Nationalism in Post War Japan," (I.P.R. 11th Conference, Lucknow, 1950).

National Diet Library. *Kowa Mondai ni Kansuru, Kokunai Roncho* 2 (Tokyo, 1951).

National Peace Council. *Views of Kagawa and Nehru on Japan's Future* N.C. 5269 (London 26 November, 1945).

New Zealand, Department of External Affairs. *Japanese Peace Settlement* No. 106 (Wellington, 1951).

——. *Report on British Commonwealth Conference, Canberra,*

26 August-2 September 1947 No. 38 (Wellington, 1947).

Oka, Yoshitake, "Outside Pressure on Government in Postwar Japan" (I.P.R. 12th Conference, Kyoto, 1954).

Oka, Yoshisato, "Pattern of Power in Japanese Democracy" (I.P.R. 12th Conference, Kyoto, 1954).

Overton, Douglas W. *The Reminiscence* (Overal History Research Office, Columbia University, New York, 1960).

Pauley, Edwin W., *Report on Japanese Reparations to the President of the US November 1945 to April 1946* (Washington, 1946).

Patch, Buel W., *Japan and Pacific Security, Editorial Research Report* 8 (Washington, 1951).

Peake, Cyrus H., *The Reminiscence* (Overal History Research Office, Columbia University, New York, 1961).

Royal Institute of International Affairs, *Survey of International Affairs* (London) from 1946-1952.

Sebald, William and Russel, B., *With MacArthur in Japan* (New York, 1965).

Secretary General, FEC. *Report, Activities of the Far Eastern Commission February 26, 1946-July 10, 1947* (Washington, 1947).

——. *Second Report, Activities of the Far Eastern Commission, July 10, 1947-December 23, 1948* (Washington, 1949).

——. *Third Report, Activities of the Far Eastern Commission, December 24, 1948-June 30, 1950* (Washington, 1950).

Shigemitsu Mamoru. *Japan and her Destiny; My Struggle for Peace* (London, 1958).

Supreme Commander for Allied Powers, Civil Information and Education Section, *Mission and Accomplishment of the Occupation in the Civil Information and Education Field* (Tokyo, 1949).

Supreme Commander for Allied Powers, Economic and Scientific Section. *Mission and Accomplishments of Supreme Commander for Allied Powers in the Economic and Scientific Fields* (Tokyo, 1950).

——. *Press Translations and Summaries* (Tokyo, N.D.).

——. Public Health and Welfare Section, *Mission and Accomplishments of the Occupation in Public Health and Welfare Fields* (Tokyo, 1949).

——. Report of Government Section, *Political Re-orientation of Japan : September 1945 to September 1948* 2 (Washington, 1949).

——. *Selected Data on the Occupation of Japan* (Washington, 1950).

——. *Summation of Non-military Activities in Japan* No. 1-35 (Tokyo, September 1945-August, 1948).

Smith, Daniel M., *Major Problems in American Diplomatic History, Documents and Readings* (Boston, 1964).

Tatsuki, Yasuo, *General Trends of Japanese Opinion Following the End of War* (Tokyo, 1948).

Truman, Harry S., *Memoirs, Years of Trial and Hope* 2 (New York, 1956).

——. *Public Papers of the Presidents of the United States* (Washington, 1963).

U.K. Ministry of Foreign Affairs. *Japan No. 1, Draft Peace Treaty with Japan* cmd 8300 (London, 1951).

——. *Japan No. 2, Amendments to Draft Treaty of Peace with Japan* cmd 8316 (London, 1951).

——. *Japan No. 3, Draft Treaty of Peace with Japan as Amended 13 August 1951* cmd 8341 (London, 1951).

United Nations, Department of Public Information, *Yearbook of the United Nations 1948-9* (New York,1950).

United States, Army Department, *Report on Economic Position and Prospects of Japan and Korea and the Measures Required to Improve Them* (Washington, 1948).

United States Congress. *House Committee on Foreign Affairs, Hearings* 12 (Washington, 1948).

United States Congress. *Japanese Peace Treaty and Other Treaties Relating to Security in the Pacific, Hearings before the Senate Committee on Foreign Relations* (82 Congress, Second Session, Washington, 1952).

——. *Senate Committee on Foreign Relations, Hearings* 20 (Washington, 1952).

United States Council on Foreign Relations. *The US in World Affairs* (New York) from 1946-1952.

United States, Department of State. *A Decade of American Foreign Policy: Basic Documents, 1941-49* (Washington, 1950).

United States, Department of State. *Analysis of the Shidehara Cabinet* (Washington, 1945).

——. *American Foreign Policy, 1950-1955 Basic Documents* 2 (Washington, 1957).

——. *Background, Pacific Security* (Far Eastern Series 48, Washington, April, 1952).

——. *Background, the Japanese Peace Conference at San Francisco* (Washington, 1951).

——. *Bulletin* (1946-1952).

——. Foreign Relations of the United States, *Diplomatic Papers, the Conferences at Malta and Yalta 1945.* (Washington, 1955).

——. *Occupation of Japan, Policy and Progress* (Washington, 1957).

——. *Japan: Free World Ally* (Washington, 1957).

——. *Record of the Proceedings of the Conference for the Conclusion and Signature of the Treaty of Peace with Japan.* (Washington, 1951).

——*Report on the Mission on Japanese Combines* (Washington, 1946).

——. *United States Relations with Japan, 1945-1952* (New York, 1952).

——. *What we are Doing in Japan and Why* (Washington, 1946).

United States, Far Eastern Command, *Japan, Friend and Ally* (Tokyo, 1952).

United States, Strategic Bombing Survey, *Japan's Struggle to End the War* (Washington, 1946).

United States, Strategic Bombing Survey, Morale Division, *The Effects of Strategic Bombing on Japanese Morale* (Washington, 1947).

World Affairs Council of Northern California, *Peace Making with Japan, Study Group Report* 2 (San Francisco, 1948).

Yoshida, Shigeru, *The Yoshida Memoirs: The Story of Japan in Crisis* (London, 1961).

Newspapers

The Christian Science Moniter, 1945-52.

The New York Times, (New York) 1946-60.

Nippon Times, (Tokyo) 1945-51.

The Washington Post 1945-55.

Books

Allen, G.C., *A Short Economic History of Japan*, (London 1962).

Axelbank Albert, *Black Star Over Japan, Rising Forces of Imperialism*, (George Allen and Unwin Ltd, London, 1972).

Baerwald, Hans H. *The Purge of Japanese Leaders under the Occupation*, (San Francisco, 1959).

Ball, MacMahon W., *Japan, Enemy or Ally?*, (New York, 1947).

Beal, Robinson John, *John Foster Dulles: 1888-1957*, (New York, 1957).

Bisson, T.A., *Prospects for Democracy in Japan*, (New York, 1949).

———. *Zaibatsun Dissolution in Japan*, (Berkeley, 1954).

Brines, Russel, *MacArthur's Japan*, (New York, 1948).

Brezezinski Zbigniew, *The Fragile Blossom: Crisis and change in Japan*, (New York, 1972).

Brands William J., (ed.), *Japan and the United States Challenge and the opportunities*, (New York University Press, 1979).

Buckly Roger, *Occupation of Diplomacy, Britain and the United States and Japan 1945-1952*, (Cambridge University Press, New York, 1982).

Bundy, McGeorge (ed.), *The Pattern of Responsibility*, (Boston, 1952).

Burton, Hugh, (ed.), *Japan*, (New York, 1950).

———. *Japan's Modern Century*, (New York, 1955).

Burton, Robert J.C., *Japan's Decision to Surrender*, (Stanford, 1954).

Cohen, Bernard C., *The Political Process and Foreign Policy, the making of the Japanese Peace Settlement* (Princeton, 1957).

Cohen, Jerome B., *Economic Problems of Japan*, (Princeton, 1952).

———. *Japan's Economy in War and Reconstruction*, (Minneapolis, 1949).

Colbert, Evelyn S., *The Leftwing in Japanese Politics*, (New York, 1952).

Cole, Allan B., and Naomichi Nakanishi, *Japanese Opinion Polls with Socio-Political Significance 1947-1957*, (Medford, Mass., 1959).

Costello, William, *Democracy vs. Feudalism*, (Tokyo, 1948).

Dallin, David J., *Soviet Russia and the Far East*, (New Haven 1948).

Dangerfield, Royden J., *The New Japan*, (New York, 1953).

Dunn, Frederick S., *Peace-Making and the Settlement with Japan*, (Princeton, 1963).

Dore, R.P., *Land Reform in Japan*, (New York, 1959).

Emerson John K., *The Japanese Dilema: Arms Yen and Power*, (New York, 1972).

Fearly, Robert A., *The Occupation of Japan, Second Phase: 1948-50*, (New York, 1950).

——. *Japan Diary*, (New York, 1948).

Feis Herbert, *Contest over Japan: The Soviet Bid for Power in the Far East*, (New York, 1967).

Franklin B Weinstein, (Ed.), *U.S.-Japan Relations and Security of East Asia*, The Next Decade (Westerview, Press 1978).

Gross, Ernest A., *Japan Between East and West*, (New York, 1957).

Gunther, John, *The Riddle of MacArthur*, (New York, 1950).

Hall, Robert King, *The Ethics of a Defeated Nation*, (New York, 1949).

Hellmann Donald C., *Japan and East Asia: The New International Order*, (New York, 1972).

——. *Japanese Foreign Policy and Domestic Politics. The Peace Agreement with the Soviet Union*, (University of California Press, 1969).

Holliday Jan and Mc Co, Mack Gavan, *Japanese Imperialism today: Co-prosperity in Greater East Asia*, (Monthly Review Press, New York, 1973).

Ito, Nobufumi, *New Japan: Six Years of Democratization*, (Tokyo, 1951).

Johnson U. Alexis and Packard R. George, (ed), *Japan the United States and NATO*, (Ballinger Pubs, 1981).

Jain Rajendera Kumar, *The USSR and Japan 1945-1980*, (Radiant Pubs. New Delhi, 1981).

Kase, Toshikazu, *Journey to Missouri*, (New Haven, 1950).

Kim Young C., *Japanese-Soviet Relations, Interaction of Politics, Economics and National Security. Vol II*, (Sage Pubs, Baverly Hills California, 1974).

Kawai, Kazuo, *Japan's American Interlude*, (Chicago, 1960).

Kennan, George F., *American Diplomacy 1900-1950*, (New York, 1963).

——, *Memoirs 1925-1950*, (Little Brown and Company, Boston, 1967).

——, *Russia and the West Under Lenin and Stalin*, (New York, 1962).

Latourettee, Kenneth Scott, *American Record in the Far East*, (New York, 1953).

Leon Hollerman (ed.), *Japan and the United States: Economic Political Adversaries*, (Westerview Press, 1980).

Lewe Van Aduard, Evert J., *Japan from Surrender to Peace* (The Hague, 1953).

Lippmann, Walter, *The Cold War: A Study in Foreign Policy*, (New York, 1947).

Maki, John M., *Government and Politics in Japan: The Road to Democracy*, (New York, 1964).

Mendl Wolf, *Issues in Japan's China Policy*, (Oxford University Press, New York, 1978).

Morely William James, (Ed), *Forecast for Japan: Security in the 1970s*, (Princeton University Press, 1972).

Muraoko Kumio, *Japanese Security and the United States* (International Institute for Strategic Studies, London, 1973).

——, *Japanese Nationalism in Transition*, (New York, 1947).

Martin, Edwin M., *The Allied Occupation of Japan*, (Stanford, 1948).

Maruyama, Masao, *Thought and Behaviour in Modern Japanese Politics*, (London, 1963).

Measland, John Wesley, *Group Interests in American Relations with Japan*, (Ann Arbor, Michigan, 1952).

Mendel, Douglas H., *The Japanese People and Foreign Policy: A Study of Public Opinion in Post-Treaty Japan*, (Berkeley, 1961).

Montgomery, John D., *Forced to Be Free: the Artificial Revolution in Germany and Japan*, (Chicago, 1957).

Morris, Ivan, *Nationalism and Right Wing in Japan*, (London,

1960).

Okubo, Genji, *The Problem of the Emperor System in Postwar Japan*, (Toyko. 1948).

O Sgood *et al Japanese and the United States in Asia*, (Jhon Hopkins University, Baltimore, 1969).

Olson Lawerence, *Japan in the Post War Asia*, (Prager Press, New York, 1970).

Packard George R., *Protest in Tokyo, the Security Treaty Crisis of 1960*, (Princeton University Press, New York, 1966).

Panda Rajaram, *An Expanding Partnership in the Western Pacific Japan and Australia 1980*, (Manthan Pubs, Rothak, 1982).

Pfultzgraff, Robert L. Jr., and Davis Jacquelyn K., *Japanese American Relations in Changing Security Environment*, (Sage Pubs. London, 1975).

Passin, Herbert, *Society and Education in Japan*, (New York, 1965).

Reischauer, Edwin O., *Japan and America Today*, (Stanford, 1953).

——. *Japan: Past and Present*, 2nd ed., (Tokyo, 1962).

——. *Japan: A Story of a Nation* (New York, 1970).

Richard Soloman H., (ed), *Conference on East Asian Security in the 1980s*, (Santa Monica, Calif, 1979).

——. *The United States and Japan*, (New York, 1965).

Reitzel, William, *et al*, *United States Foreign Policy 1945-55* (Wisconsin, 1956).

Rosecrance, R.N., *Australian Diplomacy and Japan 1945-1951*, (London, 1962).

Roth, Andrew, *Dilemma in Japan*, (Boston, 1945).

Sansom, George B., *The Western World and Japan*, (London, 1950).

Scalapino, Robert A., and Masumi Gubbosuke, *Parties and Politics in Contemporary Japan*, (Berkeley, 1962).

Sherwood, Robert E., *Roosevelt and Hopkins, An Intimate History*, (New York, 1948).

Stoezel, Jean, *Without the Chrysanthemum and the Sword, a Study of the Attitudes of Youth in Postwar Japan*, (New York, 1955).

Storry, Richard, *A History of Modern Japan*, (London, 1960).

Stuart E Johnson and Joseph A, Yager, *The Military Equation in the North-East Asia*, (Brookings Ins, 1979).

Staphen, *The Kurile Islands: Russo-Japanese Frontier in Pacific*, (Oxford University Press, New York, 1974).

Sweringen, Rodger and Paul Langer, *Red Flag in Japan International Communism in Action*, (Cambridge, Massachusetts, 1952).

Textor, Robert B., *Failure in Japan; with Keynotes for-a Positive Policy*, (New York, 1951).

Tsukahira, Toshio G., *The Postwar Evolution of Communist Strategy in Japan*, (Cambridge, 1954).

Turner, Gordan B., *A History of Military Affairs in Western Society Since the Eighteenth Century*, (New York, 1956).

Uyehara, Ceil H., *Leftwing Social Movements in Japan*, (Tokyo, 1959.

Van, Advard and Baren, E.J. Lewe, *Japan from Surrender to Peace*, (The Hague Maritime B, Nijhoff, 1953).

Vishwanathan, Savitri, *Normalization of Japanese Soviet Relations, 1945-1970*, (Lasswade Diplomatic Press, 1973).

Ward Robert, E and Shulman, Frank Joseph, comls (ed), *The Allied Occupation of Japan, 1945-1952: An annotated bibliography of Western Language* (American Association Library, Chicago, 1974).

Whitney, Courtney, *MacArthur: His Rendezvous with History*, (New York, 1958).

Wildes, Emerson Harry, *Typhoon in Tokyo*, (New York, 1954).

William, T. Tow and William, R Feency, *U.S. Foreign Policy and Asian Pacific Security*, (Westerview Press, 1982).

Willoughby, Charles A., *MacArthur 1941 1951*, (New York, 1954).

Yamaguchi, Shirokuro, *Some Aspects of Agrarian Reform in Japan*, (Tokyo, 1948).

Yokota, Kisaburo, and Tomoo Otaka, *Japan and International Organizations: A Report on National Policy and Public Attitudes of Japan toward International Organizations*, (Tokyo, 1950).

Articles

Allison, John M., "Japanese Peace Treaty and Related Security Pact," *American Society of International Law, Annual Proceedings* 46, (April 1952) 35-43.

Ball, W. McMahon, "Reflections on Japan, "*Pacific Affairs* 21, (March 1948) 3-19.

Ballantine, Joseph W., "The Future of the Ryukyus," *Foreign Affairs*, 31, (July 1953) 663-74.

Beal, R. John, "Bull's Eye for Dulles," *Harper's Magazine* 203, (November 1951) 88-94.

Bisson, T.A., "Reparations and Reform in Japan," *Far Eastern Survey*, 16 (17 December 1947) 241-7.

Borton, Hugh, "United States Occupation Policies in Japan since Surrender," *Political Science Quarterly*, LXIII, (June 1947) 250-7.

Colton, Kenneth E., George Totten and others, "Japan Since Recovery of Independence," *Annals of the American Academy of Political and Social Science* 308, (November 1956) 1-174.

Coons, Arthur Gardiner, "Neutralism: The Problem of Japan in East-West Relations," *World Affairs Interpreter* 25, (Winter 1955) 385-90.

"Criminal Jurisdiction over American Armed Forces Abroad," Notes *Harvard Law Review* 70 (1956-7) 1043-67.

Dulles, John Foster, "Security in the Pacific," *Foreign Affairs* 30 (January 1952) 175-87.

Eto, Jun, "The Bankruptcy of our Idealistic Intellectuals," *Journal of Social and Political Ideas in Japan* 2, (April 1964) 101-6.

Evatt, Herbert V., "Japan is Still a Menace, *The New York Times Magazine* (3 February 1946) 10, 46-7.

Farley, M.S., "Japan and the U.S. Post-Treaty Problems," *Far Eastern Survey* 21 (27 February 1952) 33-8.

Fukuda, Kan'ichi, "The Fate of Monarchy in the Twentieth Century," *Journal of Social and Political Ideas in Japan* 1 (August 1963) 25-8.

Fukuda, Kan'ichi, Saito Makoto, Skamoto Yoshikazu, and others, "Japanese Intellectuals Discuss American-Japanese Relations," *Far Eastern Survey* 29 (October 1960) 145-60.

Fukuda, Tsuneari, "The Intellectual Class of Japan," *Journal of Social and Political Ideas in Japan* 2 (April 1964) 21-3.

Gibson, James B., "The Occupation of Japan—Ten Years Later," *World Affairs* 118 (Winter 1955) 109-11.

Green, Leslie C., "Making Peace with Japan," *Yearbook of World Affairs*, (1952) 1-35.

Guillain, Robert, "The Resurgence of Military Elements in Japan," *Pacific Affairs* 25, (September 1952) 221-5.

Hara, Shigeru, "Who Will Promote Reforms," *JSPIJ* 1, (August 1963) 57-61.

Hayashi, Kentaro, "How to Approach Postwar Japanese History," *JSPIJ* 3 (August 1965) 67-71.

——, "Some Comments on Current Constitutional Debates," *JSPIJ* 1 (August 1963) 17-21.

Hidaka, Rokuro, "Intellectuals and Masses," *JSPIJ* 2 (April 1964) 106-11.

——, "The Role and Aims of Social Studies in Education," *JSPIJ* 1, (December 1963) 77-81.

Horie, Yoshitaka, "Japan's Self-Defense Force Today," *Orient/West* 8 (July/August 1963) 54-8.

Inamura, Junzo, "In Rebuttal of Those Who Oppose both the San-Francisco Peace Treaty and Mutual Security Agreement," *JSPIJ* 3 (April 1965) 45-8.

——, "The Peace Movement and the New Platform of the Socialist Party," *JSPIJ* 3 (April 1965) 45-8.

Irie, Akira, "The Legacy of Modern Japanese Diplomacy," *JSPIJ* 3 (August 1965) 25-32.

Ishida, Hirohide, "The Direction of Japanese Political Reorganization," *JSPIJ* 2 (December 1964) 24-9.

——, "The Vision of the Conservative Party," *JSPIJ* 2 (August 1964) 55-8.

Kaigo, Tokiomi, "A Short History of Postwar Japanese Education," *JSPIJ* 1 (December 1963) 15-23.

Kawai, Kazu, "Japanese Views on National Security" *Pacific Affairs* 23 (June 1950) 115-27.

Kawakami, Kiyoshi Karl, "America and Japan's Permanent Neutrality" *World Affairs* 112 (Summer 1949) 35-7.

Kennan, George, "Japanese Security and American Policy," *Foreign Affairs* 43 (October 1965) 90-99.

Kiichi, Saheki, "The Building of Japan's Self-Defense," *Japan Quarterly* 4 (January-March 1957) 101-10.

Kishi, Nobusuke, "Political Movements in Japan," *Foreign Affairs* 44 (October 1965) 90-99.

Kobayashi, Naoki, "The Establishment of the Constitution, An Analysis," *JSPIJ* 1 (August 1963) 14-7.

Kosaka, Masataka, "An Appeal to the Liberal Democratic and Socialist Parties: Japan, A Nation Without a Foreign Policy," *JSPIJ* 2 (December 1964) 56-9.

Kramer, R.C., "Japan Must Compete," *Fortune* 35 (June 1947) 112-3 and 176 and 179.

Levi, Warner, "International Control of Japan," *Far Eastern Survey* 15 (25 September 1946) 299-302.

Lindbeck, John M.H., "Communist China and American Far Eastern Policy," *The Department of State Bulletin* 33 (7 November 1955) 751-59.

MacArthur, Douglas II., "The Evolution of the Japanese-American Partnership," *The Department of State Bulletin* 44 (17 April 1961) 556-61.

Martin, Robert P., "Japan Rearmed," *The Nation* 172 (10 March 1951) 224-6.

Maruyama, Masao, "Japanese Thought," *JSPIJ* 2 (April 1964) 41-8.

Masamichi, Royama, The US-Japanese Security Treaty—A Japanese View," *Japan Quarterly* 4 (January-March 1957) 284-95.

Masumi, Junnosuke, "A Profile of the Japanese Conservative Party," *Asian Survey* 3 (August 1963) 390-401.

Matsushita, Keiichi, "The Conservatives and the Progressives: an Organizational Confrontation, *JSPIJ* 2 (December 1964) 46-50.

——, "Social Movements and Intellectuals," *JSPIJ* 2 (April 1964) 114-7.

McConaughty, Walter P., "The American Image of Japan," *The Department of State Bulletin* 45 (23 October 1961) 663-66.

——, "A Pacific Partnership," *The Department of State Bulletin* 45 (16 October 1961) 634-7.

Mendel, Douglas H., "Japanese Attitude toward American

Military Bases," *Far Eastern Survey* 28 (September 1959) 129-34.

——, "Japanese Views of the American Alliance," *Public Opinion Quarterly* 23 (Fall 1959) 326-42.

——, "Japan Reviews Her American Alliance," *Public Opinion Quarterly* 30 (Spring 1966) 1-18.

Menzies, Robert Gordon, "The Pacific Settlement seen from Australia," *Foreign Affairs* 30 (January 1952) 188-96.

Metzger, Stanley D., "The Liberal Japanese Peace Treaty," *Cornell Law Quarterly* 37 (Spring 1952) 382-402.

Miyahara, Seiichi, "The Japan Teacher's Union and its Code of Ethics," *JSPIJ* 1 (December 1963) 102-5.

Morley, James, W., "Japan and the USSR," in Princeton University Conference, *The New Japan: Prospects and Promise* (Princeton, N.J., 1963) 45-53.

——, "Japan's Security Policy in Transition," *Current History* 46-47 (April 1964) 200-6.

Morris, I., "Japanese Foreign Policy and Neutralism," *International Affairs* 36 (January 1960) 7-20.

Munakata, Seiya, "The Fundamental Law of Education," *JSPIJ* 1 (December 1963) 54-8.

Murthy, P.A. Narasimha, "Japan and the Bomb," *Foreign Affairs Reports* (13 December 1964, New Delhi) 183-8.

——, "The Japanese Left and the Anti-Nuclear Movement," *International Studies* 5 (January 1964) 281-95.

Nakamura, Kikuo, "Party Politics," *New Leader* 2 Supplement (New York, 28 November 1960) 22.

Ogawa, Taro, "Reflections on Postwar Education," *JSPIJ* 1 (December 1963) 24-30.

Ohara, Soichiro, "Exportation of a Vinylon Plant to China," *JSPIJ* 2 (August 1964) 107-9.

Ōi, Kai, "Toward the Formation of a New Japanese Nationalism," *JSPIJ*, 2 (August 1964) 16-21.

Oka, Yoshisato, "Political Parties and Party Government," *JSPIJ* 2 (December 1964) 14-24.

Okakura, Koshiro, "Afro-Asian Concept of Independence and Peace," *JSPIJ* 1 (April 1963) 106-8.

Okazaki, Katsuo, "The Late General MacArthur and Japan," *Contemporary Japan* 28 (September 1964) 1-9.

Okuma, Nobuyuki, "The Japanese People," 2 (August 1964) 27-31.

Ota, Takashi, "A Study of Educational Policies in Postwar Period," *JSPIJ* 1 (December 1963) 116-21.

Otake, Victor Masaru, (trans.), "Japan Looks Back on the Occupation," *Far Eastern Survey* 22 (25 February 1953) 26-32.

Passin, Herbert, "The Sources of Protest in Japan" *The American Political Science Review* 56 (21 June 1962) 391-403.

Polyziodes, A., "The Japanese Peace Treaty and After," *World Affairs Interpreter* 22 (Autumn 1951) 296-310.

Quigley, Harold S., "American Policy and Japanese Politics," *The Political Quarterly* 21 (January-March 1950) 29-39.

——, (ed.) "Post-War Politics in Japan: A Symposium," *The American Political Science Review* 42 (October 1948 and December 1948 issues) 927-69, 1149-80.

Quigg, Philip W., "Japan in Neutral," *Foreign Affairs* 44 (January 1966) 253-7.

Rawlings, C.H., "The Japanese Peace Treaty," *The Contemporary Review* 180 (October 1951) 202-5.

Reischauer, Edwin O., "The Broken Dialogue with Japan," *Foreign Affairs* 39 (October 1960) 11-26.

Saito, Makoto, "A New Beginning for American Diplomacy," 2 (April 1963) 83-6.

Sakaguchi, Akira, "The Power of the Financial World," *JSPIJ* 2 (December 1964) 115-9.

Sakamoto, Yoshikazu, "Japan in A World of Tension," *JSPIJ* 1 (April 1963) 41-6.

——, "Neutralism and the Idea of Peaceful Co-Existence," *JSPIJ* 1 (April 1963) 63-7.

Sansom, George, "Can Japan Be Reformed," *Far Eastern Survey* 18 (2 November 1949) 258-9.

——, "Conflicting Purposes in Japan," *Foreign Affairs* 26 (January 1948) 302-11.

Sato, Noboru, "Socialism, and Neutralism," 1 (April 1963) 60-2.

Shinohara, Hajime, "The Leadership of the Conservative Party," *JSPIJ* 2 (December 1964) 40-5.

——, "The Leadership of the Progressive Parties," *JSPIJ* 2

(December 1964) 51-5.

——, "Post-War Democracy and Parliamentary Politics," *JSPIJ* 1 (August 1963) 35-8.

Stratton, Samuel S., "Far Eastern Commission," *International Organization* 12 (9 February 1948) 1-18.

Stuber, Stanley I., "Japan's Problems of Self-Defense," *The Christian Century* 68 (5 September 1951) 1009-11.

Tadashi, Fukutake, "The Revolution in Japanese Agriculture: Fact or Illusion," *JSPIJ* 3 (December 1965) 16-21.

Taguchi, Fukuji, "Conservative Political Parties: A Preliminary Study," *JSPIJ* 3 (August 1965) 37-41.

Takano, Yuichi, "Foreign Armed Forces and Criminal Jurisdiction of Japan," *The Japanese Annual of International Law* 2 (Tokyo 1952) 29.

Takagi, Yasaka, "Defeat and Democracy in Japan," *Foreign Affairs* 26 (July 1948) 645-52.

Takeuchi, Tatsuji, "Basic Issues in Japan's Foreign Policy," *Far Eastern Survey* 21 (19 November 1952) 161-6.

Takeuchi, Yoshimi, "Peace and Self-Defense," *JSPIJ* 1 (August 1963) 21-3.

Takeyama, Michio, "The Emperor System," *JSPIJ* 2 (August 1964) 168-84.

Tsuji, Kiyoaki, "The Bureaucracy Preserved and Strengthened," *JSPIJ* 2 (December 1964) 88-92.

Ward, Robert E., "The Origins of the Present Japanese Constitution", *The American Political Science Review* 50 (December 1956) 980-1010.

Warp, George A., "In our Image and Likeness," *National Municipal Review* 42 (April 1953) 175-8 and 188.

Watanabe, Yasuo, "The Function of High-Ranking Civil Servants," *JSPIJ* 2 (December 1964) 92-7.

Yamada, Munemutsu, "The Development of Left-Wing Intellectuality," *JSPIJ* 2 (April 1964) 59-64.

Yoshida, Shigeru, "Japan and the Crisis in Asia," *Foreign Affairs* 29 (January 1951) 171-81.

INDEX